# OLD TESTAMENT STUDIES

*Volume 3*

# A Time For War

*A Study of Warfare
in the
Old Testament*

*by*
*T. R. Hobbs*

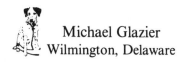

Michael Glazier
Wilmington, Delaware

## ABOUT THE AUTHOR

T. R. Hobbs is Professor of Old Testament Interpretation at McMaster Divinity College, McMaster University, Hamilton, Ontario, Canada. He studied at Spurgeon's College, London, the University of London (where he received his Ph.D.), the Baptist Seminary, Rueschlikon, Switzerland and the University of Zurich. He is the author of numerous articles in scholarly journals, *2 Kings* in the Word Biblical Commentary (1985), *Word Biblical Themes: 1 and 2 Kings* (1989), and is a contributor to the forthcoming *Anchor Bible Dictionary*.

First published in 1989 by Michael Glazier, Inc., 1935 West Fourth Street, Wilmington, Delaware 19805.

Library of Congress Cataloging-in-Publication Data

Hobbs, T. R. (T. Raymond), 1942-
   A time for war: a study of warfare in the Old Testament/T.R. Hobbs.
     p. cm.—(Old Testament studies: v. 3)
   Bibliography: p.
   Includes index.
   ISBN: 0-89453-656-7
   1. War—Biblical teaching. 2. Bible. O.T.—Criticism. interpretation, etc.
I. Title. II. Series. II. Series: Old Testament studies (Wilmington, Del.); v. 3.
BS1199.W2H63 1989
221.8'355—dc20                                 88-82460
                                            CIP

Typography by Cyndi Cohee and Mary Brown
Printed in the United States of America

Dedicated to the Memory
of
Leonard George Hobbs
(1916-1954)
Staff Sergeant, Royal Engineers

For everything there is a season,
and a time for every matter under heaven:

a time to be born and a time to die;
a time to kill and a time to heal;
a time for love and a time for hate;
a time for war and a time for peace.

Ecclesiastes 3.1-8

# Table of Contents

# Preface

This book is offered as a modest contribution to the struggle of Christians to come to terms with the issues of violence, peace and Gospel. It is not, however, a treatise on the "theology of war" in the Old Testament, nor is it a summary of what some might call the "teaching" of the Old Testament on warfare. Instead, I have tried to lay some historical groundwork, and to describe the nature of warfare in the Old Testament period within an historical framework. I have been descriptive because I believe that theories about the Old Testament and war and peace have often been formulated with little reference to the reality of ancient warfare, or with little understanding of what is to be found in the Old Testament. It is my firm belief that theories based on a lack of knowledge are less than useful. The Old Testament offers us conflicting images of human behaviour, from the compassionate and the caring, to the brutal and inhuman. Any honest chronicle of human history would offer no other picture. With the Old Testament, however, there are deeper problems.

For centuries the Old Testament has been honoured as the sacred Scripture of Judaism, and as part of the sacred Scripture of Christianity. As such it presents standards of behaviour to be emulated, and images of God which provide models of his character and activity. In both religious traditions it posssesses authoritative status. Here rests the problem. Not only is God seen as the caring shepherd, but also as the victorious warrior. Anthropomorphic representations of the deity are common and sometimes helpful in Scripture, but the sensitive reader must surely raise the question of the appropriateness of the image of God demonstrating the most violent and destructive side of human activity. To see what that image involves I have, of necessity, had to describe what it meant to be a soldier in ancient Israel.

The interpretive section of the book is left to the last chapter, not because I think it unimportant, but rather because I think the descriptive task is more important at the present time. With some of the material offered here I trust that theoretical thinkers and theologians can work to make sense of it all, and to try and draw it into the synthesis of Christian Theology.

I have approached the task from what may generously be called the "military history" angle, rather than from a theological point of view. I have consciously avoided the latter, and have sought to bring to bear on the topic the insights and analytical methods of modern military history. Those writers who have influenced my approach I name with gratitude. Apart from the classic treatises on the theory of war by Machiavelli, Du Picq, von Clausewitz and Sun Tzu, and the important works from the annals of military history, such as Caesar's *Gallic War*, Josephus's *Jewish War*, Homer's *Iliad*, Xenophon's *Persian Expedition* (the *Anabasis*), Froissart's *Chronicles* and countless other records of wars, campaigns and battles, I have been most influenced by the "new wave" of modern writers. Gwynne Dyer's popularization of the complex issues of soldiering opened up new angles of vision, as did the important studies by Elmar Dinter, and Richard Holmes, all listed in the selected bibliography. I would aiso like to thank the latter for the generous time afforded me on a brief visit to talk over matters of military history. Four books stand out as most influential. One is N.F. Dixon's *On the Psychology of Military Incompetence*, which, if the topic were not so tragic, would rank as one of the more humourous ventures into the military mind. Richard Holmes's *Acts of War: The Behaviour of Men in Battle* has presented a masterful synthesis of the physical and psychological effects of battle upon the individual soldier. Few books on military history have had such deep impact on the practice and the reading of military history as the brilliant *Face of Battle*, and more recently *Mask of Command*, both by John Keegan, and their profound effect on my own thinking needs to be gratefully acknowledged. I also wish to record my gratitude and indebtedness to my colleague and friend, Dr. P. Kenneth Jackson of McMaster Divinity College, whose patience with my obsession, and whose warm encouragement were most appreciated. The same holds true for Diane Jacobs-Malina and Bruce J. Malina of Omaha, Nebraska, who first suggested that I put down on paper my thoughts on warfare in the Old Testament period which had been accumulating over the past several years.

On the matter of footnotes I have sought to be as helpful as possible to the reader. Bearing in mind that this is not an academic thesis, I have taken the position that the footnoting of each assertion is not necessary. I have included a very small number of footnotes, usually of quotations with full bibliographical references. At the end of the book is an additional list of volumes related to the general topic, and the reader who wishes to probe matters further can consult that list.

I have never seen combat, and therefore can never know the range of emotions which such an experience evokes in the human breast. Those studies and memoirs I have consulted often fill me with a sense of thankfulness for the people who fought on my behalf in a succession of wars, and also for the good fortune of not having to have fought myself. I do not subscribe to that school of thought which regards military experience, especially combat, as a better builder of character than more peaceful dedication to the betterment of society and the lot of one's fellow human beings. Had I had the experience I might have benefitted from it and become stronger in spirit, but, on the other hand, I might have finished up, like so many men, physically and emotionally damaged almost beyond repair. To such victims of war, from the nameless Israelite spear-carrier, to the modern paratrooper, this book is offered as a gesture of memorial. To one in particular, Sergeant Leonard George Hobbs, Royal

Engineers, who fought well and honourably and had his fill of combat and excitement, this book is respectfully dedicated. He was my father, and he died too soon.

T.R. Hobbs
Divinity College
McMaster University

# Introduction

The purpose of this small book is to introduce the reader
to the historical and cultural context of warfare in the Old
Testament. In an age when warfare is a dirty word for an
increasing number, and in which there appears to be a
growing movement dedicated to peace and motivated by
strong religious feelings, the subject of this book might seem
out of place. Why take a distasteful topic such as warfare,
and from an age which has little or nothing to do with the
modern world, and expound it? It is not simply an exercise
in academic irrelevancy? I think not, for several reasons.

First, let us look at some facts. An increasing segment of
the worldwide Christian community is repulsed by warfare,
and many sensitive people find the spectre of nations and
groups organizing themselves so that their young men can be
equipped and trained to kill the young men of other nations
and groups repulsive. Further, since the Protestant Reforma-
tion in the sixteenth century in Europe, so-called "peace
churches" have arisen. Prominent among these are the ana-
baptists, later called the Mennonites. These Christians took
seriously the words of Jesus about rendering to Caesar and
to God what belonged to each. They took a stand on institutional violence. Whatever skills and abilities the members of
these churches possessed, they were determined not to use
them in destructive and violent behaviour. Article XIV of
the Dordrecht Confession puts it simply:

> Regarding revenge, whereby we resist our enemies with
> the sword, we believe and confess that the Lord Jesus has
> forbidden his disciples and followers all revenge and resis-
> tance...[1]

Alongside the Mennonites now stand the Society of Friends, historically a later group, but whose devotion to the cause of peace is well-known.

It is to groups like these, and to the thousands of individual believers who love peace and work for peace, that the first part of the Christian Scriptures, the Old Testament, is an embarrassment. Much of this collection of books is taken up with stories of conflict between individuals (Cain and Abel), and groups (the Slaughter of the Shechemites in Gen. 34); of wars between peoples (the Conquest stories of Joshua and Judges, and the battles of the books of Samuel and Kings). Not only this, but rules and regulations for warfare are given (Deut. 20) which seem particularly brutal in their effect on a defeated enemy. Psalms are written which praise God for victory in battle (Ps. 18), and bound up with the eschato-logical (final) vision for the Kingdom of God, is the violent destruction of the enemies of the people of God (Isa. 66.22-24). It is difficult to integrate this material into a theological system which holds the absence of conflict and violence in high regard. And many attempts to use the Old Testament in a theology of peace tend to be highly selective in their choice of material.

On the other hand, in spite of the admirable history of religious groups such as the Mennonites and Friends, and in spite of the noble concerns of other Christians in the "peace movement", it must be noted that in the context of the world-wide Christian community, they are probably in the minority. Other well-intentioned Christians do not think it inconsistent to be followers of Jesus Christ, and at the same time to take up arms either in defensive or offensive wars. Throughout the history of Christianity, right up to the present day, wars

---

[1] The text of the Dordrecht Confession can be found in W.L. Lumpkin *Baptist Confessions of Faith* [revised edition] (Valley Forge, PA:Judson Press, 1969):73ff.

conducted by so-called Christian countries of the world have been sanctioned by the presence of chaplains within the ranks of the fighting soldiers, and supported by the prayers of the people on the home front. This was a fact of military life not only when the "christian" armies of the crusades embarked on sacred wars against unbelievers, but also in wars in which both participants were nominally Christian. In the "Hundred Years War" in fourteenth-century Europe, the eye-witness and chronicler, Froissart, frequently refers to the celebration of the Mass before battles between Christian England and Christian France. One of the most eloquent sermons in the homilies of the twentieth-century church, Helmut Thielicke's, *Silence of God*, was preached by a German pastor to a congregation whose sons and brothers were fighting and dying for the cause of Nazism at the gates of Stalingrad. The inconsistency of priests or chaplains of opposing armies both praying for victory seemed not to have occurred to those who fought in or observed the conflict. The notion of fighting for one's way of life, particularly when that way of life is bound up with certain religious attitudes and practices, is accepted by many people, and when pressed for a reason, many will turn to the example set by the Old Testament.[2]

On the one hand then, the warlike nature of so much of the Old Testament is a stumbling block to many devout readers, and on the other hand, appeal is made to its example of violent and destructive behaviour. This is, of course, a

---

[2]See the fascinating study by F. Anderson *A People's Army: Massachusetts Soldiers and Society in the Seven Years' War* (New York: Norton, 1984), especially ch. 7 "Victory Undoubtedly Comes from the Lord", which analyses the religious disposition of many of the soldiers who fought in this war. An interesting book is J. Simmons *Winning Wars The Spiritual Dimension in Military Art* (New York: University Press of America, 1986), which puts forward the thesis that history demonstrates that the morally upright and religiously orthodox tend to win wars

During the English Civil War a volumes of exhortations was published by Robert Ram, a Parliamentarian. The title page of the volume contains the words, ". . . The Soldiers Catechisme: Composed for the Parliaments Army: Consisting of Two Parts: Wherein are Chiefly Taught: 1. The Justification, 2. The Qualifications, of our Soldiers. Written for the Incouragement and Instruction of all that have taken up Armes in this Cause of God and his People; especially the Common Souldiers." There follow quotations from 2 Sam. 10.12 and Deut. 23.9. See also the list of sermons in Anderson *A People's Army* Appendix D, pp. 257-262.

simplification of what is a much more complex issue, but it does set out the broad lines of the matter.

An additional complicating factor is that much of the literature dealing with the topic of warfare in the Old Testament tends to be less than helpful when it comes to interpretation of the topic. There are several books which deal with themes of warfare, such as the concept of "holy war", or "the divine warrior" motif, but they tend to be reworking of themes rather than interpretation. What I mean by this is that they organize material found in the text of the Old Testament in a systematic way, but avoid questions of historical meaning. For example, Why does ancient Israel have a notion of "holy war"? To what end was it used and why? What social and political relevance did a "divine warrior" motif have in the history and life of ancient Israel? Further, is it possible to see any relevance of this to Christian Theology?

There is also a number of books which purport to be "military histories" of the Old Testament period. Two facts become evident however; on the one hand they are well-intentioned expositions of the "great battles" of the time, and on the other, most, if not all of these books are written by military personnel.[3] This is no condemnation of the authors, but the reader should be aware of course that the military training that most of these authors underwent, and the "military mind" that it produced, carry with them their own set of assumptions about the nature of the world and the nature of history. It is no surprise then that those involved in the profession of arms should see the course of history dependent upon a series of "great" and decisive battles in which that profession is practised.

Finally, there are several works written to deal with the "problem" of warfare in the Old Testament, and they are written with a distinctly Christian bias, and one must add, a

---

[3]See, for example, R. Gale *Great Battles of Biblical History* (London: Hutchinson, 1968); M. Gichon, Ch, Herzog *Battles of the Bible* (London: Wiedenfeld & Nicholson, 1978); J. Liver [ed.] *The Military History of the Land of Israel in Biblical Times* (Jerusalem: Maaracoth, 1964) [Hebrew].

modern Christian bias. For example, one volume with the title *The Problem of War in the Old Testament*,[4] by the late Peter Craigie, fails to deal critically with the question begged by the title. For whom is warfare in the Old Testament a problem? It is clear from a reading of the Old Testament itself that the act of war was *not* a problem for the ancient Israelites. The Old Testament is full of examples of warfare, and there is no evidence to suggest that warfare *per se* is regarded as even a necessary evil. It is taken for granted as a part of life. For example, when Joab killed an adversary his death was ordered by David, not simply because he had killed, but because he had killed at the wrong time. He had avenged in a time of peace, blood which had been shed in war (1 Kings 2.5-6) and, what was probably worse, because of his association with David had implicated David in his deed, thus bringing dishonour to his lord. To go back to another illustration, note that in Gen. 34 the motivation for the action of the sons of Jacob, and the motivation for the reaction of Jacob to what his sons had done—killed all the males of the city of Shechem by deceit—is not "right and wrong" or "good and evil", as though these were absolute values. Rather the motivation is defence of honour. Dinah had been raped, bringing dishonour to the family. This deed had to be avenged, and it was. Jacob's reaction to the slaughter was based on his understanding that since his family had done such a serious thing to another family, he could expect revenge. So he chose to move south. We shall return to this later, but for the moment I will stress the point again: in the Old Testament killing a fellow human being in the course of an armed conflict between groups or nations is taken for granted. The notion which lies at the heart of the modern "peace movement", that killing another "child of God" is wrong, is not echoed at all in the Old Testament. The personages found within the pages of the Old Testament and the writers who record their stories cannot be treated simplistically as "people like us."

---

[4]P. Craigie *The Problem of War in the Old Testament* (Grand Rapids: Eerdmans, 1978).

This is an important point, and needs some expansion. It is a truism to say that the world of the Old Testament is different from ours. But like all truisms, it happens to be true, and the implications of its truth need to be taken seriously. Let us sketch these differences.

First, there is the obvious chronological difference. The Old Testament stories are set in a period approximately from 1800 B.C. to approximately 400 B.C., although the literature of the Old Testament comes from a later span of time. This is an age of great empires rising and falling, and caught in the middle, often like a ball in a basket, are Israel and Judah, tossed about by the giant waves of history around them. Probably the most important aspect of this time is the level of its technology. This is an age in which the only source of energy was either human or animal strength. To move from one place to another, one either walked, or—more rarely—rode in a chariot or on the back of an animal. Manufacturing, such as it was, was done with the force of the human arm aided by fire. In terms of warfare in the Old Testament period this is important. For one thing it affected the nature of the wars that were waged, and the nature of the battles that were fought within those wars. Troops went into battle mostly on foot, and the weapons they used were simple ones by today's standards, able to be powered—thrown or pulled—by the human arm alone. The quality of the materials was relatively poor. The obvious effect these factors have on the conduct of battle is that battles were much more dependent upon the physical strength of the participants than "firepower". With few exceptions, "firepower" was notoriously inaccurate and much more dependent upon factors like wind and weather. Battles were close order affairs in which the participants looked into the eyes of, wrestled with the arms of, and smelled their opponents as they fought.

Another important difference between the Old Testament age and our own in connection with our topic of warfare is the nature of the society. For most of the period we are going to deal with, ancient Israel and Judah were, to use the technical terms, "centralized bureaucracies". At the top and centre was the king and his court, and under the control of the king the resources of the land, both human and material.

This was a major change from the time before the monarchy when, according to most recent work on the period, the society was much more "egalitarian" in its goals if not its reality. An obvious effect of warfare is that the king decided, often with the aid of advisers whose positions were dependent upon the king (a kind of cleft stick), when to go to war, and with whom. He had no parliament or congress to place checks and balances on his activities. He was a despot. It is in such a social structure that "grand strategy" and "foreign policy" become possible, and instead of the defensive wars of the period of the judges, Israelites and Judaean armies move outside the borders of Israel and Judah to conquer the land of neighbouring monarchs. Thus is created an empire, which needs vast amounts of resources, in both personnel and goods, to be properly maintained. Bureaucrats are needed to run the new system, and soldiers are needed to police it and defend it.

This kind of social change imposes strains on the traditional way of life, structured more around notions of kinship. An important issue to be borne in mind is whether the new system can deal adequately with the problems it creates, with its use of the manpower of the people, in new ways.

Another difference between the Old Testament period and our own is the most important indeed. It concerns the question of the values of the society. Closely linked to questions of cultural and social values are questions of motivation. We have already noted that warfare, and other kinds of armed conflict, are taken for granted in the Old Testament world. An important question is, Why? Why did people of that society and culture choose to settle differences by fighting, and frequently killing, when to us the more reasonable course of action would be to talk out these differences, and seek a kind of compromise? The operative phrase here, of course, is "to us", and when looking at ancient historical material, such as the Old Testament, we must beware of "using the ancient world as a springboard for a [modern] . . . polemic."[5]

[5]M.I. Finley *Ancient Slavery and Modern Ideology* (Harmondsworth: Penguin Books, 1980): 63.

To explore this point a little, let us examine some assumptions in a recently published article on war and the Old Testament, entitled "War, Religion and Scripture", written again by the late Peter Craigie.[6] The article deals with the important and perplexing problem of the relationship of organized violence, religious "thought" and the role of scripture in the three great religious traditions of Judaism, Christianity and Islam. Of necessity, the article is little more than a survey of the topics, but offers some insights worthy of comment.

The article begins with an acknowledgement of the difficulty of reconciling the notion of "religion" with the warlike and militaristic character of much of the behaviour of human beings inspired by religion. There is for him ". . . a fundamental discrepancy between the tenets of the major religions and their involvement in warfare" (p. 4). For a definition of warfare, Craigie turned to a political philosopher of the period known as the Enlightenment, Thomas Hobbes, and the Prussian military strategist, Carl von Clausewitz. Hobbes's important book, *Leviathan* [7] was published in 1651, and von Clausewitz's classic *On War* [8] was published posthumously in 1832. For Hobbes, in war ". . . the notions of right and wrong, justice and injustice, have . . . no place." and for the Prussian ". . . to introduce into the philosophy of war itself a principle of moderation would be an absurdity." This creates a moral dilemma when seen in the context of religious ideals. To find a way out of this dilemma, Craigie suggests that "religious attitudes to war" must be seen in the larger context of "religious attitudes to the state" since the state is generally the unit which goes to war. In the notion of the state war might indeed be legitimate, but ". . . from the moral perspective of the majority of the religious traditions,

[6]P. Craigie "War, Religion and Scripture" *The Bulletin of the Canadian Society of Biblical Studies* (1986).

[7]T. Hobbes *Leviathan* [edited with an Introduction by C.B. MacPherson] (Harmondsworth: Penguin Books, 1968). Originally published in 1651.

[8]Carl von Clausewitz *On War* [edited with an Introduction by a Rapoport] (Harmondsworth: Penguin Books, 1968). Originall published in 1832.

violence is evil " (p. 6). Craigie's solution is to argue for a compromise between the evil reality of warfare, often necessary to the existence of a state, and the moral claims of religion, which sees violence as evil. The details of the argument to reach these conclusions are not important, because we are more concerned with the *assumptions* with which the article begins.

To make the point as briefly and as directly as possible, on the one hand it is a highly selective reading of history which can state that "... from the perspective of the majority of the religious traditions violence is evil." It is not only the fanatics who fight and kill in the name of religion, and the Old Testament bears ample testimony to religious warfare. On the other hand, Craigie treats concepts of religion and the state in a thoroughly modern way, as though religion were a free-standing institution of society, and as though the concept of nation-state is uncritically applicable to ancient Israel and Judah. In the world of the Old Testament it is anachronistic to think of "religion" as though it were organically unrelated to other institutions of society such as economy (adaptation), kinship (belonging) and polity (organization and structure), or as though it were a free set of ideas about metaphysics. These institutions are like four pillars supporting a building, each dependent upon the others. By seeing warfare in context in ancient Israel we can understand it. As Professor Michael Howard expressed it, "The roots of victory and defeat often have to be sought far from the battlefield, in political, social and economic factors which explain why armies are constituted the way they are, and why their leaders conduct them in the way they do." [9]

The culture of ancient Israel was dominated by concepts of kinship/belonging, and intimately bound up with kinship is the religious ideology of the people. After all, is not the God of Israel the God of the "fathers, Abraham, Issac and Jacob"? Is not Israel itself called a "family" (Amos 3.2) and do not familial terms predominate in descriptions of the

[9]M. Howard *The Causes of War* [2nd enlarged edition] (Cambridge, Mass: Harvard University Press, 1983), p. 196-197.

people's relationship to God? If then God is seen in some way as a "father-figure" of the people, and the members of the group or nation are seen as kin, either real, as in the exposition of the tribal system in Israel, or imagined (fictive), as in the designation "children of Israel" for the whole body, does this not lead to a rather closed view of the group? One only has project the sense of the small family on to the whole to realise what this entails. If one "belongs" to such a group, then any threat to any one member of the group is a threat to all, and, by the same token, any threat to the limits the group has established for itself is a threat to the individual members of the group. Israel captured this sense in the concept of "covenant". In such an understanding of society, "religion" in the way understood in Craigie's article is unthinkable. If there be a "religion" it is the ideology which gives the group its founding stories, identifies members of the group, and perpetuates the "sense" of the group.

Just to make the point from a slightly different perspective, think of the dominant social institution in North American society, of the ones named above. It is the concern with adaptation to our environment, in exploitive capacity, namely economics. Politics is dominated by the economy, and the rise and fall of the currency is probably of more direct concern to individuals than the intricacies of foreign policy; families are classified according to monetary income level; and the decline or rise in church membership is treated with the same presuppositions as the rise and fall of the stock market index. The institution is supported by an ideology, which has all the trappings of a "religion". Traditions are created and perpetuated to ensure that "the great spirit of free enterprise" was the dominant ideology in the minds of those who developed both Canada and the United States. The question of belonging is answered by value being placed in individuals in terms of their income and disposable wealth, and it hardly needs demonstrating that the social organization of our countries is dominated by concerns of material wealth.

Within this system warfare is thinkable and justifiable if it can be argued to be in defence of "national interests" understood in terms of the political-economic ideology. So North

Americans are willing to go to war to defend capitalism against communism, as in Korea, Vietnam and in Central and South America.

Now we seem to have come a long way from our initial concern with warfare in the Old Testament, but, on reflection we have not wandered far. In both cases, the ancient and the modern, I am suggesting that questions of warfare must be seen in a broader context than simply ideas about warfare. As I have indicated there is an historical, social and cultural context which provides a more comprehensive understanding of warfare in the Old Testament period. But this involves an enormous amount of material, so the next question is: How does one chart out this context so that the information needed can be managed in a meaningul and helpful way? The question is fraught with difficulties, not the least is that the kind of information from which we seek to develop as full a picture as possible of ancient Israelite society is sparse. The historical data afforded by the Old Testament itself are small scraps of information which do not make up a very full picture. The Old Testament was written for purposes other than informing the twentieth-century academic historian. How do we do a responsible job of understanding ancient Israelite society, when the raw data which the sociologist or historian of the modern world takes for granted are just not available? How can we talk about "culture" and "values" when we are now unable to interview the ancient Israelite "man in the street" about his opinions?

In a recent book, *Ancient History: Evidence and Models*, Sir Moses Finley states:

> "The ancient historian cannot be a cliometrician in a serious way, but he can resort to a second-best procedure through the use of non-mathematical models, *thereby controlling the subject of his discourse by selecting the variables he wishes to study*" [emphasis mine].[10]

[10]M.I. Finley *Ancient History: Evidence and Models* (New York: Viling Books, 1986):60

In other words, a reasonably responsible analysis of an ancient society can be undertaken through the use of *models* of society developed elsewhere. To continue with Finley's description,

> "A model has been defined as a simplified structuring of reality which presents supposedly significant relationships in a generalised form. Models are highly subjective approximations in that they do not include all associated observations or measurements, but as such they are valuable in obscuring incidental detail and in allowing *fundamental aspects of reality* to appear. This selectivity means that models have varying degrees of probability and a limited range of conditions over which they apply."[11]

A model then is a convenient framework within which data can be classified and relationships between data understood. Instead of allowing the historian to "tell all he knows about XX" in the fashion of school examinations, it encourages the historian to place what he knows into some kind of reasonable synthesis, and to make judgments on relationships between the data. It is an exercise in typology. The process suggests that, allowing for certain variables, similar organizations or institutions can be understood in similar ways. The use of models in this way is based on the principle of observation from which several consistent factors emerge. From these factors a basic framework is constructed within which other similar phenomena can be examined. This is a more common mode of thinking than most of us realise, and some would argue that it is universal. We understand new experiences by fitting them into models (constructs) of reality which we have unconsciously developed from past experiences. If we were unable to do this, or if we reacted to *every* new experience without any previous reference points, we would be unable to handle life and become insane. But I do not want to labour what is a fairly obvious point.

---

[11] Finley *Ancient History*: 60.

Throughout the course of the following pages we shall be using various models of society and groups which have been developed to understand our general topic of warfare in the Old Testament. But this approach does not destroy the particularity of ancient Israel and Judah, and we will need to illustrate our points frequently with evidence from these two societies. We need to look at the society of ancient Israel, both from the point of view of its social structure and its political structures. We also need to know something of the cultural values of ancient Israel, its ideological support, and finally we need to understand how the presence of a well-organised military sub-structure affects such a society. In what follows what we shall be able to do is to broaden our perspective on the topic of warfare in the Old Testament. As I stated at the beginning of this work, we are adopting a "military historical" approach to the topic because I believe that it is needed. But, looking at the familiar material in this way we shall learn new things. We shall not answer all questions that might occur to us, but we shall probably ask new ones, and in our search develop a larger picture of the phenomenon of warfare. In so doing we shall be better informed to discuss some of the theological implications of the topic.

When writers on the Old Testament talk of history they do not often make some very elementary distinctions about the precise definition of that "history". The reality of "history" exists at more than one level. First, there is the event, or series of events (actions) which are the subject of study. Second, there is the reality that the reporter, the historian, seeks to pass on to the reader. Among other things, the historian is a sifter, and an interpreter, so there is always a certain amount of subjectivity in what is done. This is no less true of the Old Testament historian than it is of the modern historian. Some would argue that it is more true of the Old Testament writer. Third, there is the reality that the record of the event creates. If the reporter/historian is concerned with answering a limited number of questions, then the reader is guided to look at the events of the past in terms of those questions alone. It should also create in the serious reader an awareness of the range of nuances in a collection of material like the Old Testament.[12] Not only was the Old Testament composed over a long period of time, but it also represents the literary output of different sectors of the ancient Israelite community. Royal scribes, priests, workers, prophets, politicians, farmers all work within different social and political restraints, and their words reflect this. Their common experience was the reality of the violent days in which they lived and the practice of warfare they would have witnessed. If they wrote about this common experience they would write from a distinct perspective with an element of subjectivity. In their further reflection on this common experience they would produce that grand "umbrella" which has been labelled "the faith of ancient Israel". But this "faith" is neither monolithic nor permanent. It changed as new experiences helped interpret the past. In the penultimate chapter we shall explore some of the possibilities of this phenomenon further.

I offer a reminder to the reader. The subtitle of this book is "An Introduction to Warfare in the Old Testament". It is no more than that, an outline of the subject, seen perhaps from a different angle, but only an outline. In the final chapter I shall explore some of the implications of what we discover for the formulation of a Christian response to warfare in the Old Testament. These are no more than suggestions, but, based as they will be on a firmer historical foundation than has thus been customary, they will be fresh and challenging.

[12]On views of history see D. Lowenthal *The Past is a Foreign Country* (Cambridge: Cambridge University Press, 1987).

# 1

# Historical Observations: The Judges

We need first to give our topic an historical context, but not simply in the sense of the correct chronology. Chronology is, of course, important, but it is not the sum total of history, and at times exaggerated claims can be made for its role in the writing of history. History should never be relegated to a string of dates or events, as though there was an unspoken connection between pieces of the chain. Rather than drawing a line through the course of history, it is better at times to pause and survey the landscape at specific periods of history. Our intention in this and the following chapter will be to sketch some of the major changes Israel experienced in those years in which the Israelites occupied the land of Canaan. We shall survey the people of Israel before and after the founding of the monarchy, and shall try to paint as broad a landscape as possible. This gives us a time frame of approximately seven hundred years, from the time when Israel appears as a people in Canaan around 1200 B.C., until the time of the invasions from the east and the incorporation of the nations of Israel and Judah into the Assyrian and Babylonian empires at the end of the eighth century (722 B.C.) and the early part of the sixth century (597, 586 B.C.). Our focus of attention will be briefly on the period known as the period of the Judges, from approximately 1200 to 1040 B.C. Then, in the following chapter we shall devote more attention to the period that Israel was a monarchy, that is from the

appointment of Saul as Israel's first king in approximately
1040 B.C., until the destruction of Jerusalem by the Babylonians in 586 B.C.

The reasons for this apparent imbalance are several. The
first is that it is at this later stage of history we first meet an
army in Israel organized in a systematic way. The second is
that the records of this period are fuller. The advent of a
monarchy meant the advent of bureaucracy, and a bureau-
crat's role is record keeping. The result is that we know far
more of this period than we do of the one that preceded it.
The third, is that we have a great deal of comparative
material from other societies surrounding Israel. Names of
specific bodies of troops, titles of officers and roles and functions of various soldiers can be illuminated by reference to
similar names and functions in the armies of the surrounding
nations. At times, where the necessary information is lacking
for Israel we can—with discretion—fill in some of the gaps
from what we know of other nations. As we shall see, there is
no indication in the Bible of the daily tasks and general lot of
the common soldier, but from some Egyptian documents
which warn of the uncomfortable life of Egyptian troops, we
can gain a fairly good idea of what it was like to be a foot
soldier at that time.

Now, having said this, we must also make clear that our
concentration on the period of the monarchy does not mean
that we will dismiss the period that preceded it, the period of
the Judges. It simply indicates that we cannot know too
much about this earlier period, for many reasons. There is a
serious academic debate going on about the reasons for the
emergence of Israel at the end of the second millennium
B.C., and it would be foolhardy to try in such a brief book to
decide one way or the other on the matter. Second, much of
the description of this period found in the literature is very
late. The so-called "Deuteronomistic History", (Joshua—
2 Kings) which contains most of our information on the
period, was put into its final form right at the end of the
period we are dealing with, that is, some time during the
exile of Judah in Babylon. It is therefore separated from the
events it describes in Judges 1 by some six hundred years. To
place this in some kind of perspective, imagine the com-

parable task of writing a modern history of the Hundred Years' War (A.D. 1337-1453) with only the barest of outlines, and the memories of eye-witnesses passed on by word of mouth over six centuries! We cannot escape the impression in one or two places that the stories of this period have been selected, rearranged, and retold in the light of later events, and perhaps in the service of later events and institutions. In some cases there is probable cause for suspecting a large dose of anachronism in the stories of Joshua.

Now, it is important to sketch some of the significant elements of this period. We begin with the stories of Joshua. The book of Joshua, part of the Deuteronomistic History, purports to tell the story of the conquest of Canaan by the Israelites under the command of Joshua ben Nun, a successor of Moses. The story as told has some features worthy of comment. In the first instance, the concern for order within the book is noteworthy. Joshua leads the tribes of Israelites across the Jordan, almost to a script, and camps them in the vicinity of Gilgal (Josh. 1-4). In chapter 5 the males are circumcised and for the first time the people eat the produce of the land.

In the following chapters is told probably the most well-known story in the whole Old Testament, the capture of the city of Jericho (Josh. 6-7). After a minor setback caused by the disobedience of Achan, the soldiers of Israel move up on to the central plateau to the north of Jerusalem and success-fully attack Ai, and defeat its army and the army of its neighbor Bethel. Following this success, Joshua is tricked into an alliance with the cities of Gibeon (Josh. 9), and he fights a pitched battle with a coalition of Canaanite kings who have come to force Gibeon out of its alliance with the Israelites. The battle results in a victory for the Israelites, and chapter 10 ends with a count of the kings defeated thus far in the campaign.

Chapter 11 recalls a battle in the north of the country against another coalition of Canaanites under Jabin of Hazor. The battle ends in victory for Joshua, and the north is secured. Chapter 12 offers a list of the Canaanite kings defeated in the complete campaign. Chapters 13-19 consist of the division of the land among the tribes. Chapter 20 tells of the establishment of cities of refuge for the protection of those who have killed another unintentionally. The following chapter lists the cities set aside for the levites, chapter 22 divides up the east side of the Jordan and the final two chapters tell of the covenant ceremony with which this whole period ends.

So much for the general outline of the book of Joshua, let us now look briefly at some of the questions which this picture of the occupation of Canaan raises. First, there is a large piece of the country, the central region known later as Ephraim, which is not mentioned in the narratives of conquest, nor are any kings from this region listed in Josh. 12. The only place where it figures is when Joshua goes to Shechem to sacrifice after the defeat of Ai and Bethel (Josh. 8.30-35). The absence of this large section of land would suggest that the narratives of Joshua are not a historical reconstruction of the conquest, since it is incomplete. There is evidence from the work of archaeologists at Shechem to show that Shechem was destroyed during the Late Bronze Age, but there is no Old Testament literary evidence to suggest that this was done by the invading Israelites. In fact, if it had been attacked by Israel, the absence of the conquest from the pages of the Old Testament is most surprising, unless the narratives have another purpose.

Second, there are some serious gaps in archaeological data in support of the story of the conquest, and this fact has been conveniently presented and analysed by J.M. Miller.[1] Most notable, probably because the story in Joshua 6-7 is the most dramatic, is the absence of any Late Bronze Age materials from Jericho and Ai. As archaeologists continue their work it is becoming clear that site after site yields no remains from this period, the very period in which Joshua is dated. To date, no satisfactory explanation of this phenomenon has been put forward. In support of the "historicity" of the book

[1]J.M. Miller "Archaeology and the Israelite Conquest of Canaan: Some Methodological Observations" *PEQ* 109 (1977): 87-93; see also B.S.J. Isserlin "The Israelite Conquest of Canaan: A Comparative Review of the Arguments Applicable" *PEQ* 115 (1983): 85-94.

of Joshua, there has been a tendency among some scholars to look for a thirteenth-century destruction level at many of the sites which have been excavated. It is argued that if such destruction levels can be found at the sites named in Joshua 12, then the historical reliability of the book of Joshua is confirmed. Unfortunately, the zeal with which this search is carried out is misplaced. One problem is the definition of "destruction level". Definitions range from thin layers of ash from burning to thick layers of destruction debris. But what if such layers are found? What do they prove? Even if thick layers of destruction debris are found at a certain site—and this is rare—how extensive are these layers? Given the method of archaeological excavation, it is very difficult to prove that the layer is consistent over the whole site. Further, what caused these layers? It is often assumed that it was the Israelites, but there are several problems with this. On the one hand there are other explanations for such destruction levels, such as a local conflagration with innocent causes, such as a domestic fire caused by the overturning of a pot. Another cause could be the attacks of the Philistines who were settling from the west at about the same time the Israelites came in from the east. And yet another cause could be the campaign of Pharaoh Merneptah, who led an army through Canaan in the same period. On the other hand, not all of the city-states mentioned in Joshua 12 were actually destroyed. "Smiting with the edge of the sword", an expression often used in the conquest stories, is what one does to armies or populations of cities, and Josh. 11.10-15 would suggest that the practice of burning cities to the ground was done very selectively. After all, why destroy what you would only have to rebuild?

A third, and more serious, problem with the stories as they appear in Joshua is that they stand in contradiction to the opening chapter of the book of Judges. Joshua ends with the old man, Joshua, "a long time after" the conquest (Josh. 23.1) calling the representatives of the settled tribes to a covenant ceremony which takes place in Josh. 24. However, Judges 1 opens with the events "after the death of Joshua", and it is obvious that the tribes have not yet begun to take what was promised them in the previous book.

Earlier scholars solved this problem either by insisting that the historicity of the book of Joshua was supported well enough by the archaeological evidence that was available, so that the "general picture" of the conquest could be maintained, or by opting for a theory of an "infiltration" of only certain of the tribes over a long period of time.[2] It was argued that somehow in the course of history the stories became retold in the light of the dominant ideology of the tribe that was in Egypt (possibly Ephraim), so that it appeared that all of Israel was in Egypt, and all of Israel took part in the "conquest."

A new alternative has been suggested in recent years. That is that most of the early Israelites were peasant farmers under the oppression of the Canaanite city-states, and they revolted against their overlords. The dominant ideology of the revolt was belief in Yahweh, the liberator from Egypt. The new society was "tribalized" and settled in the hill country to form an alternative way of living, different from the old system under which they suffered.This reconstruction, or application of a new "model" was first proposed by George Mendenhall in 1962. It was thoroughly researched and re-presented in a different form by Norman Gottwald in 1980 in his book *The Tribes of Yahweh*.[3]

We cannot argue the pros and cons of these positions here, nor do we have the space to discuss in detail the more recent approach of a number of recent scholars which attempts to see the rise of Israel in its international context, as part of the major changes which took place between 1400 B.C. and 1200 B.C. in the Middle East. These changes saw the decline of one-time great nations such as the Hittites,

---

[2]A few decades ago there was a vigorous debate between two "schools of thought" on this issue. See J. Bright *Early Israel in Recent History Writing* (London: SCM Press, 1956). In the third revised edition of his *A History of Israel* (Philadelphia: Westminster Press, 1981) Bright modified his position somewhat, but still maintained that the ambiguity of the archaeological evidence could not "flatly refute the theory of a thirteenth-century conquest" (p. 132).

[3]See N.K. Gottwald *The Tribes of Yahweh: A Sociology of the Religion of Liberated Israel. 1250-1050 BCE* (Maryknoll, New York: Orbis 1979). See also the seminal work by G.E. Mendenhall "The Hebrew Conquest of Palestine" *BA* 25 (1962): 66-87.

Mitani, the Assyrians, and the emergence of a new balance of power, and the spread of a new technology, the making of iron. The causes were varied, but the results were large migrations of population and a disruption of ancient trading patterns. It is argued by the scholars who put forward this "model", that this larger historical context suits the stories of the emergence of Israel in Canaan extremely well.[4]

We shall return to an understanding of the stories of the conquest later, but in order to understand the context of the wars of the period of the Judges we need to pause and survey the scene in more detail. To do this we move to something a little different, and try to sketch a picture of the *nature of the community during the period of the Judges.* It is easier to state what the social structure of the people of Israel in the period before the monarchy was *not* than to state with certainty what it was. As I said earlier, much of the material describing this period is from a later, literate age organized on different lines, and we have to make allowances for a certain amount of "overwriting" of older traditions. This is unavoidable. However, there are recent studies which have examined the period in detail and which offer us a wealth of information. To return to a point I made earlier, this information is not simply a listing of events in chronological order. For the period of the Judges that is a virtual impossibility, and if it were possible, would not be very helpful. We need to ask questions which elicit broader answers than these. If we want to understand some of the "why's" of warfare in this period, as well as some of the "what's", then we are compelled to look more closely at the kind of society that existed, and adopt what scholars have called a "synchronic" view of the period. Norman Gottwald's important book, *The Tribes of Yahweh*, which was published in 1980, is such a volume.

Among many other things Gottwald offers an important analysis of the catalogue of terms which are used as self-

[4]See J. Strange "The Transition from the Bronze Age to the Iron Age in the Eastern Mediterranean and the Emergence of the Israelite State" *Scandinavian Journal of the Old Testament* 1 (1987): 1-19.

designations of Israel from the period before the monarchy. Here we shall simply state the general conclusions of his work. The most important designation of Israel at this time is *people* [Heb: *'am*], which incorporates the general cultural limits of Israel. This would include the people who spoke the same language, or dialect, and who shared the same values, and ordered their lives according to those shared values. Gottwald suggests that this is to be distinguished from the more political designation of *people*, which is a translation of another Hebrew word *goy*. The word *assembly*, from the Hebrew *'edah* and *qahal* is the representative male body which made decisions on behalf of the whole. These are part of the political structure of the people.

The common word *tribe* [Heb: *shevet*], is on the one hand a technical organization for Israelite society, and is to be understood as a political subdivision associated with certain territory, but it is more than this, because the system is also patterned along lines of descent, each tribe from one father, in similar fashion to the whole of Israel. Synonyms for the *tribe* are words like *house* [Heb: *beth*] and *family* [Heb: *mishpachah*].

Beyond this, however, these latter words have other meanings. They are used to designate smaller collective units with the complete system. The *mishpachah* is a kind of "protective association", for mutual aid and assistance in times of threat to others of the group. Closely linked to this concept is the term *'elef*, "the *mishpachah* in arms." the military muster which the association could field in times of emergency. Finally, the *household* or the "autonomous extended family" [Heb: *beth 'ab*] is the smaller family unit. In diagrammatic form Gottwald sees the social structure as represented on the following page.

As we shall see, this is a different social structure from what followed during the time of monarchy. But beyond the structure itself, and the surface language used, we need to look deeper at the implied cultural values of such a society. All of the terms (house[hold], family, tribe and even *'elef*) with the exception of the term *Confederacy* are kinship terms, terms which define membership, belonging. The exception

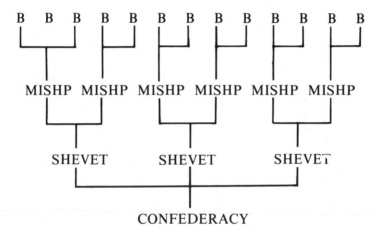

B = *beth'ab* (Household)   MISHP = *mishpachah* (Family, clan)
SHEVET = *shevet* (tribe)

however, is not a Biblical term itself, but a translation of the concept of the overall organization of the society which had cultic, military and juridical functions. The Bible incorporates this concept within the term *covenant*, the agreement which binds the groups together to each other and to God. This abundance of kinship terms is something worth pondering. Much of the debate on this formative period of Israel's history has revolved around appropriate *political* structural models, hence the concept of the Greek *amphictyony*, a confederation of separate groups for religious and political purposes, has formed the basic model for the period of the Judges in Israel. This is now being abandoned, and being replaced by other models, such as the one expounded by Gottwald. However, these models are still *political* ones. The specific terms used take us beyond the political structures to an underlying ideology of the relationships between the groups within the confederacy, and the members within the groups. The extension of family terms to the larger group is a projection of the concept of family on to the people as a whole. This means that the attitudes towards others in the larger group, and the responsibilities for others in the larger group are those one would exercise towards one's own immediate family. In the context of the ancient Mediterranean world, this has interesting implications for the way we interpret much of the Biblical material, and is of special importance for our understanding of the wars of this period. But before we examine those implications, let us look at some illustrations of the idea.

One biblical book which has been set in this early period, and which scholars believe to have retained much of the flavour of life from this period, even though its final literary form dates from a later time, is the book of Ruth. In modern thought the book appears to many to be a "romance", a story of love between a woman, Ruth, and the man she eventually marries, Boaz. But much more is going on in the story than romantic love. It is a story about belonging, about who is "in" and who is "out" of the social patterns of Israel. Ruth is left husbandless and childless, and under the ancient Israelite law, it is the duty of the brother of her dead husband to raise up children to carry on the family name. Boaz, it seems, is a close enough relative, and through the intricate customs the liaison is legitimately established, and eventually, Ruth is incorporated into the society. She marries Boaz, and gives birth to a son, Obed, David's grandfather. In this story two things are accomplished, the "Israeliteness" of Ruth and the legitimacy of David's ancestry are affirmed. The point I want to make is that the limits of the society are so well-established, that Ruth could not simply emigrate to Judaea and settle there. Literally, she had to "marry into" the tribe, and in the proper manner. In some sense her "Israeliteness" had already been granted by the fact that her former husband came from Bethlehem. Her marriage with Boaz formally sealed her membership.

With this in mind we return to the language of the socio-political structures of ancient Israel. The fact that the language of the family is used to describe this structure at this time is important. All such use of language reflects major presuppositions about how groups and societies should function. It provides a clue to the underlying values of that society. For example, today we talk often of the "social structures" or the "breakdown of society", and unconsciously we use language from engineering. Society for us westerners is more a machine than a body, or a family, as it was for the ancient Israelites (see Isa. 1, Amos 3.1). Machines can have parts replaced in the interests of efficiency. Bodies and families (at least in antiquity) have fixed limits. Within those limits the parts function in harmony, but to add something on to those entities is extremely difficult. This happened in only one way, by marriage, the making of "one flesh" of two independent human beings. A family could be enlarged by the production of more and more children, and normally marriage took place between a male and female of the same group. In this way the group's identity was preserved, and of course we must bear in mind that the "group" under discussion is not the western "nuclear family", but a much larger unit. The Old Testament abounds in illustrations of this (e.g. Gen. 24). Scholars call this kind of marriage *endogamous* (marriage within).[5]

---

[5]For a convenient study of this topic see R. Fox *Kinship and Marriage* (Harmondsworth: Penguin Books, 1967).

On occasion the group might wish to expand its relationships with others for a number of reasons. It might want to acquire land, enlarge its wealth (seen in the size of flocks), increase its security, or simply widen its sphere of influence. To achieve these ends marriage was again the means. This marriage was directed outside the group, and usually agreed upon by members of the group in negotiation with the intended partner group. This is called *exogamous* marriage (marriage outside), and a perfect illustration of this is found in Gen. 34. Note the rationale for the intermarriage between the Shechemites and the family of Jacob:

> "Then we will give our daughters to you, and we will take your daughters to ourselves, and we will dwell with you and become one people" (vs. 16).
> ". . . will not their cattle, their property and their beasts be ours? Let us agree with them, and they will dwell with us "(v. 23).

An illustration of a slightly different nature, but nevertheless making the same basic point, is found in the incident of the daughters of Zelophehad in Num. 27.1-11 and Num. 36.1-12. Here limits are placed on this kind of marriage, lest the borders become too wide.

The implications of this are that the group has a well-established sense of identity. Its limits are firmly fixed, and there are acceptable ways of extending those limits through intermarriage with another group, and the extension of the covenant to that group. As many have argued, this is an alternative way of living from the Canaanite city-state system which it sought to replace. In the period of the Judges we see this dominant group self-consciousness being supported by the social structure. That structure is tribal. The expectations of the members of the system are expressed in the story of the war between the Israelites and the Canaanites in Judges 4 and 5. In the Song of Deborah mutual aid between the tribal groups, in the spirit of Josh. 22 is expected, and those who do not fulfill this responsibility are criticized. Nor can the organization change too much. The attempt of Abimelech, the son of Gideon, to accept the position his father had

refused, that of king, meets with disaster and failure (Jud. 9).
It is necessary to make one or two further points in this
connection. Groups which are like the one described above,
having a strong sense of group identity, and clearly understood limits, have been studied in detail by various scholars—
sociologists and cultural anthropologists—and in addition
to having carefully defined limits, have a strong fear of pollution, both symbolic and actual. I have stated that the metaphor of a body figures prominently in the way the ancient
Israelites viewed their society. Such a notion, of course, is a
common one in the New Testament (see 1 Cor. 12.12-26),
but there it is not a new insight. It is found also in the
Prophet Isaiah's description of the society of ancient Judah
as a desperately ill body (Isa. 1.1-6), and it emerges from a
culture which carries this strong sense of group identity.
There is a strong connection between the way the group is
viewed and the way the individual body is viewed. Entrances
and exits to the socio-political body, which include the gate
in the walls of a city, the door of a house, and the fortresses
on the country's borders, and entrances and exits to the
physical body, which include the mouth, the vagina and the
anus, are guarded carefully in ancient Israelite culture. This
cultural stance is reflected in Old Testament laws, notably in
the book of Leviticus, chapters 13-18. What one eats is regulated, who can have sexual intercourse with whom is regulated, and where one puts bodily wastes is regulated. This
pattern has been examined by the anthropologist Mary
Douglas in her excellent book *Purity and Danger*.[6] Important in this scheme are the physical and symbolic limits placed
on the group, defined at this stage in terms of kinship. Of the
four types of groups she delineates, the society of ancient
tribal Israel resembles the "strong group" type. Characteristic
of this group is the strength of its social control, and its
definition of belonging.

[6]See M. Douglas *Purity and Danger: An Examination of the Concepts of Pollution and Taboo* (London: Routledge & Kegan Paul, 1972).

When Jesus told his disciples, "... if the eye is not sound, then the whole body is full of darkness" (Matt. 6.23), he was expressing what to an ancient Israelite, as well as a first-century Jew, would be an obvious point. Sickness, deformity or damage to one part of the body affects the whole body. Unlike the machine, this damaged part cannot be replaced. Similarly, the threat of, or actual penetration of the body by illegitimate means, affects the whole—this is the basis of the dietary laws of the Bible, and adultery (illegitimate intercourse) defiles the whole, including the land.

Against this background we can now return finally, to the questions of warfare in this period. So bearing in mind the kind of society we are dealing with, let us sketch briefly the wars (more properly battles) of this period as they are recorded in the book of Judges.

Chapter 1 provides a summary of the displacement of various Canaanite populations by the Israelite tribes, and a record of the failure of many of the tribes to take control of many of the strategic parts of the country. Most of the cities left in the hands of the Canaanites are important fortresses and trading centers along the main trunk road from Egypt to Mesopotamia, the so-called "Via Maris", which passed through Canaan. Chapter 2 begins the "rhythm" of the book in which the Israelites worship local gods, are given over into the hands of the local powers, and are then delivered by a "judge". Chapter 3 and following begins the naming of these judges, these deliverers of Israel.

We will not name them all, but select some of the more well-known ones. Ehud delivered Israel from Eglon, the invading Moabite King (3.12-20), Deborah and Barak defeated the Canaanite armies of Jabin of Hazor commanded by Sisera (4.1-5.31). Gideon defeats the invading Midianites (6.1-8.28), and Jephthah defeats the harrassing Ammonites (11.1-40). Most famous of all the judges, Samson, did his inadequate best to rid the southwest of the Philistines (13.1-16.31). Finally, although not mentioned in the book of Judges, a later incident certainly belongs in this period. These are the incidents recalled in 1 Sam. 4.1-7.11 and which concern the incursions of the Philistines north along the coastal plain, as far as Ebenezer, the loss of the Ark of the Covenant, the intervention of Yahweh and the eventual release of the Ark, and the defeat of the Philistines in the hill country near Mizpeh. All of these conflicts have one thing in common. They are defensive battles, designed to protect the group from outside attack. Such attacks had as their main goal the elimination of the group as a group from the soil of Canaan. At stake in these wars is the very existence of the new society, Israel, the people of God. In all cases there is penetration of the territory upon which Israel has settled. Eglon, with an alliance of Ammonites and the elusive Amalekites, invaded across the Jordan and took Jericho, "the city of Palms" (Jud. 3.13), to exercise control over Israel for eighteen years. Judging by the initial reaction of Deborah and Barak to the movements of Jabin of Hazor (Jud. 4.10), the strategy of Jabin was to dislodge the Israelites from Galilee. This was a repetition of the strategy in Josh. 11.

Gideon fought off invading Midianites, and Jephthah defended Gilead, in the north of the Transjordan, from attacks of the Ammonites to the south. Samson tries unsuccessfully to defend the Shephelah, the low-lying foothills to the southwest of the Judaean highlands, from the incursions of the Philistines, only to witness the shrinking of the territory of Dan in the southwest. Finally, the people lose the Ark by trying to ward off the Philistine incursion, and eventually defeat the Philistines deep in the heart of Israelite territory at Mizpeh.

Each of the invaders is a well-established, highly organised military machine. Some are led by "kings", such as Moab, Ammon, the Canaanites. Others, like the Philistines, have a well-deserved reputation for battle skills and organization, and most encounters with them from records outside the Bible are armed conflicts—a reputation they bring with them on to the pages of the Old Testament. The only exception is the Midianite army, whose equipment and organization seems a little more haphazard but whose intentions are clearly invasion and pillage. To a society like pre-monarchical Israel, which was a closely knit, clearly delimited group, such invasions were life-threatening, and needed to be resisted. We shall turn later, in another chapter, to the deeper reasons for violent resistance to such attacks. We note at present that such resistance is consistent with Israel's self-consciousness. The limits of the body are under threat, and this threat must be resisted.

There is another aspect of warfare in this period which needs to be seen in this broader context, and that is the major "civil wars" which took place apparently at the end of the period. This civil war is a conflict between the tribes within the covenant/confederacy. I am not talking here about the political tensions and jealousies between tribes or groups which are evident if one reads "between the lines" of certain stories, for example, the betrayal of Samson to the Philistines by the men of a Judaean village (Jud. 15.9-13), or even the tensions created by Gideon's fight with the Midianites and the jealousies and suspicions this aroused in Ephraim and the men of Succoth and Penuel (Jud. 8.13-28). These tensions are important, historically, but of not direct concern here. Instead I am talking of the larger tensions which resulted in open armed conflict between the tribes. The civil war under discussion is the fight between the tribes and the small tribe of Benjamin which comprises the final chapters of the book of Judges (19-21).

Now there are many dynamics to this story, some of which we can only touch upon. In the context of the book of Judges, the stories which end the book are "set up" well by what precedes it. Samson's story, despite its Sunday school romanticism, is a story of failure. Samson does not succeed in keeping the Philistine threat at bay, and his suicide leaves the situation as it opens in the books of Samuel, with the Philistines posing an even greater threat to the existence of Israel. With the story of Samson there are also hints that the fabric of Israelite society is far from whole. The villagers of Judah (Lehi) betray Samson to the Philistines (Jud. 15.9-13). The story of Samson is followed by the tale of disobedience with the migration of Dan from its allotted location on the western coastal edge of the tribe of Benjamin to the north of the territory, and the story of the Danites, brutality is told with alarming frankness. If these chapters tell an historical tale, then the relocation of Dan seems logical. In their position on the coast, they were astride the ancient trunk route and directly in the path of the expanding Philistines. But such rationalizations are not in the mind of the writer. Within the story which closes the book of Judges there are many dynamics. The traveller (a levite) and his servant and concubine decide not to stay overnight at Jebus, the "city of foreigners". In other words, he wishes to enjoy the hospitality of his own people, the Benjaminites who are bound in covenant relationship with the other tribes. The brutal fate of the concubine demonstrates the excesses to which the men of Gibeah went to abuse the principles of hospitality to a fellow Israelite and his entourage (to say nothing of the cavalier and brutal treatment of the woman in the group.) The story continues with the negotiations between the other tribes and Benjamin over the culprits and perpetrators of this serious breach in "family behaviour". The Gibeah-inhabitants are adamant, and refuse to hand them over. The result is a vicious civil war in which Benjamin is almost wiped out. The tribe is eventually saved through the kidnapping of women from Shiloh to perpetuate the name of the youngest son of Jacob.

The story is rich in so many things, and speaks volumes of the customs of such a closed society, and the need for survival. The reason for the war against Benjamin is primarily that the behaviour of the men of Gibeah, and the failure of the rest of Benjamin to live up to covenant obligations threatened the very life of the covenant community. It was as much a threat to the existence of the new society as was invasion from outside. The body was not working harmoniously, and the treatment was radical surgery. The same attitude is betrayed in Jesus' words in Matt. 5.30.

In this chapter we have looked at the type of society (so far as we can determine) that existed in the period of the judges. It was a closely knit society, defined internally in terms of kinship, and distinguished from other societies roundabout by strong symbolic boundaries. These boundaries are also expressed in terms of kinship. Such language helps to define who belongs and who does not, and any attempt to enter this group illegitimately—either through forced marriage (as in Gen. 34) or by force of arms (as in the book of Judges)—is to be resisted. In this context we are helped to see some of the "why's" of warfare in this period. In the next major period of history, while the sense of belonging is still strong, it becomes disrupted by the advent of a new political system, the monarchy. With the advent of this new system the rules change, and those who make the rules change.

# 2

# Historical Observations—The Kings

During the time that is portrayed between the end of the book of Judges and the middle chapters of the book of 1 Samuel, ancient Israel had undergone some significant social and political changes. It had moved from a non-centralized, tribally organized society into a relatively sophisticated bureaucracy with a new kind of political regime at the centre. That regime was a monarchy. Monarchical rule began in ancient Israel in approximately 1040 B.C., and lasted for several centuries. Before we look at warfare in this period, it would be well to offer a sketch of the development and decline of monarchical rule in Israel and Judah. Many of the stories are familiar, especially those of the early period dealing with Saul and his successor, David, but it is worth refreshing our memories.

The opening chapters of 1 Samuel concern themselves with the call to leadership of a young man, Samuel, who functioned in Israel—usually in the central hill country north of Jerusalem—in a number of capacities. He was a priest at the Shiloh shrine, succeeding the old man Eli. He is often called a prophet, although his prophetic characteristics are not as pronounced as those later figures we have come to know as the "classical prophets". He is also presented as a judge, last of a noble profession in Israel.

But, it was during Samuel's term of office that the Philistine pressure on Israel was renewed. Some time after the death of Samson, and the migration of the tribe of Dan, the Philistines had moved north and were now threatening the main trunk road to the west of Ephraim. A battle was fought between the well-organized Philistines (note they alone "line up for battle" in 1 Sam. 4.2), and the disorganized militia units of the Israelites. We shall discuss the tactics of this battle later. Israel was defeated. A second battle took place at which the Ark was captured, and it was some time before the Philistines were expelled (temporarily at least) from the central hill country.

Towards the end of Samuel's life a political crisis occurred in Israel. The elders approached him and asked him to appoint for them a king (1 Sam. 8.1-5). [1] In the Bible two reasons for this are given and they do not necessarily complement each other. On the one hand, Samuel's sons had disqualified themselves from holding office as judges after him by their unacceptable behaviour. They " ... turned aside after gain, took bribes and perverted justice" (1 Sam. 8.3). On the other hand, there is a broader agenda behind their request which is mentioned in 1 Sam. 8.19-20, and that is a military one. The people insisted on a king " ... so that we may be like all the other nations, and that our king may govern us and may go out and fight our battles." What we see here is a common argument for the introduction of a new political regime; the old regime is corrupt and therefore unfit to exercise power. Also, the new circumstances demand new ways for which the old regime is inadequate.

There may well be other reasons for the centralization of power in monarchy, socio-economic ones, for which Gottwald and others have argued,[2] but they do not figure very prominently in the narrative of the rise of the monarchy in Israel. They ought to be kept in mind. However, in the same vein, we ought not to forget that the people who actually negotiated the new regime with Samuel were the representatives of the covenant community, the elders.

---

[1] On this see S. Talmon "Kingship and the Ideology of the State" and "The Rule of the King—1 Samuel 8:4-22" in *King Cult and Calendar in Ancient Israel* (Jerusalem: Magnes Press, 1986): 9-38, 53-67.

[2] See esp. R.B. Coote and K.W. Whitelam "The Emergence of Israel: Social Transformation and State Formation Following the Decline in Late Bronze Age Trade" *Semeia* 37 (1986): 107-147.

The monarchy that resulted from the request of the people was, in its early stages, a modest affair. Saul ben Kish, a Benjaminite of striking appearance and displaying the kind of violent bravado attractive to the dwellers of the hill country, was chosen by Samuel. Although the relative smallness of the administration can be overstated, we must note that the shifts in political power were very clear. At Gibeah in Benjamin a palace-fortress was built, and an administrative community was established. Although Saul initially mustered the fighting men of the people with ancient methods, he soon established a standing army, reasonably well equipped (if his own personal armour is anything to go by), and was able throughout his reign to keep the Philistine threat at bay, and embark on punitive raids against old enemies to the south, the Amalekites.

For reasons now well-known from the biblical story, Saul did not establish a dynasty. He and his sons died at Gilboa in an attempt to stop the Philistine advances. Already a young man of his entourage, David of Judah had been appointed in his place. Even more than Saul, David's history is well-known by readers of the Bible. His military prowess was legendary, as were his human weaknesses, and his reign is a mixture of political and military successes beyond the borders of Israel against Moab, Edom and Ammon and a succession of domestic problems and mismanagment. By the time David died in approximately 960 B.C., a capital city had been established in Jerusalem, giving the new nation a strong symbolic centre, the Philistines had been defeated, and the territorial limits of David's kingdom had expanded to include the land from the northern end of the Red Sea and the borders of Egypt to the banks of the Euphrates. David bequeathed to his son, Solomon, the land bridge between the three continents of Africa, Asia and Europe.

When David died a civil war broke out between the supporters of Ishbosheth—all of whom appear to be the "old guard", men who had supported David from the beginning—and the new regime under Solomon, including the Jerusalem "élite". In what is something of an understatement, the Bible offers the comment that ". . . the kingdom was established in the hand of Solomon" (1 Kings 2.46b). This victory of

Solomon saw the beginning of the "house of David" as the successive rulers of Israel, and then Judah. From this point until the invasion of the Babylonians and the exile of the Judaean leaders in 586 B.C., with one small hiatus, a Davidic descendant ruled in Judah.[3]

Solomon's administration took a heavy toll on the people and latent tensions flared into open conflict with his son and successor, Rehoboam. His mishandling of the requests of the northern elders to lighten the taxation load imposed on the people led to a split between the ten northern tribes and Judah. The result as the establishment of a northern kingdom which was often a rival to the southern kingdom in Judah (1 Kings 12-14).

Many scholars have argued that in the north there was a tendency to support a more "charismatic" kind of kingship, rather than a firmly established dynastic kingship such as was practised in the south, but this is a misreading of the history.[4] What becomes evident from the history of the north is that it favoured dynastic kingship, but few of the dynasties were able to survive, and the longest-lived ones, those of Ahab and Jehu, lasted only through four successive kings. The political situation in the north was far more unstable than in the south, most probably because the north was a shaky coalition of ten tribes, each with its traditions and territories. Given this situation it is understandable that different factions wished to take over the reins of power, which they often did, but such factions were also unable to sustain the trust of the others long enough to stay in power. So the history of the north is of short-lived dynasties, *coups d'état,* and possibly rival co-regents. Not too much should be made of this apparent instability, however. Monarchy was still the accepted political system, no matter how often a king was assassinated or overthrown. As for the relatively short length

---

[3]On this see T. Ishida "Solomon's Accession to the Throne of David" in *Studies in the Period of David and Solomon, and Other Essays* [ed. T. Ishida] (Winona Lake: Eisenbrauns, 1982): 175-188.

[4]On the question of dynastic rule in ancient Israel see the excellent T. Ishida *Royal Dynasties in Ancient Israel* [BZAW 142] (Berlin: De Gruyter, 1977).

of the dynasties, one ought to remember that in the political context of the ancient Near East, the long, almost unbroken dynasty of David over five hundred years is the exception rather than the rule. By way of a modern comparison with the north one might note the number of different "houses" represented in the English monarchy since the middle of the fifteenth century.

In the north (Israel) the monarchy lasted until 722 B.C. when the country was invaded for a second time by the Assyrian army and annexed to Assyria. In the books of Kings, from 1 Kings 12 to 2 Kings 17, we have the biblical account of the north, including a long section dealing with the activities of the prophets Elijah and Elisha. The turmoil of the repeated assassinations of the early period following the death of Jeroboam was settled for a time by the accession of the king Omri in approximately 885 B.C. For the next forty years or so, the "Omride dynasty" ruled, ending with the violent death of Jehoram at the hands of Jehu. Jehu's takeover was intended as a purging of the north of foreign religious practices, which it initially was, but by the end of Jehu's reign the nation had begun to suffer loss of territories and other misfortunes. The Jehudite dynasty, however, lasted for almost ninety years, due in part to the lengthy reign of Jeroboam II (784-752 B.C.) The reign of this king is also noted for its prosperity and the expansion of territory to the northern borders of the old davidic empire. Up to this point the consistent enemy of Israel was Aram-Syria, and numerous wars, invasions, sieges were conducted between the two. However, by the mid-730s another, greater threat had emerged in the shape of the massive Assyrian war machine. Between 734 and 732, under Tiglath Pileser III, and again in 722, under Shalmaneser V and Sargon II, Assyria invaded and finally annexed the whole of the northern kingdom to its lands. In the final thirty years of the northern nation six kings reigned, indicating something of the rapidly growing political instability of Israel.

The southern nation of Judah lasted one hundred and forty years longer. The co-existence of Israel and Judah was a mixture of wars and alliances, of tension and peace. For a while after the split of the kingdoms, the northern border of

Judah and the territory of Benjamin was a frequently disputed region, and the fights for this land ended in the south's favour. Israel's attempt to regain Moab after the revolt of Mesha was supported by the southern king Jehoshaphat (?) (2 Kings 3), but under Amaziah (795-767 B.C.) tensions flared again between north and south, and the subsequent fight resulted in the sacking of Jerusalem (2 Kings 14).

In the biblical account of the reigns of the southern kings the various reforms of the temple find a prominent place. Under Ahaz, Joash, Hezekiah and Josiah, various attempts were made to change the practices at the temple in various ways. Hezekiah managed to survive an Assyrian invasion (2 Kings 18-20), but, according to the biblical account, the rot set in with his successor, Manasseh (2 Kings 21), so that even the "second David" Josiah (642-609 B.C.) was unable to stem the inevitable tide of disaster. The latter part of Josiah's reign was contemporary with the decline, and eventual destruction of the Assyrian empire, and in 609, Josiah made the fatal mistake of attacking an Egyptian army travelling north to go to the aid of the ailing Assyrians. At Megiddo Josiah was killed, and in the years following his death until 586 the nation was under constant pressure. Egypt dominated for a while, deposing Josiah's successor Jehoahaz (608 B.C.) and replacing him with the apostate Jehoiakim (608-598 B.C.). During Jehoiakim's reign the baton of world power had been passed to Babylon, and the king died during an abortive rebellion against his Babylonian overlord in 598 B.C. His successor, Jehoiachin, was exiled and followed by his uncle, Zedekiah (Mattathiah). By 586 B.C. the Babylonians had invaded for a second time and sacked Jerusalem. The age of the kings had ended for Israel.

Most crucial for our look at the phenomenon of warfare in ancient Israel is the socio-political system that replaced the old tribal system outlined in the previous chapter. What constituted a monarchy such as Israel's in antiquity? How did it differ from the old system?[5] And, more important,

[5]See Whitelam "The Emergence of Israel" for a thorough study of the method of approach to these questions.

how did this change the institution of warfare and how did the new system affect the society as a whole? These are large questions, and again we are stalled in part by the lack of necessary data. There are more data from this period than the previous one, but we are faced with the problem of the intentional *selectivity* of the ancient writers. Historical and social facts are passed on to the reader only in an incidental fashion. Only rarely is there a detailed and systematic description of ancient Israelite society found in the Old Testament, more common are implications and scattered facts from which we may draw inferences. But, as we stated earlier, this need not deter us from drawing some conclusions, since we can resort to the practice of using well-established models of typical societies. First, let us see what changes we can detect from the data available.

There are some important biblical passages which we do well to examine, and they are descriptions of administration and administrative practices in David's and Solomon's kingdoms. In 1 Sam. 8.10-18 there is a speech of Samuel in which he warns the people of the cost of kingship.[6] Now there is a debate in some scholarly circles on the "authenticity" of this passage. Did Samuel say these exact words at this precise time? Or, has the writer put into the mouth of Samuel a general critical comment about kingship which was phrased after a bitter experience with monarchy? For our purposes we do not have to decide one way or the other, since the comments offer a good description of what life under a king would be, or was, like. The general profile is accurate, even if the precise details are a little unclear.

In the passage, which comes in the context of a long and involved discussion on the request for a king, Samuel warns of the cost of having a monarch. The costs will be in terms of personnel and goods. In economic terms, there will be a severe redistribution of the [limited] resources of the people, and most of these resources will be drawn to the new centre of power, the king. In terms of personnel, Samuel warns that

---

[6]See esp. Talmon "The Rule of the King", and T.N.D. Mettinger *Solomon's State Officials: A Study of the Civil Government Officials of the Israelite Monarchy* (Lund: G.W.K. Gleerup, 1971).

sons and daughters will be coerced into the king's service. It would be helpful if we listed them as follows:

| Women | Men |
|-------|-----|
| Perfumers | Charioteers |
| Cooks | Horsemen (grooms) |
| Bakers | Runners (bodyguard) |
| | Officers |
| |    Captains of 1000s |
| |    Captains of 50s |
| | Ploughmen |
| | Harvesters |
| | Manufacturers |
| |    of weapons |
| |    of chariots |

It should be clear that in the second column a further subdivision can be made, that between "civilian" tasks and military tasks, with some overlap with the manufacturers of weapons and chariots. What is also clear is that, with the exception of the military officers, most of these tasks are labour-oriented. Administration was placed in the hands of others.

Beyond the use of personnel in this way, there is a redistribution of material resources which include human possessions, such as slaves. According to this passage, fields, vineyards and olive orchards will be confiscated and distributed among the "servants" [i.e. officials] of the king. Payment of the same officials will be made with taxes (tenths) imposed upon the grain and the wine produced by farmers. Further, servants of the landowners, along with their cattle and sheep will be coerced into service for the king.

For the moment we will leave this description and move to descriptions of administrative personnel found in the stories of the reigns of David and Solomon. In 1 Sam. 8.15-18 we find the following list of administrative personnel:

> Magistrate: David (the king)
> Commander-in-chief: Joab

Recorder (Mazkir: Heb.): Jehoshaphat
Priest (Zadokite): Zadok
Priest (Levite): Ahimelech
Secretary: Seraiah
Regimental commander: Benaiah
  of the Cerethites and Pelethites
Priest: King's sons.

In 1 Kings 4.1-6 we find a description of Solomon's personnel. The list is slightly different. Obviously some of the names have changed, but also we note that the size of the administration has been enlarged.

Priest: Azariah ben Zadok
Secretaries: Elihoreph and Ahijah
Recorder: Jehoshaphat
Commander-in-chief: Benaiah
Priests: Zadok and Abiathar
Chief of Staff: Azariah
Palace manager: Ahishar
Minister of forced labour: Adoniram ben Abda

Note that the number of priests has increased, as has the number of secretaries. The title of "recorder" [Mazkir] has disappeared, but three new offices have appeared, "chief of staff" [Heb: "over the officials"], "palace manager" and "minister of forced labour". The powers of the magistrate, which originally resided with the king, according to the first list, do not appear in the second. We will remember that the inability of David to fulfill the demands of the office of judge led to the revolt of his son Absalom. While we do not see the office listed in the second catalogue of administrators, the office does appear a number of times in the books of the prophets, who were contemporary with the kings. The prophet Amos, for example, attacked those who perverted justice (Am. 2.7; 5.12), as does his near contemporary Micah (Mic.

3.9-11). One can assume from this that the office was maintained, but probably on a local level.

It will be helpful if we tried to show in a diagram what has now happened to Israel, and we are helped in this again by a "model". The model is of the typical "centralized bureaucratic empire" (cbe) which has been extensively studied by S.N. Eisenstadt in his book *The Political Systems of Empires.*[7] Eisenstadt examined cbe's from the ancient Egyptian to the British, and covered a vast period of time and an enormous amount of information. The details need not concern us. Instead we look at the common structure that all of these empires had. It can be illustrated by the following diagram:

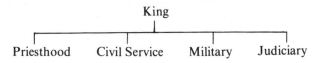

It is unrealistic to expect that every member of Israelite and Judaean society saw and appreciated such a change. According to 1 Sam. 8 the effects of this change were felt by the "average" Israelite at a very local level. What is important, however, is that this new system represents a decisive shift in the manipulation of *power* in Israel. Power is now directed from a definable centre. Edward Shils has described such a centre in the following terms:

> "The center, or the central zone, is a phenomenon of the realm of values and beliefs. It is the center of the order of symbols, of values and beliefs, which govern the society. It is the center because it is the ultimate and irreducible."[8]

Within this central core, government is managed by the establishment of the new institutions, and the incorporation

[7]S.N. Eisenstadt *The Political Systems of Empires: The Rise and Fall of Historic Bureaucratic Societies* (New York: The Free Press, 1969).

[8]E. Shils "Center and Periphery" in *The Constitution of Society* (Chicago: University of Chicago Press, 1982): 93-109.

or modification of the old. Membership in these institutions is frequently a matter of ability, and not family or kinship connections, and with the rise of these institutions comes a decline in the political power of the elders. Each of these institutions also forms a small power unit of its own, and it is the king's task—certainly to his advantage—to maintain an equilibrium between the power groups under his control so that no one of them gains too much power. The king may favour one particular institution, and in ancient Israel it was generally the army, but favour did not mean the loss of control. The king's ability to control, and play off one against the other without destroying the whole, is the art of politics.

Such a change in the socio-political structure of ancient Israel was necessary if Israel was to enter the new world of power, or at least, so the elders who approached Samuel would have argued.

Since the primary threat to the tribal community was a military one, it makes sense to see the response to this threat in terms of a new military organization. The people ask for a king "... to fight our battles for us ... ", and thus articulate the primary motivation for the new administrative development which led to the establishment of a monarchy. Kings in the ancient Near East at this time were not primarily political figures, but a mixture of warrior, priest and chief administrator. With the development of the monarchy we see the presence of a central institution devoted to the practice of warfare, the recruitment and maintenance of an army, and the execution of the political will of the central authority, the king. The development of this military presence in Israel is seen most clearly in many of the later kings, such as Omri and Jehu in the north, but it is already present *en herbe* at the beginning wih the significant changes introduced by David, and even by Saul.

In the stories of Saul we find certain clues concerning the establishment of a military institution even this early in the monarchy. In fact, it stands to reason that since the desire for a king was sparked by a military threat, then the military response should take shape early. Once Saul had established himself with his minimal administration at Gibeah, the Philistine threat increased. Philistine garrisons were established on the plateau north of Jerusalem, in the town of Michmash. The Israelites were forced to break up into small bands and hide. The tool-making industry, so vital to the success of any military establishment, was firmly in the hands of the Philistines, and the distribution of weapons was minimal amongst the Israelites.

In spite of these conditions, there are some hints of a minimal military organization among the Israelites. Saul's son, Jonathan, who obviously had some kind of military status, was accompanied by an "armour-bearer" [Heb: *nose' kli*], which, in turn, implies an amount of equipment which Jonathan would use in battle. The appositional term "*na'ar*", often translated "young man", also indicates a certain social, and military status attached to Jonathan. He was a senior officer in the, albeit depleted, army.

To build up an army to counter the Philistine threat, and to defend Israel against Moab, Ammon, Edom and Zobah, Saul developed an organization and a strategy stronger than the defensive measures we find in the period of the Judges, and this organization is reflected in the details of the campaign against Amalek (1 Sam. 15.4). Details of the story of David and Goliath betray a concern for organization and supply, as Saul is now embarked on a lengthy campaign against the Philistines. On this foundation David built an impressive military structure and continued a more aggressive foreign policy.

The pattern outlined in 2 Sam. 8.15-18, and which was firmly established during David's reign, offers us the bare bones of the social changes which were brought about to accommodate the new reality in Israel's life—a professional army. Such a professional army soon became independent of the king's leadership, although not of his political control. Some time during David's life he found himself in serious danger on the field of battle. To ensure the safety of the king, he handed over his role as chief warrior to Joab (2 Sam. 21.15-17). In light of the fact that this situation created the circumstances of David's affair with Bathsheba, the story of 2 Sam. 21 is probably misplaced, and took place early in David's reign.

In similar fashion, although it is almost the final incident in the record of David's reign, the census which David initiated in 2 Sam. 24 probably took place earlier in the reign. The motives of the census are betrayed by David's choice of the census takers—Joab, commander-in-chief of his army, and his staff [This is the reading of the Greek version. The Hebrew text mentions only Joab. In any event, Joab led the census, and could not have conducted it alone.], and the summary of the results of the census given at the end of it:

> And Joab gave the sum of the numbering of the people to the king: in Israel there were eight hundred thousand fighting men who could handle the sword, and the men of Judah were five hundred thousand (2 Sam. 24.9).

David died, having established an empire stretching from the northern end of the Dead Sea, to the "entrance of Hamath", better understood as Lebo of Hamath, modern Lebweh.[9] Its eastern borders were well into the territories of Ammon, Edom and Moab. To his successors he bequeathed the need for an aggressive foreign policy. His empire had been built on conquest and control of his neighbours. If this empire were to be maintained then it would have to be supported by an equally strong ruler, prepared to govern his dominions with a strong hand. Secondly, David left to his successors a military organization that had to be maintained and perfected. Military organizations, to be effective, have to keep up with changing technologies, shifts in battlefield tactics and the consequent needs of manpower. To remain static is to become obsolete and ineffective. David had built his empire on conquest with a good army. Again, that army needed to be maintained to keep a hold on those conquests. Thirdly, and contrary to what one might expect, he also bequeathed a heavy economic burden. Conquest of other lands in antiquity was primarily for the purpose of increasing income. This was done by controlling trade routes, and the

---

[9]On this identification see Y. Aharoni *The Land of the Bible: An Historical Geography* [revised edition] (Philadelphia: Westminster Press, 1978): 70-73.

productivity of the conquered countries. But there is a point reached when the income is outstripped by the costs. Control over larger territory calls for a larger army, defended lines of supply, and a regular maintenance of the army's efficiency through the supply of new recruits and usable weaponry. This, as we have hinted at earlier, puts a great strain on the local resources of manpower and materiel. According to the Bible, there was a "time when kings went forth to battle . . ." (2 Sam. 11.1), and this was the "turn of the year" [i.e. "spring" as in RSV], early in the month of Nisan when the barley and grain harvests were in. But this also takes away from the local scene the very men required to bring in the harvest. This, coupled with the shifts in social location of those now working for the king in his vineyards, weapons factories, chariot factories etc. (1 Sam. 8.10ff.) would place an enormous strain upon the economy which can be relieved by more conquest, for more "tribute" from enemies. Finally, with such changes as this the need for control of the local population, to ensure a steady supply of goods and services, became paramount, and, as we shall see, a necessary adjustment in life in Israel. Many of David's successors continued with an aggressive foreign policy.

# Excursus

# David and The Invention of Tradition

We have stated in the above chapter that the political, and eventual social structure of Israel changed with the introduction of the system of monarchy into Israel. The changes we have outlined must have happened at a fairly fast rate, and many of them would have been in place early in the reign of David. According to 2 Sam. 8.15-16 David's administration was a sophisticated one, and is patterned on the typical ancient Near Eastern court. Under Solomon this system is expanded and developed, and under the numerous successors further expansion and "fine tuning" must have been undertaken. Scattered throughout the Old Testament are numerous references to innovations in public works, building programmes, agricultural systems and fortifications, to name a few, which would be possible under a strong centralised authority like the monarchy.

A monarchy such as was introduced under David consists of more than structural changes. A new ideology developed alongside it which gave it its reason for existence and also its justification for continuing. This ideology has been called by those scholars who write Old Testament theology, the "David-Zion Tradition". This needs some brief explanation.

In the later period between the two world wars many scholars became disenchanted with the old-style "literary criticism", which sought to unravel the complicated (sometimes too complicated) pre-history of written documents by analysing them into numerous sources. It was not unusual in the use of this method of analysis for a single chapter to be seen as a compilation of eighteen different literary sources, consisting of earlier documents and numerous editorial comments and "glosses". This kind of study eventually fell victim to the law of diminishing returns, for the more sophisticated and analytical the method became, the greater the number of separate sources were found. This led eventually to a complete loss of sight of the original narrative with which the scholars began, and the unschooled Bible reader (sometimes the schooled as well!) became more confused than enlightened, and failed to see the purpose of it all. In the 1920s and 1930s an impasse of this kind of study was broken by an approach to the text which saw it in a slightly different light, not as the random compilations of several literary sources, but more as literary reactions to the "core religious traditions" of Israel. These traditions, often regarded as a kind of "creed", although the term is not really appropriate, were the five pillars upon which the faith of ancient Israel rested, and which formed a kind of *sine quae non* of Israelite religion. These traditions were those religious ideas which attached themselves to great events of the past or great persons of the past. They were 1) the Patriarchs, 2) the Exodus-Conquest, 3) the Sinai covenant, 4) the Jerusalem-Zion traditions and 5) the traditions surrounding the person of the king, the so-called "Davidic traditions". It can be seen at a glance that with the prominent places afforded the traditions surrounding Jerusalem and David, that the final form of the synthesis which held all together emanated from the Southern kingdom of Judah, probably from Jerusalem itself.

One other thing ought to be pointed out, and it is something which has been overlooked in studies of the religious traditions of ancient Israel. That is that only one of these traditions has at its centre a person, still living during the formulation and propagation of the tradition, who had a vested interest in its form and perpetuation. That person is, of course, the king of Judah of the line of David.

The so-called "Davidic tradition" incorporates much of the ideology of kingship found in other parts of the ancient Near East, and many studies have explored these connections. Briefly stated, some of these ideas would involve the divine election of the monarch, the special status of the king in relationship to the deity, the peculiar responsibilities of the king toward the deity and toward the people. In ancient Judah many of these items were subsumed under the tradition of the covenant with David, which receives its narrative base in 2 Sam. 7, but which is repeated in poetry in Pss. 2, 72, 89, 110, 132 in one form or another. This covenant guaranteed the perpetuity of the Davidic dynasty in Jerusalem.[1]

When we see the development of this tradition from an historical point of view, it would be wise perhaps to ask the very important question, *cui bono*? Who benefits from this tradition? The same question asked of the other traditions can be answered with "the people". The Patriarchs are the founders of the nation; in the Exodus the people left Egypt under the leadership of Moses; at Sinai, again through the mediatorial role of Moses the people entered into covenant with Yahweh their God. But all this happened without David, in fact before David had entered on to the scene of ancient Israel's history. He was a latecomer, but more than that. There was strong resistance to the innovation of the monarchy, as we have seen in the narrative of the founding of the institution (1 Sam. 8-12). Many scholars also believe that this opposition endured throughout the period of the monarchy and is to be seen most clearly in the harsh criticisms of many of the prophets. Be that as it may, some effort must have been made by the supporters of the new institution of monarchy to incorporate the innovation into the traditions of the past.

Some of the support came from some of the prophets who worked with David over a number of years, and we can detect a shrewd handling of the problem of the introduction of the new system to the old ways. Samuel himself, though warning the people against monarchy, eventually acquiesces

---

[1]See the exposition of these traditions in G. von Rad *Old Testament Theology* 2 vols. (ET Edinburgh: Oliver & Boyd, 1962), also in E.Rohland *Die Bedeutung der Erwählungstraditionen Israels für die Eschatologie der alttestamentlichen Propheten* (Unpublished dissertation University of Heidelberg, 1955). This latter study is regarded as a classic statement on the topic. See J.J.M. Roberts "Zion in the Theology of the Davidic-Solomonic Empire" in *Studies in the Period of David and Solomon* [ed. T. Ishida] (Winona Lake: Eisenbrauns, 1982): 93-108.

to the request and grants the system under certain conditions. Nathan, the prophet of David, warns against too swift a change with the building of the temple (2 Sam. 7), and suggests a postponement. But in the preceding chapters there is a fine blend of the new and the old as a neutral city of Jerusalem is chosen for the new capital, and the old symbol of the religious life of the people, the Ark of the Covenant, is brought to rest in this new capital. Throughout the reign of David, Nathan appears as the judge of the king as he condemns him for breach of the old covenant law (2 Sam. 11) with his affair with Bathsheba, and his contrived murder of Uriah her husband. Later in the monarchy, prophets appear as champions of the "old ways". Adonijah, the prophet from Shiloh, warns of the splitting of the kingdoms into two because of Solomon's apostasy (1 Kings 12), and Shemaiah the prophet stops an invasion of Rehoboam to the north to regain the kingdom taken away in judgment on the south (1 Kings 12). Finally, the verdict on the period of the monarchy, both north and south, is that the kings behaved badly "in the eyes of Yahweh" by breaking the old covenant law, and therefore brought punishment upon the people as a whole. Thus we see that the innovation was not greeted with universal enthusiasm, and remained under critical survey throughout the duration of the monarchy.

But what could David and his courtiers do to legitimise the system other than incorporate it into the already existing traditions of ancient Israel? This is primarily a matter of historical investigation, but, as we have already stated, the sources with which we are dealing tend to be biased in favour of the new system. How then are we to understand the historical dynamic of the "ideologizing" of the new political and social system of the monarchy in such circumstances? We have to adopt a model of historical investigation and to test the data, as we have it, against the model.

In 1983 the results of a symposium were published under the title *The Invention of Tradition*, edited by Eric Hobsbawm and Terence Ranger,[2] and throughout the volume

---

[2]E. Hobsbawm, T. Ranger *The Invention of Tradition* (Cambridge: Cambridge University Press, 1984). For an excellent discussion on the development of written

several historians examined the phenomena of "invented traditions" as a means to incorporate novel situations with the past. The cases under discussion ranged from the 19th-century invention of traditions about the Scottish Highlands to traditions surrounding colonial rule in India and Africa. It seems appropriate to adopt this model of historical investigation in our look at the relationship of the "Davidic traditions" to the older religious traditions of Israel and Judah. The results might be valuable. But first some exposition of the model and some definitions are in order.

Three quotations from Hobsbawm's introductory article offer us a fine description of "invented traditions."

"Invented tradition is taken to mean a set of practices, normally governed by overtly or tacitly accepted rules and of a ritual or symbolic nature, *which seek to inculcate certain values and norms of behaviour by repetition, which automatically implies continuity with the past.*"[3]

"[Invented traditions] are responses to novel situations which take the form of reference to old situations, *or which establish their past by quasi-obligatory repetition.*"

"The past, real or imagined, to which they refer imposes fixed (normally formalized) practices, such as repetition."[4]

There is, therefore, in "invented traditions" an element of self-justification of the present by means of an appeal to the past, real or imaginary. Numerous examples from history could be drawn, and the symposium volume offers several, including the "popularization" of the British monarchy in the 20th century.

The context of the development of "invented traditions" is time of social change. Transformation of society is a constant, and the fusion of the new and the old inevitably follows, but

---

propaganda during David's reign, see K. Whitelam "The Defence of David" *Journal of the Study of the Old Testament* 29 (1984): 61-87.

[3] Hobsbawm *Ibid.*, 1.

[4] Hobsbawm *Ibid.*, 2.

"... we should expect it to occur more frequently when a rapid transformation of society weakens or destroys the social patterns for which 'old' traditions had been designed, producing new ones to which they were not applicable, or when such old traditions and their institutional carriers and promulgators no longer prove sufficiently adaptable and flexible, or are otherwise eliminated"[5]

In this process the old traditions are not abandoned. On the contrary, creative use is made of the past traditions and traditional material for new purposes at a time when often the old ways have deliberately fallen into disuse because of the extent and speed of social change.

Initially two features are recognizable about "traditions". First, they are by nature impractical. Attention is drawn to the difference between customs, which change with the times and show a strong degree of adaptability, and traditions, whose intention is to foster stability and invariance. Second, tradition is weakened if an attempt is made to rationalise it, and explain it. In the realm of law and jurisprudence, there is no practical value to the wearing of gowns and wigs. Such traditions are symbolic. In military circles modern dress uniforms are relics of older battledress, as a glance at the colours and splendour of an early nineteenth-century battlefield will demonstrate. Today they have no practical value at all, except as symbols of attachment to a particular regiment or corps. They are traditions and no rationalistic explanation of them will get at the heart of the tradition. Instead, such traditions can be supported by appeal to "regimental spirit" and other intangibles.[6]

This brings us to another feature of such "invented traditions", and that is that they are supported by ritual and ceremony which might take old forms and transform them to suit the new situation. In Hobsbawm's words, "... in-

[5] Hobsbawm *Ibid.*, 4-5.

[6] On the matter of "regimental spirit" in the 19th-century British army see B. Farwell *Mr. Kipling's Army: All the Queen's Men* (New York: Norton, 1986), especially chs. 2, 3.

vented tradition uses traditional material for the construction of invented tradition of novel type and for novel purposes." The exact extent of this is difficult to detect, but the purpose of it is to create historic continuity, often by creating a past "beyond effective continuity". The net result is that a sense (often a false sense) of historic destiny is read into the past. Thus the modern British monarchy sees the tribal struggles of an Alfred or an Arthur as precursors of the later history, and the Nazi movement in Germany between the wars adopted the Germanic myths as part of their credentials. To enhance this sense new symbols are created, flags, emblems, and a strong sense of national identity.

The types of "invented traditions" vary, and Hobsbawm has offered three:

a. those establishing or symbolizing social cohesion or the membership of groups, real or artifical communities.
b. those establishing or legitimizing institutions, status or relations of authority.
c. those whose main purpose was socialization, the inculcation of beliefs, value systems and conventions of behavior.

While all three can be reflected in the changes that came about with the Davidic monarchy in Israel, it is the second which is most appropriate. The new institution needed legitimizing, especially since it was the only one introduced with a strong measure of oppostion to it.

When compared to old traditions, invented traditions appear unspecific concerning the nature of the values, rights and obligations membership in the group implies. Old traditions were specific, invented traditions appeal to general concepts of "loyalty", "patriotism" etc. However, the *practices* of the invented traditions are almost compulsory since they are symbolic. They are ". . . signs of club membership, rather than statutes and objects of the club." It is now a time for uniforms, flags and banners and for formalized language. In terms of the relationship of human beings to their past the model of "invented traditions" is extremely important, since it affects the way the past is understood:

"... the history which became part of the fund of knowledge or the ideology of the nation, state or movement, is not what has actually been preserved in popular memory, *but what has been selected, written, pictured, popularized and institutionalized by those whose function it is to do so.*"[7]

How is this process to be seen in the development of the Davidic tradition, the traditions surrounding the institution of monarchy in ancient Israel, and the literary support given to this institution? We can only sketch some of the main features. In general, there is a selectivity of past history, and the development of a continuity with the past evident in the Old Testament presentation of the Davidic monarchy. This can be seen in three areas, listed without embellishment. First, the patriarchal stories have received a "Davidic flavour" in their current form. The blessing of Jacob in Gen. 49 clearly singles out Judah as a tribe for special royal destiny (Gen. 49.9-10). Further, the early presentations of the Patriarchal promise have been overwritten with the monarchy in mind.[8] Second, the traditions associated with Sinai and the covenant and lawgiving were later incorporated into the traditions about Mount Zion[9], and scholars have long recognized the interconnectedness of the Davidic and Zion traditions. Third, the ideology of the perpetuation of the Davidic dynasty permeates the early stories of the monarchy, and has long been recognized as an *apologia* for the Davidic dynasty.[10] Work has already been done on these areas, although the connections and the significance have not always been fully

[7] Hobsbawm *Ibid.*, 13.

[8] R.E.Clements *Abraham and David: Genesis 15 and Its Meaning in Israelite Tradition* (London: SCM Press, 1967).

[9] See J.D. Levenson *Sinai and Zion* (Minneapolis: Winston Press 1985): passim, and Roberts "Zion in the Theology of the Davidic-Solomonic Empire."

[10] Argued many years ago by L. Rost *Die Überlieferung von der Thronnachfolge Davids* [BWANT III] (Stuttgart: W. Kohlhammer, 1926) now published in English as *The Succession to the Throne of David* (Sheffield: Almond Press, 1982). See also T. Ishida "Solomon's Accession to the Throne of David" in *Studies in the Period of David and Solomon, and Other Essays* [ed.T. Ishida] (Winona Lake: Eisenbrauns, 1982): 175-188.

appreciated. David's apologists needed to present the new system as a logical progression of the earlier traditions, and to develop an understandable rationale for the innovation. It needed to be seen as part of a divine plan, and in the ways outlined above the necessary continuity with the past is established.

But, we need to see how this affects the military history of the monarchy. We have argued above that the innovation of the monarchy was, first, a response to a military threat, and second, resulted in a deliberate militarization of the people of Israel. In turn, the style of warfare changes from a strategy of defence of home and one's own, to a strategy of offensive warfare in which surrounding nations are subdued and brought under the control of Israel and/or Judah. Thirdly, in keeping with the processes we have outlined above, new symbols are developed, and new loyalties expected under the new regime. We can do little at this stage beyond offering a sketch.

On the question of the shift from defensive to offensive wars under the monarchy, already begun by Saul in his war against Amalek, reasons need to be found for this change. The innovation of monarchy does not necessarily result in the declaration of war against neighbouring countries. The initial reason for the request for a king is *defensive*. For the offensive wars economic and larger strategic reasons can be found in the literature on the history of ancient Israel (e.g. the securing of trade routes), but such reasons do not amount to needed justification of war. In the annals of warfare few wars are publicly justified on grounds of crass economic gain, even if some would argue that this is the sole justification of warfare. Other reasons are announced, such as the evil nature of the enemy, or the need to redress some serious wrong done in the recent or distant past.

Thus it is that in the epics produced during the monarchy, known in the so-called Yahwist source of the Pentateuch current enemies are seen in that history as ancient enemies. Amalekites resisted Israel's exit from Egypt; Edom is the jealous half-brother of Israel; the forerunners of Aram and Moab sought to prevent Israel's approach to the promised land. All fall victim to Israel's expansionist policy during the monarchy, and other enemies are chosen because of slighting of honour, such as was the case with David's war against Hanun of Ammon (2 Sam. 10). In justification of these actions a "... continuity with a past beyond effective continuity ..." is created.

Accompanying this invention of tradition at the time of the monarchy is the shift in the focus of loyalty of the common Israelite. We have pointed out already that the Davidic-Zion tradition is the only one of the five religious traditions of Israel which concerned a living human being, and a viable institution attached to that human being. It appears then that loyalty to the king takes the place of dedication to the covenant ideal, at least at the political level. At the secesssion of the north the Israelites declare that their loyalty cannot be given to David (1 Kings 12.16), something which was not demanded under the old covenant regime. In many Psalms the focus of attention is the king, especially in the so-called individual psalms of lament. No prayers were ever offered for the old covenant leaders, such as priests, judges and prophets, but with advent of monarchy intercessions come into the psalmody of Israel/Judah whose political intention is to offer support for the king, and especially the king in battle pose. Israel's enemies now become his enemies, and at that symbolic centre of society stands the monarch. The political will of the people is now able to be expressed by the private will of the king, so it is he who goes to war against his enemies, taking along with him the conscript army, and justifying his actions by virtue of his new-found place of power in society, at the centre.

Such observations as these point out that the monarchy in Israel/Judah, coming as it did at a time of rapid and widespread social change, infiltrated itself into the history of the tribes as an innovation, but an innovation with a past. It is supported by repetitive rituals, such as coronation, and temple festivals in which the royal figure plays a prominent role. Soon the full trappings of monarchy are embedded in Israelite society. From the political perspective the king is accompanied by an administration. From the symbolic point of view other elements are introduced, from the crown on the king's head, the distinctive robes in battle, to the develop-

ment of the idea of the sanctity of the royal person, an idea
which one of the "old school", in the person of Joab, found
difficult to understand, but his younger colleagues did not (2
Sam. 18.9-15). In distinction from this, and sometimes in
opposition to this, the popular memory preserved a different
history, a different past, and hoped for a different present. It
is perhaps in the words of the prophets, often so critical of
the monarchy, that the popular voice can be heard.

# 3

# Men of War

Warfare in any age involves a struggle between human
beings, usually to the death, or at least to the submission of
one to the other. It is a matter of debate whether this deadly
struggle is innate to human nature, or whether it is learned. I
would suggest that since some of the earliest depictions of
human activity involve organized combat,[1] the scales would
tip in favour of the innate tendency to violence in humans.
What we do know is that soldiers have fought against each
other from the beginnings of human social development.
The Old Testament, with its violence and warfare, constitutes
little more than additional pages in this catalogue of human
aggression. Throughout their history ancient Israel/Judah
were involved in warfare. To do it better, armies were
organized, men were trained and equipped. In this chapter
we shall look at some aspects of this organization and
training.

## A. Organization and Recruitment

Any army that enters the field of battle must be organized,
however simply. Even before the monarchy in Israel there is
evidence of a tactical plan in many of the battles, which

[1]See A. Ferrill *The Origins of War: From the Stone Age to Alexander the Great*
(London: Thames & Hudson, 1985). The debate on the origins of human violence is
a long and a complicated one. For one perspective on the issue see A. Montague
*The Nature of Human Aggression* (Oxford University Press, 1978).

implies the basic elements of battle order such as leadership, logistics, weapons supply, command, communications etc. All of the elements are necessary on the field whatever the level of sophistication of the organization. Those that enter the field have to be told what to do, and when, and need to be under some element of control if the fighting is to be conducted with any degree of success. The need for control increases the more complicated the battle order, and the supporting social system become. But even in the period before the monarchy in Israel we can find evidence of a relatively primitive, but nevertheless effective organization of able-bodied men into an army.

It is customary to call the army which was mustered at this stage in Israel's history a "militia", which is a proper, but sometimes ambiguous word. What it means in this context is a task-oriented fighting force which was mustered when a special need arose, and disbanded when the problem had been dealt with. This is not quite what a militia is today, or even in the early part of the "modern period" of warfare since the seventeenth century. The main difference is that modern militia units—the "territorials" in the British system, the "national guard" in the United States, and the "militia" in Canada—are used to supplement already existing regulars. Militia units today demand a certain amount of time of their members for training. Uniforms are worn and the members of the militia are subject to the rules and regulations of the regulars.

In ancient Israel this was not the case. Militia units were not raised to supplement regular forces of professionals, they comprised the entire army. Such a "citizens' army" presupposes a way of life which is not primarily oriented to war and conquest, but rather to peaceful and necessary activities, such as the growing of food and cultivation of the land. This way of life—subsistence agriculture—is too labour intensive to allow for the maintenance of a regular army. It cannot supply the manpower needed for such an army—the men are needed in the fields and at home—nor can it provide enough surplus production to be able to support such an army in the field of war. In Israel's premonarchical days there was just not enough centralization of power to effect the necessary redistribution of production to this end. As it was, the men involved in this relatively simple agricultural way of life were seconded for limited periods of time for the defense of territory, a city or a related group of people. This fact would shape an army in this early period in more ways than many would imagine. Recruitment would be, of necessity, on the very local level. Leadership and battle organization would also be controlled from the local level. The men who did the fighting would undoubtedly have more confidence in a leader they knew and respected locally, than in a stranger. It is clear then that we are not dealing with large numbers of fighters, or large fighting units. There would not be extensive and continuous control on the field of battle, nor would tactics be very complicated. Lengthy (and costly) campaigns would be out of the question, and this in turn rules out any concept of a "grand strategy". Tactics would be influenced by the familiarity of the fighters with the terrain, and the fighting units would not wander too far afield. Wars would tend to be defensive. This is the picture we get from the book of Judges.

As we have seen in an earlier chapter, the wars of the period of the judges were defensive wars. An army was raised to deal with specific intrusions by an enemy, or the attempt of a more powerful neighbour to dislodge the Israelites. In the case of the invasion of Moab (Jud. 3.12-20), Ehud the Israelite assassinated the Moabite leader, Eglon, in Jericho and called together an army from the hill country of Ephraim to expel the Moabite force from Israelite territory. The exploits of Shamgar (Jud. 3.31) must also be seen in the context of the pressure exerted by the Philistines in the southwest, pressure which would not be relieved until the time of David, and which also forms the background for the stories of Samson (Jud. 13-16). Similarly, the armies called up by Deborah and Barak and by Gideon, were for the defence of Israel against attacks by Canaanite cities in an attempt to dislodge Israel from the hill country of Galilee on the one hand, and to repulse an invasion of invading Midianites on the other (Jud. 4-5, 6-7). In none of these cases is there an attempt to invade the territory of another.

Scattered throughout the stories of Judges there are some

details which enable us to reconstruct—at least in part—the methods of muster and recruitment of soldiers for these ad hoc armies. There was no central authority with the power to demand military service as there was later in the monarchy. Instead the levy of troops was done on a small, local scale, yet it was done efficiently. According to the story of Deborah and Barak's conflict with Jabin of Hazor and the Canaanite chariot army, Barak mustered a force of ten *'elafim* from Zebulun and Naftali in the north (Galilee) to fight the Canaanites (Jud. 4.6). It is not clear from the story, or even from the poem which accompanies the narrative account of the battle, whether all of the tribes were summoned. However, in Jud. 5.14-15 there appears to be a sarcastic reference to the failure of at least Ephraim, Benjamin and Reuben to become involved, and in 5.17, Gilead (not a tribe), Dan and Asher are clearly criticized for not fighting. Gideon pulls together another coalition of northern tribal units, thirty-two *'elafim*, made up of Abiezrites (his local clan), Manasseh, Asher, Zebulun and Naftali (Jud. 6.35). The method of muster is simple. Messengers were sent out throughout the tribal territories to call the fighting men to arms (Jud. 6.35; 7.24).

How were these early armies organized? In answer to this question we have to guard against reading back into the early period designs and battle orders of later ones, or against drawing too close a parallel between Israel and her neighbours as a substitute for lack of evidence from within Israel. For example, it is a common assumption that the armies of the period of the judges were organized according to the decimal principle, that is in multiples of ten. Now this is possibly true of the later monarchical armies, but the evidence is lacking for the same detailed organization in the early period, in spite of the many claims to the contrary made by scholars.

To be sure, in Exod. 18.21, 25 there is reference to "captains of ten" alongside "captains of thousands, hundreds and fifties". However, here there is no reference to a specifically military organization. The issue is rather the appointment of judges who can dispense justice on behalf of Moses. This new organization allows the dispensing of justice which is fair and fast, and if there is a parallel between these early judges and the so-called "military judges" of Jehoshaphat, listed in 2 Chron. 19.5-11, then the account in Exodus is anachronistic. On the other hand, it is a moot point whether the residence of Jehoshaphat's judges in "fortified cities" implied that they held military rank or office. In the case of Deut. 1.15 we are dealing with a reading back into the early history figures of an organization that belongs to the period of the monarchy. The evidence is lacking for the organization of the early armies of Israel into units of ten, fifty, one hundred and one thousand men, in ascending order of importance. The evidence suggests a far looser organization. Where there is specific reference to organization for war (Num. 31.14, 48, 52, 54) the figures are of "thousands" and "hundreds".

To make any sense of these figures we have to be clear what is meant here by the word translated "thousand" in these early stories. There is every reason to suspect that the word is not so much a numerical designation (10 x 100), but rather a socio-political designation. Two textual clues for this reading can be found in Mic. 5.1 (Evv. 5.2) and Jud. 6.15. The first of these reads:

> But you, O Bethlehem Ephrathah, who are little to be among the clans (*'alfe*) of Judah, from you shall come forth for me one who is to be ruler in Israel.

The second is in Gideon's response to his call to service and reads:

> ... And [Gideon] said to him, "Pray, Lord, how can I deliver Israel?" Behold my clan (*'elef*) is the weakest in Manasseh, and I am the least in my family (*beth 'av*). ...

These texts have two things in common. On the one hand both talk of weakness and smallness. On the other hand it is the word which is translated as "clan" (*'elef*), which is described as small or weak. In the first text Micah cannot even belong to the clans (*'elafim*) of Judah, and in the second, Gideon's "clan" is the weakest of several clans in Manasseh.

This is the word which is elsewhere translated as "thousand(s)". In both cases there is clear indication that the term refers to a subdivision of a tribe (Manasseh or Judah), and in the latter, it is a division greater than the "house" (*beth 'av*).

In an important article George Mendenhall[2] examined this socio-political designation and suggested that not only should it be understood as the sub-unit of a tribe, as it is in these texts, but in military contexts it should be understood as a unit of men able to be mustered into the early army in cases of emergency. It is also clear from some texts, like 1 Sam. 9.20-21, that the term *'elef* and the term *mishpachah* ("family") are to be equated. In this latter text the same style of self-deprecation used by Gideon is used by Saul. According to Mendenhall, the *'elef* is the armed *mishpachah*, a unit of eligible men of military age.

Exactly how many men each *'elef* would contain is open to question, but a clue is found in the census lists of Numbers 1 and 26. The result of Mendenhall's study of these lists is that the phrase "... xx thousand nn hundred ..." should be understood as appositional, and read "... xx *'elafim*, that is, nn hundred...." The reference to the *'elafim* would be to the number of armed units available for muster in a given tribe. The second number would be a qualifier, giving the total number of individual men eligible for the tribal muster. Mendenhall's thesis has great merit. It treats the two texts from Judges and Micah seriously, and enables us to make some sense of otherwise exorbitant figures in these tribal lists.

If this is the case, then it is possible to gain an idea of the average number of men in an *'elef* simply by dividing the total number, in hundreds, by the number of *'elafim*. There must be a caution, however. In these census lists, which come from a relatively late date, not all of the families (*mishpachoth*) of these tribal regions are listed. It is possible then that these lists refer to some kind of "selective service" roster. In Numbers 1, the average size of an *'elef* would be as follows:

[2]G.E. Mendenhall "The Census Lists in Numbers 1 and 26" *JBL* 77 (1958): 52-66.

| Tribe | Units | Men | Size of 'elef |
|---|---|---|---|
| Reuben | 46 | 500 | 11 |
| Simeon | 59 | 300 | 5 |
| Gad | 45 | 650 | 15 |
| Judah | 74 | 600 | 8 |
| Issachar | 54 | 400 | 7 |
| Zebulun | 57 | 400 | 7 |
| Ephraim | 40 | 500 | 12 |
| Manasseh | 32 | 200 | 6 |
| Benjamin | 35 | 400 | 11 |
| Dan | 62 | 700 | 11 |
| Asher | 41 | 500 | 12 |
| Naftali | 53 | 400 | 7 |
| TOTALS | 598 | 5550 | 9 |

The size of the average *'elef*, if an "average" ever existed, would be nine men. What we have here is probably a list of the maximum number of men eligible for military service at a certain time. From various tribes the numbers of these units eligible for the muster would vary and be dependent upon the population of the tribe at a given time, and the number of eligible males available.

However, population of the tribes is an extremely difficult thing to calculate, not only because we lack the raw data of a thorough census of the country during this period, but even with the best available evidence some of the calculations made by geographers and historians are not always reliable. The calculations are made often by taking the amount of available space in a village or town which has been excavated, and subjecting it to a formula of "persons per square metre", and working out an answer which is projected over the whole site. This seems a fair method of working, but it is probably not accurate, and certainly not objective. For example, what constitutes "available space", or, to put it another way, How much space do people need to live in? It is here that the subjectivity creeps in because it is tempting to answer the question by basing the calculations on the amount of space we might need to live in. But such a need is determined by our culture which often sets our personal toleration of other people. Use of space is culturally determined, set by that

culture's values. Some cultures—a nomadic one, for example—
need large expanses of space for relatively small populations.
Others show a remarkable tolerance for what we might con-
sider overcrowding. If the problem is understood from this
perspective it becomes clear that the level of tolerance for the
proximity of others is far higher in the Middle East than it is
in the west. This suggests that the levels of population in
ancient Israelite centres were probably a little higher than
have thus far been calculated by western scholars.

One recent attempt to study this issue is that of Lawrence
Stager in his article "The Archaeology of the Family in
Ancient Israel".[3] In the very detailed and valuable information gathered for this study are some population figures for
the hill country of Ephraim in the period of transition
between the judges and the monarchy. These figures are
based on a study of three sites, Et-Tel (Ai), Khirbet Raddana
and Meshash. Based on the presupposition that one person
needs ten square metres of space in which to live (a decidedly
generous allotment in my estimation), then the average household at Ai would vary between 4.1 and 3.0 persons, at
Raddan between 4.3 and 2.3 and at Meshash between 7.2
and 4.5. Several other variables are built into these calculations to allow for the differences in the final figures. These
figures would provide for an approximate population at each
site of between 320 and 240 for Ai, between 202 and 108 for
Raddana and between 955 and 598 for Meshash. This work
is undoubtedly valuable, but must be tempered by the caution
offered above. It is quite possible then that these figures are a
little low.

Regarding the *'elef*, we quote the work of another scholar
whose study of the social organization of the period of the
judges has become a classic, "... the *'eleph* was a military
unit in old Israel, but did not contain one thousand men, nor
indeed any fixed number, but rather a very much smaller but
variable number of men actually mustered or promised for
muster by a *mishpachah* in order to supply a round number

[3]L.E. Stager "The Archaeology of the Family in Ancient Israel" *BASOR* 260 (1985): 1-36.

of troops for the *shevet* for all-Israel wars."[4] Although it is tempting, as both Gottwald and Mendenhall have done, to see parallels here between ancient Israel and other societies like Mari, Ugarit and old Egypt, which were organized along regional or "tribal" lines, the parallels are not exact. The main difference is that in Israel there was no centralized power controlling policy or manpower at this time, whereas in these other societies there was a king and a court.

The age of the combatants in time of war in this period was the same as that for soldiers throughout the ancient Near East, twenty years of age or older. The upper limit is not given and was undoubtedly flexible. Need would often determine eligibility for warfare, and it is likely that in times of extreme emergency, any able-bodied man would be called up to fight. An illustration of this is the muster of the Moabites in 2 Kings 3 who call together men not normally used in defensive warfare. The lower age group seemed to be adhered to, and often appears in biblical and non-biblical material as the military "age of majority."[5] It is the basis for the census lists in Numbers 1 (Num. 1.3). Beyond this it is very difficult to calculate exactly how many men of military age there would be in a community. A town the size of Ai with between 240 and 320 inhabitants, that is 70 "average" families, according to Stager's calculations, would not be likely to muster more than two eligible men per family. This would give a total of one hundred and forty men, or eighteen *'elafim*. In a later list the number of men in an *'elef* is larger than that calculated in Numbers 1 and 26. Simeon is able to muster a total of one hundred men, which is equal to seven *'elafim*. This gives an average of fourteen per unit (1 Chron. 12). Note, however, that in the same list Judah, with six units has over eight hundred men, an average number of one hundred and thirty-three per unit! The variation in these figures would have a lot to do with the fact that in some of

---

[4]N.K. Gottwald *The Tribes of Yahweh: A Sociology of the Religion of Liberated Israel, 1250-1050 BCE* (Maryknoll, New York: Orbis Books, 1979): 271.

[5]In the Egyptian "Instructions of Meri-Ka-Re" it appears as though Egyptians were recruited into the army in their twenty-first year. See *ANET*: 415.

these lists the precise geographical boundaries of a *mishpachah* are not given, nor do we have here a complete number. Note, for example, that Dan is listed as having only one family (Num. 26.42), yet can offer for muster four hundred soldiers! We must also bear in mind that there was rarely such a thing as an "all-Israel" war in the period of the Judges when all the available troops would rally. There is no record of all the tribes going to war to defend their territory. The long exception is the full muster of the tribes against one of their own, Benjamin (Jud. 20-12).

Some idea of the normal tribal muster in this early period can be gained from the figures found in the stories of Gideon and Deborah and Barak. From three tribes, and his local area, Gideon initially mustered thirty two *'elafim*, and from the tribes which came to the aid of Gideon, there were possibly forty *'elafim* (Jud. 5.8). But the precise number of men in each unit is impossible to calculate.

It can be assumed that at this time the dominant method of fighting was on foot, and that battle organization was relatively simple. The *'elafim* went into battle commanded by their local leader, but under the temporary command of the "general", such as Barak, Gideon or Jephthah. Certain tribes were noted for their specialized skills, and these were used in fighting. The Benjaminites contained several slingers who were famous for their accuracy, and were almost the cause of the defeat of the other tribes who attacked Gibeah (Jud. 18-20). In 1 Chron. 12 other tribal units who had deserted to David in his outlaw days had developed reputations as soldiers, and many (e.g. Zebulun and Gad) could handle any weapon of war.

Once in battle units could be controlled (but exactly how well is not clear) by the use of runners and messengers, but, as the reaction of the Ephraimites to Gideon's command shows (Jud. 7.24-8.3), such a loose system of command had its drawbacks, and could not deal effectively with tribal units who did not wish to fight—as in the case of Reuben and Asher and others in Jud. 5, or those units who wished to get in on the action sooner and resented being called on at the last minute. This feeling would have certainly been exacerbated if the commander, like Gideon, came from one of the non-descript households in one of the smallest clans of Manasseh! Local pride, and local resentment of others were clearly present in the army of the Judges.

Before moving on to a survey of the monarchical organization of the military, we ought to look at the question of supply of troops in the field during times of war. The evidence is again scant, but it is possible to draw some conclusions from some of the stories in the book of Judges, and in some of those from the very early monarchy. Together these stories reflect the changing circumstances of warfare, and the changing methods of supply as the needs arose.

The first point we must make is that wars of this period were relatively short-lived affairs. Here we do not have long campaigns conducted by Israelites abroad. As we have stated above, these were defensive wars, on local ground, and rarely, if ever, far from local (and friendly) sources of food. Not only were the wars themselves shortlived, but it is most unlikely that the battles of this period were much more than extended skirmishes which would have lasted a minimum of minutes, and a maximum of hours. We ought to note that battles of later centuries, for example, those of the American Civil War or the Thirty Years' War, with vastly superior numbers and complicated battle plans, formations and systems of control, rarely took longer than a day. Further, such battles would not have employed all the troops at the disposal of the general in command. With such a comparison in mind it becomes clear that the problems of supply for the ancient Israelite army of the period of the Judges were not acute. Three incidents reveal something of the way in which the problems of supply were dealt with. They are the attack by the other tribes on the Benjaminites at Gibeah (Jud. 19-21), Saul's pursuit of the Philistines after the battle of Michmash (1 Sam. 14), Saul's confrontation with the Philistines in the Valley of Elah—the setting for the story of David and Goliath.

The tribal armies that gathered together against Benjamin at Gibeah adopted a relatively simple method. Supply of food, weapons, and presumably reinforcements was prearranged. By taking a certain percentage of the population and assigning them the task, the "provisions" (*tsedah*) for the besieging troops were guaranteed. The arrangement had been at a gathering of "all Israel" at Mizpah, with the tribal representatives making the necessary decisions. Such materiel needed to support the siege would have come from the various tribal territories, and have been pooled before the battle. The story of Jonathan's defeat of the garrison at Michmash (1 Sam. 14) is well known and the details do not need to be repeated here. Jonathan's surprise tactics resulted in a panic-stricken flight of the Philistines down the notorious Beth Horon "pass" to friendlier territory. In an attempt to ensure the utter defeat of the enemy by keeping up the pressure of his army on the Philistines, Saul placed a ban on the eating of food throughout the pursuit (1 Sam. 14.24). Jonathan, Saul's son, ignorant of the ban, ate some honey he found by chance in a wood. The man was spared. His justification for his action does make reference to a method of supply which would have suited the period well:

> How much better if the people had eaten freely today of the spoil of their enemies which they found ... (1 Sam. 14.30).

The practice of using the enemy's supply of food and weapons, especially if it was better than one's own, is taken for granted, and one might assume that it was a common, if erratic, method of supplying early Israelite soldiers. David also used it in his outlaw days (1 Sam. 30).[6]

The third incident reflects the conditions of a better organized army, but does add another element which might well be a remnant of an earlier system of supply. As we have seen in the previous chapter, David's visit to the battlefield at Elah was to bring supplies from his household to his brothers (1 Sa. 17.17-18). These supplies were put into the charge of the "baggage master" (*shomer haklim*). These supplies would

---

[6] In 6th century B.C. China it cost "one thousand gold pieces a day" to keep an army in the field. See Sun Tzu *The Art of War* [Eng. trans. S.B. Griffith] (Oxford University Press, 1963): 72.

be distributed later according to need. This method of home supply of food is not uncommon in ancient armies, especially in the case of a drawn-out confrontation, as is the case with the "stand-off" in the Elah valley.

In none of these cases is the method of supply a permanent one, in the sense that a regular system of setting aside provisions was maintained in case of war. Like the mustering of troops, the supply of food and other necessities was made possible only when the need arose. Transport of these supplies in this early period would have presented little of a problem since most of the battles were fought on "home ground" and communication would have been easy.

When considering matters of organization and recruitment in the monarchical army, we must be aware of the major shift in Israelite society that took place. We have outlined this in chapter two. Not all of the changes happened overnight, but the structure of society was so reshaped around a new centre that change was inevitable. The military developments have to be seen in the context of the major political and economic reorganization under the monarchs with the creation of a centralized bureaucracy of priests, lawyers, civil servants and generals (2 Sam. 8.15), each having a discrete role to play in the new system. In addition a new political factor has to be acknowledged, namely the personal political ambitions of the king, especially those ambitions directed beyond the borders of the country, and the measures taken internally to support those ambitions in a material and ideological way. For the moment we note what some of the measures were.

David's census (2 Sam. 24) must be considered of course as a symbol of the power and ambitions of the leader of the new regime. David's son, Solomon, undertook an extensive revision of the political boundaries within Israel (1 Kings 4.7-19), which disregarded the older tribal divisions (Josh. 13-18). In this way, Solomon ensured a regular supply of provisions for the royal household and its agenda. Solomon's son, Rehoboam, undertook a revision of the territory left to him after the secession of the north (2 Chron. 11-12), and the intention of this was for internal control. Finally, we note the extensive building programme undertaken by Solomon and his successors of the border fortresses of Judah. All of these factors provide some context for the military changes undertaken during the monarchy. Simply put, these changes consisted of the professionalization of the army, the construction of a supporting administration, controlled recruitment and the development of a sophisticated "battle order" employing a greater number of troop types under a central command for strategic and tactical purposes. Let us now add some colour to this outline.

Reference to the professionalization of the army is found in several passages pertaining to the monarchy. One of the clues is the frequent reference to the *sar tsaba'* (lit: "prince of the host"). The term *sar* is a bureaucratic term meaning "officer" and is often used to designate civilian functionaries, such as the "city governor" (*sar ha'ir*). In the military context it designates the senior officer of a unit, and the *sar tsaba'* is the commander-in-chief of the army. Such an office presupposes, of course, the existence of a standing army. It was the title given Phicol, commander of Abimelech of Gerar's forces. It is also the ascription of Sisera, the commander of Jabin of Hazor's forces (Jud. 4.2,7; 1 Sam. 12.9). In all of these cases the immediate, and only superior of the *sar tsaba'* is the king himself. In David's administration, Joab was the first commander-in-chief (2 Sam. 8.15) and the reference to him in the context of the bureaucratic structure of the new kingdom shows his position to be a bi-product of the centralized form of government. Others to bear the title are Amasa, Saul's commander, and Omri.

A standing army needs a staff and administrative support, and it is clear from the evidence that early in the monarchy these were put in place.

A professional army needs careful organization and a sophisticated command structure. As this happens the balance between "front line" troops and "support" troops changes in favour of an increase in the latter. This, in turn, would increase the burden of support imposed upon the local population. Some examples from non-Israelite countries, roughly contemporary with the Old Testament, would be helpful at this point.

The records of the kingdom of Mari,[7] a large city state on the Euphrates River, which thrived during the eighteenth century BC, shows that the army was a highly organized and stratified system of command. At the head of the army, as commander-in-chief, was the king. Other officers and senior ranks were:

| Term in Mari | English translation |
|---|---|
|  | staff officers (king's sons) |
| GAL-MAR-TU | Generals (Lit: Great Ones) |
| redum | aide de camp |
| DUB-SAR-MAR-TU | administrative officer |
| suqaqu | regional commander |
| nasiqum | guard |
| GAL-KUD | troop leader |
| UGULA-IO-LU | section leader (10 men) |
| GIR-SIG-GAR | bodyguard, attendant |
| alik pan | standard bearer |
| baddum | reconnaissance officer |

This is not a complete "order of battle" of the general staff of the army of Mari, but rather a selection of named officers from the records. Neither are they in order of importance. The *alik pan*, for example, who led troops into battle carrying the standard of the army, was a prestigious position, and usually given to a senior officer.

From a period a few centuries later, the Egyptian army of Thutmoses III (15th century BC) consisted of divisions of five thousand men each. Each division carried its own divisional name. The division was subdivided into twenty battalions of two hundred and fifty men each. These were further subdivided into companies of fifty each, five companies per battalion. Officers named in the Egyptian records include

---

[7]On the army organization at Mari see J.M. Sasson *The Military Establishment at Mari* (Rome: Pontifical Biblical Institute, 1969). On Ugarit see A.F. Rainey "The Military Personnel at Ugarit" *JNES* 24 (1965): 17-27.

the general of division, the assault officer, the chariot commander, the standard bearer and the company commander. Of course at different times during Egypt's history the order of battle would be different depending on several variables such as political organization of the country and the nature of the military pressures on the army. Neither of these two examples is complete, nor would the order have remained static. An army must develop according to the political structure and the political ambitions of the commander-in-chief, and keep up to date with available technology. But these examples do show the growing complication of a standing, professional army. Since it is clear from the record that Israel chose to go this route, then we must expect to find at least traces of similar organizations in the text of the Old Testament.

The basic divisions in the monarchical army in Israel were along similar lines to those of neighbouring countries. Not only did the *'elef* become a unit within the army, but this is further subdivided. 1 Sam. 22.7 betrays an early division into "thousands" and "hundreds" as Saul refers to his ability to appoint his men as commanders of these units. A similar order existed in the Philistine army (1 Sam. 29.2), and it is possible that David commanded such a subdivision. This basic order David clearly incorporated into his fledgling army, as is illustrated by his battle order during the revolt of Absalom (2 Sam. 18.1). The "hundred" (*me'ah*) is a fixed unit in the mid-monarchy, and *sar me'ah* seems to be used as a rank designation for palace officers. The evidence for this is hidden in some English translations (RSV), but retained in others (NEB), of 2 Kings 11.

By far the most common designation is that of the "fifty" (Heb: *chamishim*). It is found, for example, in the frequent references to the fifty who "run before" a military or political leader (e.g. 1 Sam. 8.11; 2 Sam. 15.1; 1 Kings 1.5) and is presupposed in the military reorganisation under the monarch in 1 Sam. 8.12. The position seems well established in the mid-monarchy, and such a unit (three in all!) plays a prominent role in the attempt to arrest Elijah in 2 Kings 1. The leader of such a group has the formal rank of *sar chamishim*.

Although the term *sar eser* (commander of ten) appears in Deut. 1.15 as a designation for the head of a sub-organization of a tribe, there is little evidence to suggest that this was a formal rank in the Israelite monarchical army. This is unusual since the unit of ten men received prominence in battle formations from the Romans on until the modern-day "squad". It is never mentioned in the Bible as a military unit, with the exception of what appears to be an informal grouping of men in the incident of David's dealings with Nabal of Maon (1 Sam. 25.5). The same figure is mentioned in the slaying of Absalom (2 Sam. 18.15). It is possible that chariots were organised into squadrons of ten (2 Kings 13.7), but the evidence for the unit of ten men in the army is absent, although such a unit seems a logical possibility.

One further subdivision is to be noted, and it occurs in a poorly translated passage in 2 Kings 11. The setting is a revolt against the usurper queen Athaliah, organised from within the palace by Jehoiada the priest. In v.7 the RSV translates: "... and the two divisions of you, which come on duty...." The word translated "divisions" is *yadoth* "hands". It seems a reasonable conclusion that such a unit would consist of five men. However, this is the only reference to such a unit, and it appears to have been restricted to the guards on duty in the royal palace.

Within the monarchical army in Israel, as with contemporary armies there was a formal division among the "arms of service". That is that soldiers with different training and skills were organized under different commands, and used in concert with others on the field of battle. The basic divisions were those of *infantry*, *chariotry* and *cavalry*.

Israelite infantry can only be reconstructed from scant references in the Bible, but one can assume on the basis of this slender evidence that the infantry was subdivided among the four common branches of spearmen, swordsmen, archers and slingers. Each would necessitate a distinct training and the acquisition of a distinct skill. While there is a possibility that some soldiers would be good "all around" fighters, able, like the men of Zebulun and Manasseh, to handle all weapons of war (1 Chron. 12.33,37), there is also evidence of specialized skills, such as the spearmen of Naftali (1 Chron.

12.34) equipped with spear and shield, and the slingers of Benjamin, who were expert shots, and who wrought havoc among the attacking tribes (Jud. 20.15-16), and the men who "drew the sword". The context of these references is stories about the period of the judges, but it is clear that such skills were prized in the monarchical army, and organized into specialized troops. The swordsmen, able to be used in close fighting, are referred to in 2 Sam. 24.9 and in 2 Kings 3.26. The slingers are able to effect the fall of Kir Haresheth in the combined campaign against Moab (2 Kings 3.25), and the equipment of the rebel soldiers in 2 Kings 11. consists of "spears and shields", like that of the men of Judah whom Asa mustered to fight against the Ethiopian king Zerah (2 Chron. 14.7). It is, of course, quite possible, that an armed soldier, ready for battle would be equipped with more than one weapon. This was standard practice throughout the ancient Near East at this time, but there were also areas of expertise, and special skills which were cultivated among the infantrymen of contemporary armies.

One final note here on slingers. Lest the comments about the accuracy of slingers should be doubted, one should check the position of slingers in the famous relief of the siege of Lachish by Sennacherib. In the battle order, the slingers stand behind the archers, presumably a testimony to their greater accuracy.

Archers, equipped by now with the standard composite bow, would also comprise a branch of infantry. There are few references to archers in battle in the Bible, but sufficient to show them to have been a discrete unit within the infantry. It appears that archers were also protected by a shield (2 Chron. 14.7), and the shield here might not be the small "buckler" carried by spearmen. The small shield allowed for quick and easy movement on the field of battle and would be for minimal protection of the warrior. The archers' shield is depicted in Assyrian reliefs, and is a large wicker canopy-like structure which the archer stood behind, and which would enable the archer to stand his ground while firing. The respective value of these branches of the army will be dealt with below under tactics.

Infantrymen, of course, travel on foot, but there is evidence

of a more mobile force of soldiers in the armies of the monarchy in Israel, the cavalryman and the charioteer. The foot
soldier is only minimally hindered by the lie of the land and
the roughness of the terrain. By climbing and scrambling, an
infantryman can advance and attack over the roughest land,
and in the annals of military history several battles have been
won by the adventurous thrust into enemy territory by men
on foot, who attacked where they were least expected. This
is more difficult to do with the mounted fighters, whether on
horseback or in chariot.

There is little doubt, however, that a cavalry and a chariot
force did develop in Israel during the monarchy, and were
used to great effect in fighting. One question, difficult to
settle, is: When were they introduced? And another question,
impossible to answer, is: What was the balance between
mounted men and foot soldiers in the Israelite army? The
answer to the former depends on an historical judgment on
the available evidence, the speculation regarding the latter
can be constructed from what we know of the relationship of
infantry to cavalry and chariotry from other nations of the
time. The first recorded use of chariots in the Israelite army
is found during the time of David. In 2 Sam. 8.4, David took
from the king of Zobah enough horses for one hundred
chariots (chariots were usually drawn by two horses).
Whether this is a simple measurement, or whether this indicates that David himself had a fledgling chariot force in his
army is unclear. There is no record of David or his army
actually fighting with chariots. Absalom acquired a chariot
(2 Sam. 15.1), but this appears to be a status symbol, demonstrating his desired rank, rather than a war vehicle. In the
battle between David's army and the rebels, Absalom chose
the more conventional transport of a mule (2 Sam. 18.9). It
appears that it was Solomon who developed a strong chariot
wing of his army, according to 1 Kings 10.26-29, but since
Solomon was engaged in no serious wars throughout his
reign the exact purpose of this chariot force is unclear.

Whatever the date of the introduction of the chariot into
Israel's army, it is clear that by the mid-ninth century BC,
chariots were common vehicles of war. In the days preceding
the rise of the Omride dynasty, we encounter Zimri "com-

mander of half of [Elah's] chariots" (1 Kings 15.8), who led the revolt against the king. From this time on chariots appear frequently in battle reports. Charioteers, it seemed, developed a reputation for recklessness and rebellion because it was another chariot general, Jehu, who led the coup against the last of the Omrides, Joram (2 Kings 9). Jehu was also noted for his hard driving (2 Kings 9.20). It is interesting to note that Jehu makes a special effort to gain the support of Jonadab the charioteer (2 Kings 10.15-17).

## B. *Leadership and Motivation*

Armies are made up, among other things, of leaders and followers, and these relationships are generally formalized in organized armies into officers and soldiers. It is expected of officers that they will possess certain qualities and strengths of character which will inspire the mass of the troops to obey them, and to put their lives in mortal danger. The relationship is like no other. The "art of battle" is to inflict as much damage on the forces of one's opponent as possible, which means often killing as many of his men as possible. But this is done at a cost, and rarely do two antagonists achieve their ends without considerable cost in lives lost. In battle everytime a soldier obeys an order to engage the enemy the chances of him getting killed increase. It therefore requires a particular kind of individual to ask others to expose themselves to such great danger, and a particular kind of individual who will willingly accede to the request. In exploring these dynamics we enter the difficult field of studies into leadership and motivation.

These are vast areas of knowledge, and we have to keep in mind that we are trying to examine the phenomenon of warfare within the Old Testament period. There are many modern studies which have been conducted on qualities of leadership, and many theories have been expounded on the nature of leadership. We could move from some of these general models of leadership to the particular of the Old Testament world, but what we have to avoid is the tendency to modernize. Unfortunately, many portrayals of military leaders in the Old Testament have been turned into pictures of modern battle heroes with decidedly modern interests. We have to look carefully at the particulars of the Old Testament world, and whatever models are used must accommodate those data drawn from our primary source, the Old Testament.

A study conducted in the recent past of qualities of leadership drew up a list of characteristics which leading managers in business thought would be appropriate for a good leader.[8] There were twenty-five characteristics in all, and the list included items such as the ability to make decisions (#1), integrity (#), analytical ability (#7), enterprise (#13) and single-mindedness (#21) among many others. The list contains some commendable characteristics, which most would covet. But a few comments are in order. First, it is an ideal list, something like a Christmas list, in which one would put what one most desired as a gift, but in reality one would be content with a few items on the list. In other words, no one person would possess all of these characteristics. Second, the list was drawn up by businessmen, and while modern armies rightfully place great emphasis upon organization and management skills because of the growing complexity of the modern fighting unit, it is unlikely that these characteristics were prized in antiquity as much as others which are notably absent. For example, missing from the list are physical abilities, stamina, physical dexterity and strength. Even today, in some types of warfare such qualities are valued highly. Also missing are less physical and more psychological qualities like cunning, as exemplified in the stories of Jonathan and Gideon, and, although attempts have been made to control excessive violence in warfare, the qualities of a leader must include the ability to be at times quite insensitive to suffering in the interests of "getting the job done". It would be inappropriate then for us to develop a modern, and perfectly viable model for the modern age, and to read it back into the Old Testament when looking for qualities of leaders in battle.

---

[8]Cited in J. Adair *Effective Leadership* (London: Pan Books, 1983): 201.

One of the greatest writers on the "art of war" was the Prussian theoretician and practitioner of war, Carl von Clausewitz (1780-1831). In his famous book, *On War*,[9] published in 1832, he sketches some qualities of leadership, amongst which he places the indefinable gift of "genius". Genius is accompanied by "energy, firmness, staunchness, strength of mind and character", and the combination of these and other characteristics leads him to offer the following comment:

> As the forces in one individual after another become prostrated, and can no longer be excited and supported by an effort of his own will, the whole inertia of the mass rests its weight on the Will of the Commander: *by the spark in his breast, by the light of his spirit, the spark of purpose, the light of hope, must be kindled afresh in others:* in so far only as he is equal to this, he stands above the masses and continues to be their master: whenever that influence ceases ... the masses drawing him down with them sink into the lower regions of animal nature which shrinks from danger and knows not shame.[10]

This, or course, puts an enormous weight of responsibility upon the shoulders of the leader, whose character must be equal to the task (character, incidentally, which escapes non-civilized cultures, according to von Clausewitz.) In turn, this presupposes an attitude on the part of the regular soldier in battle, namely that of looking at all times to the inspiration afforded him by his commander, an inspiration which provides him with sufficient motivation for dangerous and deadly action. Such a construct, while it may contain certain elements of truth in it, is idealistic in the extreme, and the literature of warfare does not support the theory of leadership expounded here, nor the corollary, the image of the follower. Particular leaders may inspire confidence, loyalty and even love in their men, but this is no guarantee for victory, and it cannot be generalised.

[9]Carl von Clausewitz *On War* (Harmondsworth: Penguin Books, 1968): 144.

[10]Clausewitz *Ibid*: 145

Another "model" of leadership which has been used frequently when discussing Old Testament characters is that of "charisma", especially the way in which it was expounded by the sociologist Max Weber. Again the literature is vast, and we cannot delve too far into the discussion, but this model has been seen as appropriate to military leaders in the Bible. Weber offers the following comments about charisma:

> The term 'charisma' will be applied to a certain quality of an individual personality by virtue of which he is set apart from ordinary men and treated as endowed with supernatural, superhuman, or at least specifically exceptional powers or qualities. *These are such as are not accessible to the ordinary person*, but are regarded as of divine origin or exemplary, and on the basis of them the individual concerned is treated as a leader.[11]

Apart from vague definitions of charisma as out of the ordinary or beyond the profane, we find little in Weber's description that enables us to pin down this quality further. Since, as he suggests, it is a quality normally recognised by the followers or disciples of the person concerned, it possesses a kind of secret quality, and most of us are left in the dark. Further, application of such a characteristic to some well-known and successful leaders in history, shows the model to be less than adequate. In the case of the Old Testament, we shall see, in fact that there are other elements of leadership which have to be considered, and which do not necessarily fit Weber's model.

Any study of leadership must take into consideration the expectations, and thereby the standards of the community to which the leader and soldiers belong.[12] What constitutes a model leader in one culture does not necessarily transfer to

---

[11] M. Weber *The Theory of Social and Economic Organization* [Eng. trans. Talcott Parsons] (New York: Free Press, 1947): 358-407. Idem *Ancient Judaism* [Eng. trans. H.H. Gerth] (New York: Free Press, 1952): 17-19.

[12] This notion is well expounded in J. Keegan *The Mask of Command* (New York: Viking, 1987).

another. Kings or general-kings regarded by their people as gods would have an easier time of leadership than one whose reputation had to be hard-earned. One of the dangers of studying the Old Testament material, as we have stated, is that of reading back into the past standards of our own day and culture. It is the danger of westernization and modernization. It is necessary then to look at the Old Testament material itself to see what constituted a leader in ancient Israel. At the same time we need to be aware of the kind of society in which these leaders functioned, and further, the values and standards which are contained within the literature of the society. One can assume that the stories of old heroes and leaders, their rise and fall, reflect certain expectations of what a good leader should be, and what a bad leader is. In one major sense we have an advantage here over the material from the surrounding cultures, because the Old Testament literature offers a broader angle of vision of the characters who walk on its stage. By way of contrast, the notion of leadership we might gain from Egyptian literature comes from the self-conscious, if not self-serving, records of an Amosis I as he recalls the expulsion of the Hyksos from Egypt [13], or the records of Thutmosis III fight at Megiddo.[14] From Assyria we are dependent upon the annals of a Shalmaneser III[15] or an Esarhaddon.[16] The image of the ideal battle leader each portrays is himself. It would be far more valuable from the historical perspective to have an alternative, or an independent view of Thutmosis's generalship and ability to inspire his men. All we have in his records from Karnak are his own words on the matter!

The Old Testament is a remarkable collection of literature in that its portrayal of leaders, kings and others is much more complex, and less one-dimensional. We must remember, of course, that the society with which we are dealing is much more tightly controlled than ours. Its borders are well-

---

[13]See *ANET.* 233-234.
[14]*ANET.* 234.
[15]*ANET.* 276.
[16]*ANET.* 289.

defined, and its standards of behaviour are carefully delineated.

There are certain characteristics which are mentioned in the Old Testament, either directly or indirectly which suggest qualifications for a leader of men in battle. First among these is the ability to kill the enemy in battle. Saul had killed his thousands, but David had killed ten times that number. The source of these comments and the jealousy it aroused in Saul indicates that they put David in a good light, and qualified him for leadership, a role he later took to himself. In Psalm 18 similar sentiments can be inferred from the praise offered to God for the ability granted the psalmist to "thrust his enemies through" when their backs were turned. Subsequently, numerous kings are praised by their historian for their "great deeds" (*gedoloth*), no doubt actions of warfare. The collection of thirty-seven men who fled to David at Adullam were such fighters and killers, and were eventually rewarded with positions of power in the future administration of the king. Note that the characteristic of the "mighty" (*gibbor*) was the ability to slaughter enemies (2 Sam. 23). So one of the qualifications for leadership was the ability to kill on the field of battle.

A second qualification, both for battle leadership, and for eventual political leadership, concerns the public display of honour. In this sense honour would encompass those values which the community held as central, and would be reflected in behaviour which met the expectations of the general population. In the case of the "strong group/high grid" society of ancient Israel, this would mean "going by the book" and exemplifying those characteristics—obedience to the Torah among them—which demonstrated that the person in question was an ideal Israelite. Soldiers are, after all, protectors of the society. Symbolically, they expel invasions, stand on its borders and regulate what enters and leaves the territory of that society, thus ensuring, to the best of their ability, the survival of the way of life to which they belong. It is fitting then that they should be seen as exemplifying the best of that society's values. Thus, some heroes, such as Moses and Joshua are praised for such an attitude. Others, such as Samson and Saul are condemned for the lack of it, and still others, like Solomon, are warned that such obedience is expected of them if the people are to prosper under their leadership. What is to be noted here, however, is that the military role of the leader is becoming less and less, and in the case of Solomon, nonexistent. With Jehu, however, his initial loyalty to Yahweh qualifies him in part for the task as leader of the revolt against the house of Ahab.

A third possible qualification for leadership comes under the category of "courage". However, this is a flexible concept and does not necessarily mean the same thing from culture to culture, nor even in the same culture. Some believe [17] that the concept has to do with the Hebrew word *chayil*, also translated "strength", "army", "valour" etc. The term, however, is used in contexts which have little or nothing to do with warfare (Gen. 47.6; 1 Kings 1.42, 52), or used so frequently and indiscriminately of men involved in warfare, that it can simply mean "soldier" (Josh 8.3; 1 Sam. 14.52; 31.12; 2 Sam. 11.16; 13.28; 17.10; Nah. 2.4; Ps. 76.6). It is, on occasion reserved for special leaders such as Jephthah (Jud. 11.1), David (1 Sam. 16.78), Benaiah, who later became a general in David's army (2 Sam. 23.20) and Naaman (2 Kings 5.1). It is also used of Gideon (Jud. 6.12), a quality which he promptly disowns! The possession of this same quality by Jeroboam ben Nebat brings him to the attention of Solomon, but what is most surprising is that it is never used of either Moses or the greatest military leader in Israel, Joshua. The terms normally translated with the English "courage" etc. are again not exclusively military in their application, but a frequent admonition to Joshua in the stories of the conquest. This is not so much a quality of leadership alone, but a demand placed on all soldiers in the line of battle (Deut. 20).

A most important qualification for leadership in the Old Testament rests not so much in the individual qualities of the person of the leader, but comes from outside. It is seen as divine choice, and a choice often confirmed by a prophet. Also common to such choices is the frequent tendency of the

---

[17]For example, see P.E. Davies "Courage" *IDB* I:712-713.

person thus singled out to resist the choice, or for the choice to be most unlikely. For example, Saul, the first king of Israel is noted for his physical appearance, yet comes from the tribe of Benjamin and acknowledges that he, of all people, is least qualified for the position given him by Samuel (1 Sam. 9.21). In one tradition of his rise to power David is likewise an unlikely candidate for the position of Saul's successor. Samuel is informed that physical appearance is not to influence his choice of the young man (1 Sam. 16.7), and by his own admission, David is not qualified to be a fighter (1 Sam. 17.31-40). Adonijah selects Jeroboam ben Nebat, undoubtedly a "man of valour" but on the basis of divine choice (1 Kings 12). Elisha selects Jehu (2 Kings 9) and Hazael (2 Kings 8), notwithstanding their military abilities, because of divine choice.

In the annals of military history the qualities which suit a leader are many. In retrospect few great military leaders have been of extraordinary physical strength, except in the age of the local hero, such as portrayed in the Iliad. More common are the men, smaller than life, and who in different circumstances often fade into the background. For every Caesar, Napoleon, Frederick the Great or Eisenhower, who were able to combine military prowess and leadership with political acumen—at least for a while—there are hundreds of former generals who either faded into oblivion in civilian life, or nostalgically clung to vestiges of the past military glory. There is, in fact, no one characteristic of leadership which can be universally applied as a standard, then recognized in individuals. Ability to kill, if pushed to the point of a pathological behaviour eventually repulses followers rather than attracts them.[18] Examples of battlefield courage can be praised as examples to follow, but can also turn to objects of ridicule as a commander is seen by tired troops as exposing

---

[18]See the fine exposition of this in G. Linderman *Embattled Courage: The Experience of Combat in the American Civil War* (New York: Free Press, 1987), esp. pp. 156-168.

himself and them to unnecessary danger.[19] At times, even the values prized highly at home as justification of the fighting cause, and often providing hopes for the final outcome of an armed struggle, can turn sour and lose their sweetness in the midst of incessant campaigning and the privations which go with it. The Egyptian soldier of Papyrus Anastasi seemed to sense no desire to "rally to the flag" or the cause in his campaigns through Canaan. His concerns degenerate into the need for survival, the location of water, the protection of his kit and food, and his personal safety from hostile and marauding locals.[20] These would be conditions which affect all fighting men of the Middle East, including Israel. The question of leadership then is how to take men with such concerns and make them fight and stay fighting. This brings us to the question of motivation of the fighter himself.

By motivation we mean the ability to remain in the field of battle, and fight when one's life is in mortal danger, and when the most reasonable and sensible thing to do would be to run away. The danger was as acute in ancient times as it is today in battle. Numbers of the slain in ancient records were often greatly exaggerated, especially when the records were left to us by the victor, but it cannot be forgotten that in these ancient battles, large numbers of men did die, and at times, when the line broke and the soldiers fled, reasonably organized tactical struggles degenerated into wholesale slaughter. This is clear from the setting of the story of Jonathan's eating of the honey in 1 Sam. 14, and Joshua's pursuit of the

---

[19]It is doubtful whether the sentiments of the modern western combat soldier can be transported back into the ancient Near East. The differences in the nature of the cultures and the societies make it a hazardous venture. However, historians of modern combat have an advantage in that they have now very full records of the thoughts and opinions of the modern combat veteran. For the ancient Near East, the combat veteran is forever silent. One can only speculate that the thoughts and feelings during combat were similar, and that at times in ancient Israel, as later in World War 2 the Falklands/Malvinas or in Vietnam, the powerful urge to self-preservation asserted itself, and potentially dangerous orders might have been disobeyed. For a modern description of such an attitude see J.O. Brende, E.R. Parsons *Vietnam Veterans: The Road to Recovery* (New York: Signet, 1985): 49-52. See also Linderman *Embattled Courage*: 229-234.

[20]Translation is found in A. Erman *The Ancient Egyptians: A Sourcebook of Their Writings* (New York: Harper Torchbooks, 1961): 194-195.

Canaanites along the same route in the story of the conquest (Josh. 9-10). Contrary to the practice of some oriental armies which were advised to let the enemy leave the field with honour, the biblical battles were a game of killing. If the opponent's line broke and his troops fled in panic, then the killing was easy, but troops must always have lived with the fear that their own lines would break and they would panic and flee, pursued by an enemy equally thirsty for their blood. How did the soldier cope with this kind of pressure?

This is an important question, and one which has received a great deal of attention in the circles of modern military history. A classic in the field is S.L.A. Marshall's important work *Men Against Fire*[21], published after his studies of fighters during the Second World War. Recently published has been Richard Holmes's *Acts of War: The Behaviour of Men in Battle*[22] (also published under the title of *Firing Line*), and Elmar Dinter's *Hero or Coward: Pressures Facing the Soldier in Battle*.[23] Even more recent is the masterful work of Gerald Linderman, *Embattled Courage: The Experience of Combat in the American Civil War*.[24] These books offer a fascinating insight into the mind of the combat soldier, his fears, hopes, and indeed some of the motivating factors that keep him "brave". But they have an advantage over our sources in that they deal with combat in the age of the literate combat soldier, who in a time of no censorship, could write home his true thoughts and feelings on the experience of battle, or on reflection would open up to an historian or psychologist and speak from memory of his reactions to combat. But this has happened only since the nineteenth century, and has been justifiably exploited by the modern historians named above.

Our sources are not so forthcoming. Dependent as we are on the written records contained in the Old Testament and

---

[21]S.L.A. Marshall *Men Against Fire* (Washington: Combat Forces Press, 1947).

[22]R. Holmes *Acts of War: The Behaviour of Men in Battle* (New York: Free Press, 1986).

[23]E. Dinter *Hero or Coward: Pressures Facing the Soldier in Battle* (London: 1986).

[24]G. Linderman *Embattled Courage*.

other ancient Near Eastern literature, we are forced to rely on the words of an elite. The role of scribe was a court role, and few would dare to present an unfavourable picture of the court for public scrutiny. Even fewer would think it worthwhile to describe the anxieties and hopes of the combat soldier, who, being recruited or conscripted from the illiterate strata of society, who would be regarded as a virtual nonentity. Even the Old Testament, which tends to be highly critical of the central power system of the monarchy, records with a distinct lack of passion the slaughter of thousands of nameless and unsung soldiers on both sides of a conflict. In the words of a later Israelite writer:

> ... there are some who have no memorial, who have perished as though they had not lived; they have become as though they had never been born, and so have their children after them (Sirach 48.9).

In the catalogue of named ones which follows we find the noble, the faithful heroes of the faith, and only one soldier, Joshua. The fact remains that thousands did fight, some to live to fight another day, others to die anonymous deaths in battle, and it is important to search for an answer to the question, Why? The answer must be devoid of an unreal, romantic picture of the past. While it is impossible to listen directly to the voices of the past, perhaps they can be passed down to us in the experience of their comrades in arms through the ages. We can listen to the records that do exist, and with the appropriate tuning hear the echoes of the nameless thousands who died on ancient Israel's hills and in her valleys.

One of the motivations to fight is, simply put, bravery. This is the decision to stay and endure and overcome in spite of a knowledge of the danger involved. It is coupled with a sense of duty, "getting the job done", a certain self-effacement when the task is accomplished. The records of battles are full of accounts of young and old, well born and peasant, the brash and the shy, committing acts of incredible bravery and exposing themselves to serious danger in the process with no thought for themselves. It would be a strange anomaly if this quality were not present on ancient Israel's fields of battle. As we have seen the term for "soldier" was a "man of valour" (*gibbor chayil*), and there are certain expectations in that epithet. But courage and bravery are not universal qualities. Not every soldier possesses them, as Marshall discovered. Further, the more organized the fighting unit becomes, as it did in Israel under the monarchy, and the more the battle develops into a "set-piece" affair, the less room there would be for individual acts of bravery, which might appear noble, but whose results were often less than desired. In the American civil war exposure of officers to enemy fire increased chances of death, robbed the unit of a brave leader, brought down enemy fire on the unit and often resulted in the demoralising of the men. "Man of valour" is a general designation in the ancient Israelite army, as we have seen, and it is enjoined in Deut. 20.3 and elsewhere as a desirable quality in battle. But allowances are made for its lack in the same chapter, and the soldier preoccupied with a new house, a new crop of vines and an unbedded wife, is permitted to withdraw from combat. The reasons for this law are intriguing. Was this phenomenon of uncommitted soldiers a common one in a land now settled? What we can be sure of is that behind the law is the fear that such a lack of bravery is contagious and will affect the fellows in the same line (Deut. 20.8). Further, the opposite of courage and bravery, namely, fear which causes panic is also mentioned in the Old Testament. Frequent references are found, usually in the form of curses on one's enemy, that he will become "like a woman in travail", or to the effect an invasion has on the soldiers of Israel and Judah (Ps. 48.6; Isa. 13.8; Isa. 21.3; Jer. 6.24; 13.21; [Mic. 4.9]). One guesses what this means from Isa. 21.3, which certainly gives it vivid content:

> ... my loins are filled with anguish: pangs have seized me, like the pangs of a woman in travail; I am bowed down so that I cannot hear, I am dismayed so that I cannot see. My mind reels, horror has appalled me; the twilight I longed for has turned for me into trembling (Isa. 21.3-4).

This is a picture of weakness, helplessness, extreme physical discomfort in the gut and lack of control. Many a soldier has attested to the physical effects of fear in battle [25], and they have been catalogued as "a sinking feeling in the stomach, uncontrollable trembling, a cold sweat, a feeling of weakness or stiffness and vomiting ... involuntary urination and ... involuntary defecation." [26] This seems remarkably close to what the prophet is describing here. Of course, one would wish this upon one's enemy, and do everything to encourage these symptoms, but since such symptoms are quite common among soldiers before and during battle, they have to be controlled. Once the individual succumbs to such feelings of fear and terror he becomes quite ineffective as a soldier, and although not common, there are examples of ancient Israel's army fleeing from the field of battle in terror and with the cry "to your tents, O Israel" (1 Sam. 4.10; 1 Kings 12.6; 2 Kings 8.21 and 14.12), or helped on their way by some frightening demonstration of alien power (2 Kings 3.27). How then are men in such state to be controlled?

The French military theorist and writer Du Picq suggested a simple solution. Troops in line should be motivated by fear, but by a greater fear of their own commanding officers than by fear of the enemy. This, of course, brutalizes men, but war is a brutal business, and such sentiments do not seem out of place for Du Picq. In fact, it is certainly possible that something approaching this policy was present in the Egyptian army. Our anonymous soldier in the Papyrus Lansing appears to have had his will to resist his officers crushed by hard work, and his colleague mentioned in Papyrus Anastasi is clearly frequently beaten into submission.[27] There is no evidence for such harsh discipline within the ancient Israelite and Judaean armies. However, breaches of military rules of behaviour in battle were dealt with very harshly, as is seen in the punishment of Achan and his family (Josh. 8).

[25]See J. Dollard *Fear in Battle* (Westport, Conn: 1944), and the comments of Du Picq cited in J. Keegan *The Face of Battle* (New York: Vintage Books, 1978): 71-74.

[26]Holmes *Acts of War*: 205. See also Brende, Parsons *Vietnam Veterans*: 46.

[27]Erman *Ancient Egyptians*: 194-196.

In addition to these factors, there are others which motivate the fighting soldier. The first is religion. The second is the psychological effect of battle on an individual soldier, and the third is the relationship which is developed between a soldier and his fellows, which is characterized, among other things, by what the "PBI's" (poor bloody infantry) chronicler Ernie Pyle called "the camaraderie of misery".

Let me remind you again that at this point we are not talking about motivation which might come from fighting for "the cause" in the grand sense. Such sentiments belong in the area of grand strategy to which the more appropriate question is "Why go to war?" No, in the present discussion we are more concerned with the question addressed to the individual, "Why stay and fight?" There is no doubt that, at least in the early stages of an armed conflict between groups, the sense of "cause" and the rightness of one's cause is present among soldiers. It manifests itself often in terms of trust in and loyalty to one's leaders. They, after all, must know what they are doing.

However, when we look more closely at the role of religion in individual motivation we see a narrowing of the focus from thoughts of the grand divine plan, or the sense that the army is the agent of the divine will, to a reflection on the immediate matters of personal survival. Into this most individual of all concerns comes a religious sense, but this sense is not "theological." There is little or no intellectual reflection here. It is much more instinctual. Ancient Israelite soldiers did not go to war, according to the evidence, believing in a sweet afterlife as the destiny of the departed faithful. Such a concept was hardly beginning to develop in the Old Testament period. In fact, in those cultures surrounding Israel in which the concept of an afterlife was quite highly developed, there is no understanding of that afterlife as a reward for death in battle. Concepts of glorious resurrection which have undoubtedly played a role in the ferocity, if not bravery of some fighting men, cannot be appealed to as motivating factors of religion in the Old Testament period. It would be wrong to equate the zeal of the Crusaders, motivated no doubt by a sense of divine reward for their valour, or the fanaticism of some Islamic soldiers with the fighting spirit of the Old Testament warrior. Both the former were spurred on by thoughts of resurrection to a more glorious and happy life. This same attitude prompted a Union soldier surveying the thousands of dead on the field of Chickamauga to exclaim, "What a harvest of souls in Paradise!" Such was not the case in ancient Israel, and could never be the case. On the contrary, as we have seen, nameless thousands died with no memorial, and there are no psalms in the Old Testament singing the virtues of the premature death of the righteous. If the narratives of Josiah's demise reveal typical attitudes to such deaths, then premature death of a righteous man on the field of battle was a disaster and not a blessing, and the loss of soldiers in battle a sign of judgment.

The concept of religion, or piety and battle motivation is a personal one, and it has clear limits. Religion guaranteed victory on the one hand, and personal protection on the other. This can be read out of the "law on warfare" in Deuteronomy 20. The combatants are not to be afraid since they are accompanied into battle by Yahweh, the God who delivered them from Egypt. "... let not your heart faint, do not fear, or tremble or be in dread of [the enemy]; for the Lord your God is he that goes with you, to fight for you ... and *to give you the victory*" (Deut. 20.4). What follows clearly personalizes this general appeal by the priests to the line of soldiers ready for battle. The irrationality of this position is not worked out in the pages of the Old Testament.[28]

Numerous psalms which touch on matters of warfare and battle demonstrate further that the religious element in battle is mostly a matter of personal protection. From the initial

---

[28]The role of religion in combat is an important study in itself, and its proper understanding depends upon so many variables. The chaplain is often the centre of focus for this topic, but the expectations placed upon the chaplain by the officers on the one hand, and the men on the other, are quite different. Private religious attitudes among the common soldiers are also quite different from the attitudes of the officers. The whole matter has yet to be studied in detail. For some preliminary comments see Holmes *Acts of War*: 241-242, 287-290; Anderson *A People's Army*: 196-224; Linderman *Embattled Courage*: 102-103; Kellett *Combat Motivation*: 193-195. In spite of the fact that it does not figure prominently in the works of Machiavelli, Hobbes or von Clausewitz, religion has, and still does, play an important role in the complex phenomenon of warfare.

terror of the conflict in which the writer is faced with the possibility of death (Ps. 18.4-5), the tone of the poem moves to a celebration of the victory given by God's marvellous display of power (vv. 7-15), the slaughter of the enemy (vv. 37-38) and the sense of deliverance from danger (vv. 46-48). In Psalm 21 skill and prowess in battle are married to God's activity on behalf of the combatant to culminate in victory and deliverance. Psalm 25 concludes with a prayer for personal protection (vv. 19-21) and a generalization of that prayer (v. 22). The poet of Psalm 27 expresses an irrational confidence in the presence of the encamped enemy (v. 3) because he knows his God will "... hide me in his shelter ... conceal me under the cover of his tent ... " (v. 5).

Such confidence, perhaps born out of a sense of the rightness of one's cause, has interesting side effects. Throughout the Psalms the enemy become the "wicked", "the aggressors", "men who devise evil against me", and the conflict is seen in terms of good and evil, right and wrong (e.g. Ps. 34.19-22), with the right always on one side. It is such an attitude, of course, which encourages the confident warrior, for what God would allow the cause of the "Lord's servants" (Ps. 34.22) to fail? Coupled with this is the display of certain attitudes toward the enemy which amount to a dehumanizing, what military historians and psychologists have termed a "pseudo-speciation" of the enemy. The enemy of Ps. 35.5, and indeed throughout the psalm are treated in this way. They are worthless "chaff before the wind", who are snared and trampled down by the (inevitable) righteous victor. We, of course, are at a loss to know precisely which enemy is in mind here. We can assume that it was "pagan" nations pressing in ancient Israel or Judah from outside, but this would be a dangerous and perhaps false assumption to make. Wars were conducted between Israel and Judah throughout the history of the monarchy, and the enemy in mind might well be former allies from the ten tribes north of the border. As with many armies, the enemy is always the aggressor, the criminal. It is he who "... draws the sword and bends the bow, to bring down the poor and needy, to slay those who walk uprightly" (Ps. 37.14-15). Such dehumanizing has the military advantage of lessening the qualms about killing, and adding justification to the act of killing itself.

"The very business of war is to produce results by death and slaughter" are the words of General William Tecumseh Sherman, and this raises another question of motivation. Why, in battle, do men do what they would normally refrain from doing in another context? In a society like ancient Israel, which paid so much attention to the care of orphans, widows and strangers, which prided itself on justice and which looked forward to the golden age of universal justice, it is anomalous to find dispassionate records not only of the killing of enemy soldiers, but also the accounts of the wholesale slaughter of civilian men, women and children by Israelite soldiers. Part of the answer to this puzzle can be found in the training of soldiers, which, while not prominent in the Old Testament, was certainly a part of the life of every soldier. Saul's response to David when he volunteered to take on Goliath concerned his lack of skill as a warrior (1 Sam. 17.31-40), and references to training are scattered throughout narrative and poem. The Reubenites and Gadites of 1 Chron. 5.18 are "trained in war" (Heb: *lemudey milchamah*). The term implies teaching. Benjaminites were well-known for their skill with the sling. It stands to reason that an organised army would be a trained army, disciplined, and skilled in battle. But such training is only part of the answer. The kind of killing that went on after the flight of an enemy, as exemplified in 2 Chron. 14.9-14 (EVV), and the kind of killing which went on after the fall of a city (2 Kings 8.12) takes a particular kind of attitude on the part of the fighting soldier which goes beyond reason. It is indiscriminate and wholesale, intent on the spread of slaughter and destruction. What motivates men to these extremes?

Group psychology can be appealed to as a contributing factor. As sure as panic spreads like a bush fire throughout an otherwise organized army, so does the lust for blood in pursuit of a fleeing enemy. Men trained to react to situations with violence will, in circumstances when they sense danger, react in this way with more vehemence. But the killing often goes beyond the level of "justified", that is, the killing of enemy combatants, to the level of atrocity, where defenseless civilians become the victims, and it is here that another kind of mental attitude takes over. It is what some military historians have called "the delight to destruction", and which one combatant described as "battle fever", an unreal state when anything remotely resembling an enemy becomes hateful. It is a state when personal safety will count for nothing, and men will behave as though intoxicated, and only when the fury is spent will reality return. Such states of mind can be reinforced by the dehumanizing of the enemy, itself an encouragement to unreality, and the prebattle speeches about inviolability and sure victory.

In a society which has a strong sense of group identity, and which sees itself threatened by enemies on the outside, in other words, a Strong Group/ High Grid society, the evocation of such a state of mind will probably be easier. As we have seen, many Psalms see the enemy as the aggressor, the criminal, and worse, a threat to the very life of the covenant community. They are the wicked, the evil. They are deserving of death and destruction because the realm beyond the community limits is a realm of dirt and death. The unleashing of this battle fever on an enemy less than human is, in the group's view of things, then, not only understandable, but necessary.

In the stress of battle and the boredom of the campaign a soldier develops strong ties with those closest to him under those circumstances. Many combat veterans of recent wars have attested to the nature of the small group around them as a family, who share much more than the average family would ever share. In some military traditions this sense of "belonging" is enhanced officially and semi-officially through a number of means. In the British army, especially in the 19th century, being a member of the "regiment" became an important symbol of this belonging, and regimental ties were extremely strong. Regimental insignia were developed, and numbered regiments eventually took names to distinguish them even further from each other, but also to give them an attachment to a particular locality. In some cases this was quite artificial because many of the members of the regiment did not necessarily come from the region in which the regiment was stationed.[29] Beyond this attachment to the larger organizational unit, many soldiers attest to the close ties they developed in combat with the ten or so men they lived with, fought with, and sometimes died with. These ties were unlike anything formed in civilian life, and became a major factor in combat performance. Because of these strong ties many men were driven to accomplish tasks in combat out of a fear of letting their comrades down, or what William Manchester called "a determination not to shame themselves in front of others." The literature of warfare, especially the literature of recent conflict in which the opinions and feelings of the fighting man have become valued, is littered with references to this strong band of camaraderie, which could be broken, but then only in part, by death.

As far as the Old Testament is concerned, we have practically no evidence for these sentiments at all, not because they did not exist, but rather because of the nature of the literature itself. It was written by those who did not value the opinion of the common soldier, and therefore it is ignored. But it is hardly likely that a strong sense of belonging was absent from the ranks of Israel's ancient warriors. In the period of the judges, troops were mustered from villages and regions, and fought in their mustered units. Those in line would then have been one's neighbours in time of peace. Knowing what we do about the strong sense of community identity which was encouraged in this period, and the values of family and home which were fostered, we can conclude that the troops fighting an invader were conscious of a strong sense of unity. Not to fight would have endangered one's home and family, and those of one's neighbours. On occasion certain language is used to offer an insight into this sense of belonging. Fellow soldiers are "brothers" who share a mutual responsibility for morale (Deut. 20.8), and the description of panic and discord

[29]See B. Farwell *Mr. Kipling's Army: All the Queen's Men* (New York, Norton, 1986): 23-31; also the unpublished paper by J. Keegan "On the Invention of Military Traditions" (1978). This paper is known to me only through conversations with Dr. Richard Holmes. I have been unable to obtain a copy.

in a rank of soldiers is "to slay one's neighbour" (2 Kings 3.23).

During the period of the monarchy the emergence of a professional army in which men from different parts of the country fought alongside each other, this closeness might not have been possible to the former degree. But in such an organized army other symbols of belonging are used. Recruitment and conscription enforces a transition from civilian to soldier on many young men. Drill, uniforms, new postings, obeying of orders, take away an old identity, but offer a new one. In this state, what Victor Turner has expounded as "liminality" (*limes*="threshold" Lat.), new limits are imposed, new sets of values are espoused, and a new kind of life is forged.[30] To survive in such conditions one becomes a part of the group. The organized, regimented, trained and disciplined monarchical army would have shaped a new kind of camaraderie, which in its own way would have brought further motivation to combat.

---

[30]For an exposition of this concept see V. Turner *The Ritual Passage: Structure and Anti-Structure* (Ithaca: Cornell University Press, 1969): 95-96.

# 4

# The Materiel of War

## A. Weapons[1]

If war is an extension of a nation's political will upon another by use of force, then battle is the art of forcing one's physical will upon the army of the enemy. This is done best when one army kills more enemy soldiers than does the other while maintaining a certain sense of control over the proceedings. The art of killing another human being in battle has long been practiced by members of the human race, and one of the by-products of our evolution is that people spend a great deal of time and energy on making the act of killing more efficient. Even the bare hand can be a weapon if used

---

[1] This topic is not so well covered as studies of weaponry of other ancient Near Eastern societies. There are many similarities between Israel's weaponry and that of her neighbours and also some differences. For comparative studies the following literature is recommended. J.K. Anderson *Ancient Greek Horsemanship* (Berkeley: University of California Press, 1961); H. Bonnet *Die Waffen der Völker des alten Orients* (Leipzig: J.C. Hinrichs, 1926); T.N. Dupuy *The Evolution of Weapons and Warfare* (Indianapolis: Bobbs-Merrill, 1980); R. Gonen *Weapons of the Ancient World* (London: Cassell, 1975); P.A.L. Greenhalgh *Early Greek Warfare* (Cambridge: Cambridge University Press, 1973); R. Hardy *Longbow: A Social and Military History* (Portsmouth: The Mary Rose Trust, 1986); M.A. Littauer, J. Crouwel *Wheeled Vehicles and Ridden Animals in the Ancient Near East* (Leiden: E.J. Brill, 1976); J. Moyer "Weapons and Warfare in the Book of Judges" in T. Dowley [ed.] *Discovering the Bible* (Grand Rapids: Eerdmans, 1986): 42-50; A.M. Snodgrass *Arms and Armour of the Greeks* (Edinburgh: Edinburgh University Press, 1967); W. Wolf *Die Bewaffnung des altaegyptischen Heeres* (Leipzig: J.C. Hinrichs, 1926); Y. Yadin *The Art of Warfare in Biblical Lands* 2 vols. (New York: McGraw-Hill, 1962).

correctly, but the possession of an artifact as simple as a rock or pointed stick which can either be used as a substitute for the hand, or an extension of it, gives the wielder a distinct advantage. It removes him, even slightly, from danger by extending his reach, and gives him an edge over the unarmed opponent by increasing the power of the blow, the cut or the thrust. If his opponent is armed then the soldier is trained to outwit him by sharpening his skills in handling the weapon, and by using protection such as body armour and/or a shield. The needs of the moment determine the size of the weapon— the spear cannot be too long or it becomes unwieldly, and the sword cannot be too heavy or it becomes a burden, and the body protection cannot be such that it hinders movement and flexibility. Thus is born a compromise between defence and offence, between the need to protect and the desire to attack and kill. From what we know of ancient Israel, in the age of massed and organized armies, the compromise was in favour of the ability to attack and kill rather than protect. Armour was worn, but it seems to have been minimal, or symbolic. Much more stress was placed upon the ability to inflict damage on one's enemies. The weapons used to do this can be catalogued only for the sake of convenience, into two categories, those the soldier held and wielded in close contact with the enemy, and those he projected, either with the arm, or with the aid of some other power source such as the elastic power of the bow string, or the centrifugal power of the sling.

As with many of the items associated with warfare in ancient Israel, there is a distinction to be made in the use of weapons in the period before the monarchy, and the period during the monarchy. References to weapons used by Israel in the book of Judges are few and far between, and it is clear that Israelite warriors were ill-supplied with "conventional" weapons of the day. There are no references to Israelite spears, bows, shields, javelins, axes, maces in this early period, and there is no reference to protective body armour (Jud. 5.8). The traditional enemies of Israel at this time, the Philistines and the Canaanites were well armed. Philistine warriors depicted in Egyptian reliefs of the thirteenth and twelfth centuries are uniformed, covered with minimal body armour, carry shields and wield swords, shoot arrows from bows and carry spears. Goliath, apart from his size, might be a typical example of this kind of warrior. In the period of transition between the judges and the monarchy, Philistines use chariot forces in the hills to control the local population. Canaanite warriors also mentioned in the book of Judges, such as the forces of Jabin of Hazor, are noted for their "iron chariots" (1.19; 4.3), which were undoubtedly used as transport and firing platforms. None of these weapons were available to the Israelites. Instead, noted Israelite warriors used unconventional weapons such as an ox goad (Jud. 3.31), used by Shamgar to great effect in a feat which is equalled by Samson's use of an ass's jaw bone by which he killed a number of Philistines (Jud. 15.15). Even traditional non-combatants showed remarkable ingenuity, as was the case with the woman in Thebes who killed Abimelech with a millstone dropped from the wall. The blow was quite as effective as a well-handled club or mace!

The battles Israel fought in this period were a combination of surprise tactics and panic caused by the use of these tactics, so that the confused enemy inflicted more damage upon himself than did the Israelites. Two such incidents are seen in Gideon's attack on the Midianite encampment (Jud. 7.19-22) and Jonathan's attack on the Philistines at Michmash (1 Sam. 14). The only common weapon among the Israelites at this time was the sword, seen especially in the civil war against Benjamin (Jud. 20) in which the Benjaminites suffer the same fate as the cities in the Book of Joshua, to be "slain with the edge of the sword" (Jud. 20.37). Once the Benjaminites had been tempted away from their defensive positions into close combat their favourite weapon, the sling, was ineffective.

When the monarchy was introduced into Israel, weapons became much more numerous. The introduction of a standing army entails the equipping of that army with the correct and effective weaponry, and once the Philistine control over the manufacture of metal objects was broken by their defeat and subjugation by David, the weapons industry passed into the control of the king. As a matter of course, Samuel warns the people of the practice of the monarch to demand the service of the young men and women of the country in the making of (among other things), "... his weapons of war and the equipment of his chariots" (1 Sam. 8.12). These weapons, as we have stated, can be divided into two categories, the hand-held and the projected.

1.  Hand-held weapons
Hand-held weapons were used at close range, and in the set-piece battle would be the main weapon of combat when the lines of opposing armies clashed. Through the use of such weapons a soldier in line would hope to overpower one or more of the enemy facing him, and to inflict as much damage upon the body of the enemy so that he would be either killed outright (a rarity) or incapacitated enough so that he would fall down or back and be dealt the final death blow. In such a line of battle, space would be limited, so wide swings with weapons would be impractical, and dangerous for one's fellows. In close-order combat, moves were restricted to the downward blow, the cross blow, or the thrust. Close order weapons were designed and handled accordingly, and consisted in antiquity of the sword or dagger, the mace, the axe and the thrusting spear or javelin.

a.  The sword
By far the most common weapon mentioned in the Bible is the sword (Heb: *chereb*),[2] a metal weapon, made of bronze or iron, with a point or blade and a handle finished in either wood or bone. Unlike the spear or javelin, the handle of the sword was much smaller than the blade. Its function was twofold, to inflict stab wounds which would penetrate vital organs of the body, or to cut or slash, which would incapacitate the victim by severing muscles and/or blood vessels.

---

[2]On the ancient sword, see further Gordon "Swords, Rapiers and Horseriders" *Antiquity* 27 (1955): 67ff; G.H. Odell, F. Cowan "Experiments with Spears and Swords on Animal Targets" *Journal of Field Archaeology* 13 (1986): 195-212; S. Rosen "The Canaanean Blade and the Early Bronze Age" *IEJ* 33 (1983): 15-29. In early 1986 a complete iron sword, dated in the seventh century B.C., was discovered at Vered Jericho, a fortress-like structure to the north of modern Jericho. The weapon is about one metre long, had a wooden handle, and a bronze haft. The weapon was badly corroded, and nothing of it, except two photographs, has yet been published. See *BAR* 12 (1986):35.

Judging by the more than forty references to the use of a sword in such a way in the Old Testament, the Israelites favoured the slashing sword, designed with one or two edges. Numerous individuals, armies and city populations are "slain with the edge of the sword" (Gen. 34.26; Exod. 17.13; Num. 21.24; Josh. 11.12 etc.). In contrast the verb for "penetrate" or "thrust" (*machatz*) is used hardly at all in the contexts of battle. In a rather unfair encounter, Ehud assassinated Eglon of Moab with a thrusting blow of a small dagger (Jud. 3.16), and the Psalmist of Ps. 18.39 (repeated in 2 Sam. 22.39), thanks God for the opportunity to stab his enemies in the back as they are running away from the field of battle. Beyond this references are metaphorical.

This literary preference is reflected in the archaeology of such weaponry. Few rapiers (thrusting swords) have been discovered from the Iron Age in Israel, whereas many more slashing swords (cutlasses) of various kinds have been found. "Sea Peoples", Philistines and Sherden, are depicted in many contexts as using the sharp-pointed rapier, such as the mercenaries in the army of Ramses III in a thirteenth-century battle against Libyans. But the Egyptian troops accompanying them are armed with the edged, sickle-shaped swords. The Old Testament makes only occasional reference to the "double-edged" sword or dagger. Ehud's dagger was such a weapon, which was also very effective as a thrusting blade, and the same weapon is mentioned in Prov. 5.4 as a simile of the sweet, but dangerous talk of the city woman. Psalm 149.6 wishes such a weapon for the army of Israel in order to "... wreak vengeance on the nations and chastisement on the peoples...." Presumably the weapon was known, not very common but highly prized.

The early preference for slashing swords instead of piercing swords is probably one born of a desire for efficiency. More common, and more effective as a piercing weapon was the javelin and/or spear. The chances of wielding the sword to cut and slash were probably far greater than the chances of piercing and hitting a vital organ. In any event, a slash on an arm, shoulder, neck or leg, with the blade then being drawn across the wound to make it deeper, would be easier to inflict, and incapacitating for any victim. Sickle swords seem to dominate in Egypt before the thirteenth century, and after this time they are found in Egyptian reliefs alongside straight-pointed swords. These straight-pointed swords are found mostly in the hands of clearly identifiable "Sea Peoples", although not exclusively so. Pharaohs are commonly depicted as slaying enemies with a sickle sword, and this attests to its common use and favoured position over the rapier. It was much later, in the Roman army, that the close-order, carefully drilled movements of the Roman army made the thrusting, stabbing sword the standard blade of the infantry. In their invasion of England at the battle of Medway (A.D. 43), against the less disciplined forces of Caractacus and Togodumnus who used the slashing sword technique, the Roman style of tightly organized lines, well protected by shield and body armour, proved the value of the stabbing sword. It later became an axiom of training that the stab or thrust was much more effective than the slashing movement. However, this is a relative judgment, because by this time the Roman protective body armour of fitted plates, and the large shield, and close order of advance precluded the use of wild swings with the slashing sword, which needed much more room and exposed too much of the body when the arm was raised to strike.

Even as late as the writing of the Iliad, the sword is seen as primarily a slashing weapon, and numerous combatants in Homer's account of the Trojan War are seriously wounded by the use of the sword in this way. For example, the unfortunate Hypsenor has his arm severed with one cutting blow from the sword of Eurypylus. The sword, though, is a weapon generally used as a secondary, or "back-up" weapon, in much the same way that the bayonet was used in later warfare. First to be used in the line would be the missile weapons, the sling, the bow, the spear and javelin. Then when the lines closed, the sword would be drawn and used, as in the fight between Hector and Aias. Nowhere is this more clear than in times of siege. The famous relief of Sennacherib, showing his attack on the city of Lachish in 701 B.C., depicts for us one of the finest examples of siege warfare in Palestine from the time of the monarchy. Among the attacking and defending warriors, none has his sword drawn.

The smiting of the city "with the edge of the sword" would begin when the wall was breached.

b. Axe and mace
   One of the more common weapons found on Egyptian reliefs is the battle-axe. It varied in shape and design. Early axes were bronze blades fastened with binding to a straight shaft. At this stage no socket was made for the shaft to fit into. Later models were the "eye" axe and the "epsilon" axe, so named because of the shape of the heads. The heads were of one piece with curved edge and a socket. They resembled a large cursive capital "E", hence the second name. A further development was the straight head, with a socket similar to the modern axe-head, and decorative variations on this form. Egyptian tombs, drawings and paintings, archaeological discoveries in Egypt and Palestine and references in non biblical literature all bear testimony to the use of the axe as a weapon of war from the earliest times right into the time of the monarchy. Its effectiveness as a close-order weapon was limited, since the cutting edge was small, and it demanded very close contact for its proper use. It would, however, inflict serious damage to the head or shoulders if wielded correctly, and later designs in which the head is narrowed, or decorated with spikes, would increase the penetrating power of the weapon. It could crush the skull, penetrate a helmet, and smash a shoulder.

The remarkable thing is that the axe (*garzen*) is never mentioned in the Old Testament as a weapon of war. It appears fourteen times in the Old Testament as a tool for cutting wood or for other labour, and once in the context of war (Deut. 20.19), but never as a weapon. In the Siloam Tunnel inscription it designates a digging tool. It would, of course, be an effective weapon if used as such, and a law in the Old Testament does attest to the fact that an axe head can kill (Deut. 19.5), but only accidentally. This does not necessarily mean that it was never used, but it does suggest that, unlike the Egyptian practice, the Israelite infantryman did not include it among his standard equipment.

The situation is similar with the mace, although the evidence suggests that it was more extensively used as a weapon.

Numerous mace-heads have been found in Palestine from the Middle and Late Bronze Age, and there are occasional references in the Old Testament to the item as a weapon of war. The word translated "hammer" or "club" in some translations is *mapitz*, which is derived from the verb *putz*, to scatter. It occurs frequently with reference to the scattering of people, especially Israel and Judah among the nations in judgment. However, the substantive noun is found only three times, and here it is clearly meant to refer to the war-club or mace. In Ezek. 9.2 the "weapon for destruction" of v.1 is described as the "weapon of shattering" (*kli mapatzo*). In Prov. 25.18 the word is used in company with sword and arrow, and in Jer. 51.20 the effect of the use of the weapon is to smash all and sundry. How widespread the use of this was in battle is impossible to say since there are no references to its use in specific conflicts. The clearest indication of its use in monarchical times is in the graphic description of Sennacherib's attack on Lachish. Many of the Assyrian soldiers hold maces in their hands, but not in battle formation. They are the guards of the surrendering Judaeans. Nowhere, however, is the mace in use as a weapon. Had it been used, the intent of the user would be to stun his enemy, or to knock him senseless so that he would not be able to defend himself, then to deliver the death blow. Smashing someone's head in, especially if he is wearing even the minimal head protection, is a long and messy business, so the mace would have limited usefulness in battle.

c. Spears and javelins

In graphic presentation, literature and archaeology the spear is a most common weapon.[3] In its simplest form it is a long pointed stick, and in its more sophisticated form it is a long shaft of wood topped by a metal head. The head was designed, either from bronze or iron, with a socket into which the shaft of the spear fitted, or with a tang—a long

---

[3]For a comparative study on the making of spearheads see J.W. Balthazar "Cypriot Hook-tang Spearheads and Riveted Daggers—Manufacture and Use" *AJA* 91 (1987): 321-322; see also Odell and Cowan "Experiments with Spears and Swords".

thin tail—which fitted into the shaft and was held with binding. Often the tangs were bent at the end to ensure a firm join with the shaft, and to stop the shaft coming off in battle. Earliest depictions of warriors from Sumer show a phalanx of uniformed and armoured spearmen advancing into battle. This method of warfare persisted well into the eighteenth century A.D. until increased firepower of the gun made such frontal advances too costly.

However, in antiquity the march of a line of spearmen was a formidable sight, and in close order such a line would be virtually impenetrable. The only counter to it was to form a line of one's own with men armed with longer spears, but again, there are limits to the weight which an infantryman can carry into battle and remain effective. The spear had the advantage of keeping an enemy at a certain distance, at least for a while. If the line of spears could be maintained in order, and if the spears stayed horizontal, then the enemy line would be forced to retreat. In later Greek warfare, the use of the hoplite was predicated on this idea of battle. But the giant shoving match of the ancient pitched battle would often preclude such neat tactics. The tendency of the spears on contact would be to rise, and once the point had passed the first line of the enemy, the spear itself became useless. It could not be used in close contact because it was too long—usually between two to three metres—and could not be manoeuvered successfully.

The spear, though, was a common weapon of antiquity, and was used as a striking weapon by individual soldiers, and a throwing weapon. But used in this fashion it belongs more to the age of heroes than to the age of pitched, organised battles. If the spear did strike home then it was certain to inflict serious wounds on the enemy. With the strength of the arm of the spearman himself, supported by the pressure from the rear from the second and third line of men, the unfortunate victim would be skewered by the weapon, and if not killed, rendered quite helpless and ineffective. The graphic descriptions of the fighting in the Trojan War in Homer's Iliad offer vivid evidence of the damage done by a well-thrust spear at an opponent. The human skull can be pierced, and a spear in the chest frequently went through the body to come out at the back through the shoulder blade, piercing lungs and/or heart. Lower thrusts ruptured the intestine and resulted in agonising death. Unlike the wounds inflicted by the slashing sword, the spear wound was often deep and fatal, an effect fully appreciated by David's companion Abishai when they came upon King Saul asleep in his encampment (1 Sam. 26.7). Only one thrust with the spear would have pinned the sleeping victim to the ground.

The difference between the spear and the javelin is mainly a matter of size, slight difference in design, and use in battle. Whereas the average spear was approximately two to three metres long, and generally hand held, the javelin was shorter, sharper, and designed for jabbing or throwing at the enemy. The metal heads of the javelins which have been discovered tend to be simple and narrower than the spearheads, without the flanges. Being slightly smaller than the spear, the javelin did not necessarily inflict the kind of wounds that were immediately fatal. In the Old Testament the javelin is the "dart" [King James Version of 2 Sam. 18.14,] and the incident in which the weapon appears illustrates well its use and effectiveness. As the helpless Absalom is hanging in the tree, Joab used three javelins to stab him. The wounds, though serious, were not necessarily fatal, because the bodyguard of the commander-in-chief, ten young men, finish off the hapless youth with their swords.

2. Projected Weapons

By projected weapons I mean those weapons by which a missile can be propelled at the enemy using more than the power of the human arm. A spear, a javelin and even a rock can be thrown to good effect, but these weapons are handheld, and limited by the strength of the soldier. Projected weapons use additional power, and among them we list the bow, simple and composite, and the sling. Both are distance weapons, enlarging the gap between the lines of soldiers, and both add a dimension to battle lines beyond the cut and thrust of the hand-to-hand combat. They bring into the battle greater uncertainty, and add to the already present element of fear. They also provide the user with an advantage over his enemy because he is now no longer limited by his size. In a slightly later era and in a different part of the world, bows were restricted in their use to the noblemen and swords were regarded as the weapon of the serf and ordinary soldier. It was unthinkable in 6th century B.C. Chinese society that a serf should have the tactical advantage over a nobleman afforded by the bow.[4]

## a. The bow

The invention of the simple bow is lost in the past.[5] Sharpened flint "arrowheads" have been found in Europe dating from the ninth milennium BC, suggesting that the bow was a common weapon then and some scholars think that the bow was in use as early as 15,000 BC for the hunting of animals, and the defence of one's own. Rock paintings of prehistoric hunters show them armed with bows. Its design was simple, a suitably shaped piece of pliable wood which would not break if too much pressure were placed on it, and a string, made of gut or leather which was attached to the bow looped over "nocks" at each end. Most early, prehistoric bow remnants show that the weapon was made of yew, elm, or less commonly, pine. Some early remnants were reinforced with leather bound around the body of the bow itself. The composite bow is referred to in two Egyptian texts which praise the physical strength of the Pharaohs Thutmosis III and Amen-hoteph II, who reigned during the fifteenth century BC in Egypt. According to both these texts the power of the bow was such that an arrow fired from it could pierce an ingot of copper and "fall to the ground" on the other side!

The composite bow was a lamination of wood, sinew and horn, glued together. Its length was approximately 120cm (4 ft) and it obviously took a great deal of strength to use it in battle. and indeed to string it, since it was made to be strung opposite to its inactive shape. This bow, however, was known long before its use by our boastful Pharaohs, and fragments of one have been found in Siberia from one thousand years before. The Old Testament itself attests to the need for well-

---

[4]See Sun Tzu *The Art of War.* 32-38.

[5]Hardy's study *Longbow* is an excellent introduction to the manufacture and use of the bow. See also Tubb "A Bronze Arrowhead with Engraved Marks from Gezer" *PEQ ROM* 112 (1980): 1-6.

made and accurate bows (Ps. 78.57), since here the wickedness of the rebellious heart is likened to a bow that will not shoot straight!

Used with bows were arrows, which originally would have been made with flint heads, soon replaced by metal ones of bronze and iron. This latter move aided and speeded up the process of mass production. Such heads were, like many of the spear heads, tanged, to be bound upon a straight shaft. The shaft itself would be fletched with feathers and secured with glue. One can only speculate on the method of manufacture of the arrows themselves. They were obviously wood, and made as straight as possible with a consistent weight to ensure a consistent rate of fire in battle.

The effectiveness of the bow went beyond that of the sword and other close-range weapons, including the spear and javelin. All of these weapons were dependent upon the power and strength of the human arm for its effectiveness. The sword and the dagger could inflict damage commensurate with the power behind the cut or thrust, and the speed and distance a spear or javelin could travel were dependent upon the arm of the carrier. Further, speed and distance on the one hand and accuracy on the other were often incompatible. The accuracy of a spear was limited to about 30m. Estimates of the distances reached by arrows fired from simple and composite bows vary. The simple bow's range has been estimated at between 80-100m. and the composite bow between 250 and 300m. The former's range is about the same as the sling, but the latter's range is far greater. The advantage of the bow is that the archer can be lined with his fellows and concentrate harassing fire on an enemy line before they have come into close physical contact. The closer the line comes the more accurate and damaging such firepower can be. Another advantage of the bow is that it can be used on terrain of the archer's (or his commanding officer's) choosing. Man-for-man an archer is no match for a heavily armed and armoured infantryman, but the archer does not have to take that chance. He can retreat and still fire at his enemy, as Xenophon found to his disadvantage, or he can harass a stronger enemy and eventually defeat them on his own terms. In the Peleponnesian Wars, the Athenian hoplite proved no match for the Aetolian archer when the archer dictated the terms of the confrontation.[6]

Another feature of the bow's effectiveness in battle is the speed with which arrows can be dispatched. Our proud Pharaoh, Thutmosis III, claims to have killed seven lions with his bow "in the completion of a moment", and his successor, Amen-hoteph shot four arrows through hanging copper ingots while charging at them in his chariot.[7] Although self-serving, the records of such feats show the respect which was given the bow and arrow as a weapon of battle. Armed with such a weapon, complete with a full quiver an ancient bowman could maintain a rate of fire and accuracy greater than that of a line of Wellington's musketeers at the battle of Waterloo.

Given these facts of history on the effectiveness of the bow it is surprising that there is no record of an archer corps in the ancient Israelite army, as there was in the Egyptian, Assyrian and Babylonian armies. There are in the Old Testament sufficient references to the power and effectiveness of the bow that it is obvious that it was used extensively in warfare. The Lachish relief shows Judaean archers trading firepower with the attacking Assyrians from the ramparts of the besieged city. The bow appears here as an ideal defensive and offensive weapon. It keeps the enemy off guard, and forces the enemy to take measures to protect himself. Therefore, the Assyrians are to be seen either firing back from behind the shields of heavy infantrymen, whose protection is studded with the arrows from the walls above, or crouching behind the siege engines as they batter away at the walls, or even firing from behind large man-size wicker shields. To the left of the relief are the long-range archers, no doubt equipped with the heavier composite bow firing from the protection of the forest that surrounded the city.

Among the other enemies of Israel, the Philistines employed archers in their battles. Ramses III, the expeller of the sea peoples from Egypt depicts these sea peoples firing

[6]Thucydides *Peloponnesian Wars* III: 94-98.
[7]*ANET*: 243-244.

arrows at the Egyptians, with little effect since these paintings show no Egyptian dead! In 1 Sam. 31.3 the Philistine archers effect the defeat of the army of Saul and wound the king himself thus forcing his retreat and eventual suicide. The death of Ahab in battle with the Syrians is caused by the chance strike of an enemy arrow (1 Kings 22.29-36), which mortally wounded him.

In the Old Testament there are occasional references to the use of bows, and presumably regiments or companies of archers in the Israelite army in battle. The most notorious of the Israelite archers was Jehu, who, after being anointed king by the companion of Elisha (2 Kings 9.1-10) returned quickly to Jezreel and assassinated Joram of Israel and Ahaziah of Judah with the bow and arrow. One other feature of Jehu's military role is that he was a charioteer (2 Kings 9.26), and his use of the bow indicates that the chariot forces of Israel used the vehicle as a mounted firing platform, in similar fashion to the contemporary troops of Assyria, and the earlier troops of Egypt. Among the royalty of Israel, Jonathan (2 Sam. 18.22), Joram (2 Kings 6.22) and Jehoash (2 Kings 13.14-19) were all armed with bows and arrows, as well as swords. The Reubenites, Gadites and some of the Manassites mentioned in 1 Chron. 5.18 were skilled in archery, suggesting some formation in the Israelite army of archers, although the evidence is sketchy.

The effect of the bow on the line of soldiers in battle was both disconcerting and disabling. It was disconcerting because, as we have indicated, it could be used at a distance where the hope of retaliation was futile. The arrow outdistanced the spear and javelin, and if a line of infantrymen was diverted to deal with an attack from enemy archers they might be drawn away from their original intention, and by the time they had reached the spot where the archers were, the enemy would have fled. A case of such tactics is recorded by Xenophon in his famous *Anabasis*.[8] Greek heavy infantry were suffering casualties from flanking fire from enemy archers. However, when a line of hoplites and peltasts were

---

[8] Xenophon *Persian Expedition* III: 3.

sent to deal with this nuisance, the enemy withdrew, firing as it went. The skirmish was inconclusive.

There is little evidence to suggest that a wound from an arrow caused instantaneous death. A shot from a composite bow could, as we have seen, pierce a copper ingot, so the power of such a weapon was obvious. However, to maintain the kind of accuracy in the midst of battle against moving human targets as one could against immobile copper ingots, and in circumstances in which noise and dust would have destroyed concentration, was extremely difficult. It is doubtful that the Pharaoh could have truthfully claimed 100% accuracy in such conditions. The well-placed shot could do serious damage, and Ahab's death was clearly due to the severance of a major artery by an arrow, and he slowly bled to death propped up in his chariot watching the course of the battle (1 Kings 22.29-36). Similarly, Joram of Israel was shot by Jehu's arrow which pierced his heart, and he died instantly. However, his colleague, Ahaziah of Judah, though wounded by the same weapon, managed to reach Megiddo several kilometers away before he succumbed to his wounds and died (2 Kings 9.21-28).

Judging by the numbers of archers present in the Lachish relief,[9] the number of times the bow and the arrow are referred to in the Old Testament and the large numbers of arrow heads unearthed by archaeologists, the bow was a very common weapon. It was also a weapon to be feared, because alongside the sword it is used metaphorically of emotional pain, a sense of danger and a threat of judgment (Ps. 7.13; 38.2; 45.5; 64.7). The sense of loss at the destruction of Jerusalem is, to the writer of Lamentations, like an arrow to the heart (Lam. 3.12). In defence of his person the king can turn his arrows (his archers?) against his enemies (Ps. 21.12), and the removal of danger is likened to the breaking or burning of both bow and arrow (Hos. 1.5; 2.18; Jer. 49.35; Ps. 46.9; 76.3; Ezek. 39.9). Even some of these quotations reveal that the arrow wounds, hurts, but does not always kill (Ps. 64.7).

---

[9]See the latest edition of the relief in D. Ussishkin *The Conquest of Lachish by Sennacherib* (Tel Aviv: Institute of Archaeology, 1982).

In the Iliad, which offers graphic descriptions of the wounds inflicted in battle by various weapons, we find references to the effect of arrows on the human body. In Pandarus's fight with Diomedes, he is wounded by an arrow which pierces his cuirass, but the wound is not fatal and the arrow is eventually removed. Similarly, Hades is wounded in the shoulder, and Euamon is struck in the leg, but neither of the wounds proves fatal. An exception is Harpalion's wound. An arrow pierced his buttocks, and went through his bladder subjecting him to painful, poisoned death. Paris, shooting at Diomedes had hoped to hit him in the belly, thus wounding him fatally, but he was unsuccessful. Diomedes's response is interesting. He berates Paris for using a sissy weapon, and suggests that had he used the weapons of close combat, he would not have survived. In the heroic age, such sentiments were valid. The bow gave the advantage to the combatant who did not wish to engage in close combat, thus disclosing his cowardice. However, in an age of massed armies with anonymous troops regimented to concentrate the killing force, the bow proved to be an effective and often deadly weapon.

b. The sling

It is probable that the sling was invented as a weapon of war at the same time as the simple bow.[10] The advantage of the sling was that there was little in the way of manufacturing that was required to make it effective. All that was needed were two leather thongs linked to a small pouch in which a stone could be placed and from which it was projected. A variation was a single piece of leather which was tapered at the ends. The average slingstone was approximately six centimetres in diameter, making it slightly smaller than the tennis ball. Its effectiveness was deadly. Of all weapons of the Old Testament period the sling was the most "cost-efficient". The raw materials were readily available, it was remarkably accurate at great distances, and the impact of a slingstone

---

[10]On the sling see Korfman, "The Sling as a Weapon" *Scientific American* 229 (1973): 34-42; D. Schlesinger "Slingstones" *QAD* 15 (1982): 116; idem "More on Slingstones" *QAD* 17 (1984): 89. These latter two are in modern Hebrew.

would smash bone, knock an opponent insensitive, or even kill. Later armies would perfect it by developing it into the catapult. The stones themselves gave way to smaller, shaped projectiles, or even to lead weights [11]. The advantage of this development, according to Xenophon,[12] was that the missiles carried much farther than the large, fist-sized stone. Presumably, if the missiles were tapered, then they would penetrate rather than bruise or smash. It remained constant throughout this period.

Slingers are referred to rarely in the Old Testament, but what references there are testify to the deadly accuracy of the sling, and to the fact that slingers were organised into units within the army of the monarchy. The metaphorical references are few. As an act of judgment God will "sling out the inhabitants of the land" (Jer. 10.18) as a sign of his displeasure, an image used again in 1 Sam. 25.29. Before Leviathan slingstones are turned to ineffective stubble (Job 41.20, EVV 41.28), and in anger God will destroy the slingers of the Greek army (Zech. 9.15). All of the other references are to factual occurrences of the use of the sling.

The Benjaminites were noted for their skill with the sling. They were, incidentally, left-handed, and were able to "sling a stone at a hair, and not miss" (Jud. 20.16). In the battle that is described in this chapter, the Benjaminites inflicted serious casualties upon the armies of the attacking tribes, felling twenty *'elafim* (ca. 180) on the first day, and eighteen *'elafim* (ca. 165) on the second day. It is not stated that these were all casualties of the slingers, but two features of the story suggest that they were. First, it is rare that specific units of an army are mentioned, unless they do something special in battle. For example, it was the Philistine bowmen who "found" Saul at Gilboa and precipitated his retreat and suicide. Second, the tactic of the Israelites on the third day was to draw the Benjaminites out into the open, and in this way they defeated them. Presumably the Benjaminites had in-

---

[11] See D. Schlesinger "A Slingshot from Dor" *QAD* 15 (1982): 116.

[12] Xenophon III:3.

flicted the serious casualties on the rest of Israel from a secure, protected position, ideal for slingers.

The second incident in which a sling is used is, of course, the most famous of all the stories in the Old Testament, the battle between David and Goliath (1 Sam. 17). Not only is this story told as a story of faith, but from the point of view of military history it represents a battle between the old-style local hero (Goliath of Gath), who, like the later Greek hoplites was armed and armoured from head to toe, and the lighter armed fighter. In hand-to-hand combat Goliath's size and strength would have served him well. However, he does not have the chance to exercise his strength. He is faced by a new kind of enemy, reminiscent of the light "peltast" of the Greek army who gained success after success against the older-style hoplites. One important feature of this confrontation of styles is that the lighter armed combatant needs greater control and regimentation, and his arrival on the battle scene reflected a greater centralized control and regimentation.

In any event, David's skill with the sling won the day. It distanced him from a "greater" warrior, and his accuracy doomed his enemy. Stunned by the shot, Goliath fell down, and before he had a chance to recover he was decapitated by David. The conflict represents different styles of fighting, different social systems. The story also demonstrates the effectiveness of the sling, and its style of use. It incapacitated its opponent, then allowed other weapons to finish off the stunned or wounded enemy.

The third incident involving slingers is the campaign of the three kings of Israel, Judah and Edom against the rebellious Mesha of Moab, recorded in 2 Kings 3. The historical background of the story can be investigated elsewhere.[13] The slingers receive brief mention towards the end of the story when it appears that the Israelites met with initial success in the south of Moab, surrounded Kir-haresheth, and ". . . the slingers surrounded and conquered it" (2 Kg. 3.25).

---

[13]See T.R. Hobbs *2 Kings* [Word Biblical Commentary: 13] (Waco, TX: Word Publishing, 1985): in loc.

The activity of slingers in a siege is attested, among other descriptions, in the Lachish relief of Sennacherib. In this relief, to which we have referred frequently because it supplies us with a stylized, but eye-witness account of typical siege warfare of our period, the attacking forces consist of heavy infantry, battering rams, archers and slingers. The rams are attacking the city walls and behind them crouch the heavy infantry, ready to enter through the breach. Behind the heavy infantry stand the archers, concentrating harassing fire up to the ramparts, and *behind* the archers stand the slingers. The slingers are in pairs. At their feet are small piles of slingstones. The slinger is a "sharpshooter", using a stable platform, and relatively unencumbered by other weapons (all carry a sword), with even his missiles at his feet. To carry these missiles would weigh the slinger down. The fact that he stands behind the infantry and the archers would suggest that his firepower is more accurate than theirs. From the ramparts a few slingers are seen returning the fire—a feature well attested in the recent archaeology of Lachish.

## B. Armour

Did Israelite soldiers wear armour into battle? References to the armour of Goliath and Saul ( 1 Sam. 17), and metaphorical uses of armour in poetic texts (Isa. 59), might give the impression that they did, and there are many paintings and other illustrations in books which offer the same impression. However the literary and archaeological evidence is slight. Soldiers were probably uniformed, but extensive use of body armour was both costly to a land with few resources, and probably unnecessary. First, let us look at the Old Testament references to armour, then we will examine whatever archaeological evidence is necessary.

As a starting point we shall begin with the description of Goliath's armour. It must be borne in mind that this is a description of the armour of a non-Israelite, but it is a suitable place to start. According to 1 Sam. 17.5-7 Goliath was armed in the following manner:

He had a helmet of bronze upon his head, and he was armed with a coat of mail, and the weight of the coat was five thousand shekels of bronze. And he had greaves of bronze upon his legs, and a javelin of bronze slung between his shoulders. And the shaft of his spear was like a weaver's beam, and his spear-head weighed six hundred shekels of iron; and his shield-bearer went before him.

Later in the same chapter (vv. 38-39) David tried on similar armour belonging to king Saul, but rejected it in favour of his skill with the sling, and the obvious mobility he would enjoy without a large weight of bronze pulling him down. Goliath's defensive armour consisted of a helmet, coat of "mail", greaves and a large shield. Let us examine the terms more closely, and the occurrence (if any) of the terms elsewhere in the Old Testament.

The word translated "helmet" is *koba'*, which appears to be a non-Hebrew word incorporated into the language. It obviously means some kind of head covering. A homonym, a word which sounds the same, but which is spelled differently, *qoba'*, is used with similar meaning in Ezek. 23.24. But since the same homonym is used in 1 Sam. 17.38 of Saul's headgear offered to David, the terms refer to the same item, and the difference in spelling is understandable if it is a foreign word. Foreign words transliterated into another language are often spelled many different ways. For example, is the city called "Beer Sheva" or "Beer Sheba"? In both 1 Sam. 17.5 and 38 the term is qualified with the word "*nochesheth*" (of bronze) which raises another question. Were bronze helmets widely used, or were they restricted to important personnel, such as the king?

In answer to this question we are limited to what we know of military garb from archaeology and inscription reliefs of other countries. Archaeology tells us virtually nothing. The number of bronze helmets uncovered in Palestine is small, and most do not appear to be Israelite or Judaean, but rather the remains left behind by an invader. But with reliefs we have more to go on. In many reliefs depicting soldiers from the many countries of the ancient Near East there is little evidence that helmets of metal were widely used.

Egyptian soldiers from the earliest times wore very little protective body-armour and seemed to depend a great deal on the protection of the shield. In many tomb drawings and models of soldiers some wear distinctive headgear, or hairstyles, but none are wearing helmets. The headdresses are fabric or leather caps worn covering the head and ears, and often topped by a tassle. Few Egyptian enemies wear anything resembling a helmet, although the hairstyles of the southern tribes, such as the Nubians are elaborate. Sumerian soldiers of the mid-third millennium BC were highly organized both on and off the field of battle, and wore distinctive uniforms, but their head coverings were leather caps tied under the chin by thongs. The famous gold helmet of the same period of King Eannatum (ca. 2500 BC) is more for ceremonial or symbolic purposes than defence. A soft gold helmet would be quite ineffective against a well-placed blow.

Later Hittite warriors wore crested helmets, but by far the most distinctive helmet-wearing troops were those of the sea-peoples, and the later Assyrians. Two groups of the sea-peoples figure prominently in Egyptian art, the Sherden and the Philistines. Both were well armed and armoured. The Sherden wore a simple, bowl-like helmet, topped by a disk, and carrying its most distinctive feature at the sides—two horns. The Philistines wore a very distinctive headgear which is still the subject of great debate. In the reliefs it looks like a headband into which have been secured fronds of material. Several reliefs depict these warriors, the most famous being the depictions of captured sea-peoples at Medinet Habu, and the remarkably detailed scenes of the great naval battle between Egypt (under Ramses III) and the Philistines and Sherden. No archaeological evidence of this distinctive headgear has been found, but Trude Dothan, a leading authority on the Philistine culture, describes it as "... a leather cap and an ornamental headband from which a row of slightly curving strips stand upright to form a kind of diadem...."[14] It is obvious from the vigorous discussion continuing in the

---

[14]See T. Dothan *The Philistines and Their Material Culture* (Jerusalem: Israel Exploration Society, 1982): 12.

scholarly journals that there is no consensus on the materials used or the purpose of this piece of headgear at all. Was it protective, or was it simply a part of the Philistine warrior's uniform? In any event, it is unlike anything found in reliefs of Semitic warriors.

The Assyrian army used helmets to a considerable degree, and the most famous relief of the fall of Lachish, to which we continually return, shows a number of Assyrian soldiers wearing distinctive headgear which most have correctly interpreted as helmets. They are of two types. One is a cone-shaped helmet with flaps that covered the ears and the side of the face. Many archers and slingers are wearing these. The other type is more rounded, with similar ear-flaps, but with one distinctive feature. It is topped by a crescent-shaped crest, similar to the piece discovered at the site. The wearers of this type are all spearmen. Other headgear, worn by various archers and attendants appear to be a kind of wrap, or turban.

Of the Judaeans manning the walls and resisting the attack, none are wearing crested helmets, and most are wearing the wrap or turban-type headgear, similar to those worn in Sections 1 and 2 of the relief, by two Judaeans going into exile. These two characters are obviously old, and this raises the possibility that the defenders wearing such headgear on the walls are not soldiers, but civilians. Others are wearing cone-shaped helmets similiar to those worn by the attackers. Since there are no archaeological remains to inform us of the material out of which these helmets were made, we cannot assume that they were made of metal. The possible crest discovered at Lachish was metal, and this would indicate that the certain regiments in the Assyrian army wore metal headgear, although this is not certain. The fact that on occasion the Biblical writer deems it necessary to add the word "bronze" to the use of the term "helmet", would suggest that the headgear was not normally made of metal.

The term used here for coat of mail (Heb. = *shiryon qash-qashim*) is unique as a phrase. *Shiryon* occurs in v. 38 of the same chapter indicating a piece of Saul's armour. It was worn by Ahab in his last battle (1 Kings 22.14). During the rebuilding of the walls of Jerusalem after the return from exile, some of Nehemiah's men were set aside to prepare weapons and defensive armour (*shiryonim*) in anticipation of attack. It is used metaphorically in Isa. 59.17. In only one other place does the term occur. In 2 Chron. 26.14 in a description of Uzziah's reorganization of his army and its re-arming, coats of mail (*shiryonim*) are included in the list of newly made weapons. This is the only reference which would hint at a widespread use of "coats of mail" in the Israelite army.

The term *qashqashim* properly means "scaled", and it is this kind of armour that is in mind in 1 Sam. 17.5, rather than the chain mail (a series of linked metal rings) of the later Roman army and used during the medieval period. The technology of making chain mail is quite sophisticated, and was probably beyond the capabilities of Israelite metal-workers. Scaled armour, on the other hand, is widely attested in antiquity, and although the term *qashqashim* is not used in the Old Testament of armour apart from 1 Sam. 17.5, it is generally assumed that the term *shiryon* is to be understood as scaled armour. It was commonly used by Hittite charioteers from the 13th century BC. Fragments of metal (bronze) scales were found in the 14th-century tomb of Amenhoteph III at Thebes, and a complete coat of scaled armour was discovered in the tomb of Ramses III (12th century BC). Thutmosis III lists two coats of scaled armour as prizes of war at Megiddo. Later Assyrian soldiers, particularly mount-ed archers are depicted in what appears to be scaled armour. A number of the attackers at Lachish wore such armour, and several pieces have been discovered during the excava-tions there. The method of making this was simple. Small plates of bronze about 10-15cm in length, and about 6cm wide were sewn on to a fabric base, possibly of leather or quilted cloth. The garment covered the whole torso down to the knees and the shoulders and upper arms. In some scenes it appears to be belted, and from the belt is slung a sword. The weight would have been considerable (Goliath's probably weighed close to 120lbs.!), and the wearing of such a piece of armour would have greatly hindered mobility. It is under-standable then that, apart from the use of the coat of Goliath, who obviously had the physical strength to wear such a garment, the only other occurrence of the use of such a coat in battle (1 Kings 22.34) is by a charioteer. Outside the Old Testament Hittite charioteers used such a coat, and Assyrians used it on horseback, and on foot. Assyrians at Lachish wearing scaled armour are foot-archers (though not all), guards, some spearmen, and what appear to be unmounted cavalry-archers. Its effectiveness was limited, however. The vivid description of Ahab's death in 1 Kings 22.34, in which he is wounded "between the scale armour (*haddebakim*) and the breastplate (*shiryon*), is a poor translation. The term *debbakkim* comes from a root meaning "to join", "to cling to", and a better one is "between the joins and the scale armour". Ahab was unfortunate enough to be struck where the scales had parted. As far as the interpretation of the Lachish relief can depict, none of the Judaeans defending the city were wearing such scale armour, and there does not appear to be any in the loot that some of the Assyrians are presenting to the enthroned Sennacherib. The scarcity of reference, and the absence of such armour in the Lachish relief would suggest that average Israelite and Judaean soldiers were not equipped with such armour. It appears to be the equipment of a king in battle.

One of the items of Goliath's armour can be dealt with quickly. The text mentions that he wore "greaves of bronze on his legs" (1 Sam. 17.6). Several problems exist with this reference. In the first place the exact meaning of the word *mitzchah*, which is translated "greaves" is unknown. Second, the word as it appears in the Hebrew text is in the singular, so the translation of "greaves" is unconventional. The attempt of some of the later versions to change it to a plural only highlights the problem. Third, the use of leg coverings by Philistines is nowhere attested in the paintings of Philistine warriors of the period and earlier. According to the Assyrian relief of Lachish and others, some Assyrian soldiers wore leg coverings, but there is no evidence that they were used at all by the Israelite or Judaean armies.

The shield, however, is a different matter. Second only to the term "sword" (Heb: *chereb*) in its frequency in the Bible are the words for "shield" (Heb: *shelet* and *magen*). *Shelet* is a "loan-word" related to the Akkadian word for the same item *saltu*, the second is a Hebrew word derived from the verb *ganan*, which means "to fence round", "to protect", providing us with a good idea of its purpose. We can treat occurrences of either word as referring to the same piece of equipment. The shield was widespread throughout the ancient Near East, and while the shape and style varied from time to time and place to place, it was used by most armies of the region. Its purpose was simple, to provide the infantryman with protection in the event of attack.

We do not have the space to look at the development of the shield in the ancient Near East in detail. Suffice it to state that early depictions of Egyptian soldiers from the Old Kingdom (ca. 2900-2200 BC) through to the period of the New Kingdom (ca. 1550-1100 BC) and beyond show them using shields, varying in shape from the old rectangular shields to the "round-top" shields of the later periods. They were made of wood and covered with hide. Sumerian warriors are depicted with large, rectangular shields marching in formation and later Hittites used distinctive shields of small rectangular shape, or "ox-hide" shape, but with the coming of the Philistines the smaller, round-shaped shield is introduced into the region. Numerous Egyptian drawings and paintings of Sea-Peoples show them all using the distinctive round shield, reminiscent of those of the warriors of the Aegean region from which they came.

References to Israelite and Judaean shields are many in the Old Testament, and the only difference between the usage of the two words *shelet* and *magen* is that the former is never used metaphorically of Yahweh, whereas the latter is. Of the seventeen references in the Psalms to the *magen*, all but one refer to Yahweh as protector, and a common designation is ". . . a shield of those who take refuge in him." (2 Sam. 22.3,31 [// Ps. 18], Prov. 30.5).

As a defensive item of a soldier's equipment, both terms are used frequently in such references as 2 Kings 11.10 (// 2 Chron. 23.9), 1 Chron. 5.18; 2 Chron. 14.17; 32.37; Jer. 46.3, 51.11; Ezek. 23.24, 27.10, 38.4-5 and Nah. 2.14. Further, the shield, particularly if it was embossed with precious metal, was used decoratively, as in Solomon's decoration of the Temple and Palace (1 Kings 10.17). Shields taken in battle were also displayed as trophies (2 Sam. 8.7 [// 1 Chron. 18.7]; 1 Kings 14.26-27). Being faced with a wall of shields, in similar fashion to the Assyrian attackers at Lachish, was a symbol of siege (2 Kings 19.32). Some of the references deserve added comment though. In 2 Chron. 23.9 there is a reference to the "large and small" shields which were distributed by the High Priest Jehoidsa during the *coup d' état* against Athaliah, a detail omitted from the account in 2 Kings 11.10. The possibility here is that the writer is referring to shields for different types of soldiers, but this is only a possibility. Second, there is the curious reference to hanging shields on walls. The Song of Songs alludes to the fact that the Tower of David in Jerusalem had space for one thousand shields to be so used (Song 4.4), and Ezek 27.11 refers to the same practice. The significance of this is not clear, but there is one possibility. In the Lachish relief the battlements of the walls and towers of the besieged city are festooned with the shields of the defenders, in much the same fashion as pictures of the old Viking longships. This served two purposes. First, it enabled the owner to be free from its weight, yet still enjoy a measure of protection, and second, it protected the battlements themselves from missiles and general wear from the outside. At the same time the shield could be taken up for hand-to-hand combat when needed. This is possibly the secret to the allusion in Jer. 51.11, where a proper translation of the text should be:

Sharpen the arrows! Fill the shields!

The shield, once laid down, is now taken up and "filled" with the left arm of the owner ready for combat.

One further point on the references to shields is the unusual comment in the lament of David for Saul on the "shields, not anointed with oil ... " (2 Sam. 1.21).[15] Although anointing is commonly used as a sign of special status, there is probably nothing of that in mind here. There is no other hint

---

[15]See A.R. Millard "Saul's Shield not Anointed with Oil" *BASOR* 230 (1978): 70.

in the Old Testament that weapons were anointed or blessed before battle. The answer lies probably in the nature of the make-up of the shield. There are references to gold or bronze shields in the Bible, but these, as we have seen are mainly decorative. If they were made of solid, cast metal then they would have been too heavy to handle in battle. If they were beaten gold or bronze they would have been quite inadequate for protection. Most shields known from this period were made of wood, covered with hide and containing the minimum functional metalwork. Such was the case with Egyptian shields, and in the Lachish relief the shields of the attackers appear to be made of strips of laminated wood, covered with hide. The anointing with oil could well have been an attempt to preserve the wood and hide against the elements. Dry wood hide would easily split when struck.

One final point concerns the historical use of shields. None of the references to the military use of shields is found in texts dealing with the period before the monarchy, so the evidence suggests strongly that the use of shields in formations of soldiers was a mark of an organized, centrally controlled army. This is a fact borne out by the passing reference in the Song of Deborah (Jud. 5.8) that the battle was won against the Canaanites by a poorly equipped army without shields and spears.

## C. Raw Materials and Manufacture

Equipping an army during the time of the monarchy put an enormous strain on available resources. The "militia-type" field forces of the period of the Judges fought with a minimum supply of weapons, no uniforms, and for short spans of time. With the organization and maintaining a standing army in the latter period, things changed considerably. It is difficult to estimate the number of a "typical" monarchical army. Externally, there are two extremes of comparison. The expeditionary army of Thutmosis III consisted of three divisions of 5,000 men each. This would give him a total of around 15,000 plus camp followers. At the other end of the scale, Shalmaneser III fielded an army of 120,000 men during his western campaigns in the mid-ninth century BC.

For ancient Israel and Judah, beyond some figures which might or might not be accurate, we are in the realm of speculation. Shalmaneser's record states that Ahab contributed a force of 2,000 chariots and 10,000 infantrymen to the Aramean coalition at the battle of Qarqar (ca. 853 BC). Yet, according to 2 Kings 13.7, Jehoahaz's army consisted of the same number of infantry (10,000), 50 cavalry and 10 chariots. This was deemed a disaster. This would suggest that the 10,000 infantrymen fielded by Ahab at Qarqar did not comprise the entire Israelite army. This was simply an expeditionary force. Many men would have stayed in Israel for duties there such as the guarding of cities, fortresses along the main routes and possibly civilian control. In Judah, the staffing of fortresses along the southern border would have been a perpetual problem, and eventually, according to the Arad correspondence, this task was done by Greek mercenaries.

Although 1 Kings 4.26-28 and 10.26-29 offer information on Solomon's "chariot cities" and construction of horse stalls for large numbers of chariots and horses, these do not appear to be for Solomon's domestic army, but rather for export to the Hittites and the Syrians. It is difficult to know exactly what proportion of different kinds of troops there were in the armies of ancient Israel and Judah. The figures for Qarqar indicate a 1:5 ratio of chariots to infantry, but it is unlikely that this was typical at home. Chariots are campaigning vehicles, and of little use in the hill country of Samaria or Judah. Even the 1:5 ratio is a generous one when compared to a Chinese campaigning army of two centuries later. According to Sun Tzu, the ideal ratio is 1000 chariots to 100,000 foot soldiers (1:100), and the chariot unit was broken down into a chariot containing three armoured soldiers, 72 infantry and 25 camp followers such as cooks, grooms, baggage men and wood and water carriers.

There were two main materials which organised armies depended on for equipment, wood and metal—either bronze or iron.[16] The normal consumption of wood of a campaigning army was considerable. Wood was needed for fuel for campfires, for building of encampments. On some marches trees would have to be cleared to allow access to certain areas, and according to Deut. 20, when a city or region was attacked, trees would be cut down, probably for a punishment. During sieges the mounds of earth built up against cities were reinforced with wooden beams, as is seen at Lachish. Frequent reference to the making of towers in connection with sieges in the Old Testament, indicates that tall wooden firing platforms were also built for use during a siege.

By far the most important use of wood was for the manufacture and repair of weapons. The average Israelite soldier was equipped with a shield, a spear, and possibly a sword. In each of these there was a large amount of wood. Shafts for spears were smoothed straight by craftsmen, and a constant supply would need to be kept in case of loss or breakage during a campaign. Sword hilts were encased in wooden handles, bows were either composite—wood, sinew and bone—or simple, one continuous piece. Arrows, like spear and javelin shafts, needed to be straight, and were made as such through filing and smoothing. Enough wood was needed to manufacture and maintain such weapons, and the amount must have been quite large. We have no figures at all on the amount of wood needed over a given period of time, but we can surmise that the need was always there, and increased during times of extensive campaigns.

In addition to the normal weapons of war, such as swords, spears and bows, any supply train accompanying an army on campaign (such as in 2 Kings 3) would have used wood in the shape of wagons and chariots. It is possible that pack animals substituted for the wagons, but that brought on additional problems of supply. In any event, even a relatively

---

[16]On these materials in the Mediterranean world see R. Meiggs *Trees and Timber in the Mediterranean World* (Oxford Clarendon Press, 1982) and J.D. Muhly, T.A. Wertime *The Coming of the Age of Iron* (New Haven, Conn: Yale University Press, 1980).

small chariot force needed much wood for the manufacture and repair of chariots, which have been described as having ". . . a light framework of wood, covered with hide or wickerwork and mounted on a sturdy axle with two wheels." Numerous references to forests and trees in the Bible and elsewhere indicate that the land was much more heavily wooded in antiquity than it is today. However, the needs and practices of the army, the growth of agricultural land, and the use of wood for fuel in metal melting would have made significant inroads into the forests. The whole process also needed organizing and staffing.

In addition to wood, vast amounts of metal were needed for the maintenance of an army. If each bowman carried a quiver of between 15 to 20 arrows, a spear and a sword or dagger, then he could be considered a significant consumer of metal. Metal would be needed for arrow heads, spear and javelin heads, blades and possibly axes or maces. Shields were often studded with metal, and chariots had some metal parts, as did the controlling equipment for horses. Some of this, of course, could be captured from the enemy dead—a practice common throughout the history of warfare—but to ensure a steady and reliable supply some means of manufacture or importing of the materials was needed. It appears that weapons were made out of both bronze and iron. Archaeological excavation has uncovered bronze and iron swords, bronze and iron arrowheads and spearpoints from not very different periods. Early iron, which came to be used as a dominant metal at the early part of the first millenium, was soft-wrought iron, and quite unsuitable for cutting or stabbing. Later the technology was developed for its steeling, or hardening, and it became much more widely used.

Supply and manufacture was a constant problem. We know from Job 28 that metals were mined from the earth in Palestine, but we have few examples of actual mines. Numerous furnaces have been found at various archaeological sites, but they are often scattered too widely to talk of a smelting "industry" at many sites. The furnaces are more often than not used for local needs. However, there are some areas where smelting was done on a large scale. In the southern Arabah Valley several sites have been uncovered. Tel el-

Keleifeh, discovered first by Nelson Glueck had extensive smelting activity during its history, but the latest research shows that it was used in the Chalcolithic period (pre-3000 BC), the Late Bronze Age (14th-12th centuries BC) and in the Roman period, not during the time of the monarchy. At other sites, such as the Wadi Amram, Wadi Feinan, Wadi es-Sabra, remains have also been found of extensive metal work, but these sites are in modern Jordan. The largest site in northern Jordan at Mugharat Wardeh is dated too late to be of relevance to the Old Testament period.

Enough references are found in the Old Testament to smelting procedures to show that it was a familiar site in some cities of ancient Israel and Judah. Where the metal came from is not fully known. According to 2 Sam. 8.8 it was valued as a prize of war, but the fact that the sources of metals were, for the most part, in the Transjordan, might help to explain the need for Israel and Judah to control this territory. In any event, the need for wood and metal altered the shape of the geographical and social landscape in Israel and Judah permanently.

# 5

# The Art of War

It is customary, and proper in writing a study of military history such as this to make a distinction between "strategy" and "tactics", although the two are often confused. The differences are for some only a matter of degree, but there is more to it than this. In one sense strategic matters deal with the "big picture", whereas tactics are concerned with local details. This is true, but the very nature of these differences in size affects the very character of strategy so that it cannot be construed as simply a larger version of tactics. The German military theorist, Carl von Clausewitz, described strategy as "... the employment of battle as the means towards the attainment of the object of War."[1] He continues:

> "... it must therefore give an aim to the whole military action, *which must be in accordance with the object of the War*; in other words, Strategy forms the plan of the War; and to this end it links together the series of acts which are to lead to the final decision, that is to say, it makes plans for the separate campaigns and regulates the combats to be fought in each."

Further he states:

[1]C. von Clausewitz *On War* (Harmondsworth: Penguin Books, 1968): 241-243.

"... in Strategy everything is very simple, but not on that account very easy. *Once it is determined from the relations of the State what should and may be done in War*, then the way to it is easy to find...."

This requires, of course, a special kind of mind and "genius" to make the right kind of decisions. But the main difference between Strategy and Tactics becomes clear from these quotations. Whereas the tactician, be he general, colonel, or captain, is concerned with the deployment and use of his forces for the achievement of an immediate military goal, the winning of a battle, the strategist, plans the execution, by military means, of the imposition of the political will of his leaders on the enemy state. Not only does the strategist need a significant amount of political experience and expertise, according to von Clausewitz, but he also needs a stronger character and will of his own to make what are much tougher and far-reaching decisions. The political will of a people or nation emerges from its ideology and self-understanding, and is expressed in attitudes and policies towards other peoples and nations. In the case of the Union States in the American Civil War, the political will was expressed as a desire to crush what they regarded as a rebellion of the southern states. To this end an army was raised, equipped and trained. Campaigns were organized, and resources of manpower and materiel were distributed accordingly. Battles were planned so that the enemy might be engaged at strategic points of geography. It is at the local level of the battle that tactics are used with the deployment of limited forces to achieve the simple objective—defeat of the enemy on the field, at a particular place and time. I think it helpful to maintain this distinction in our study in this chapter, even though at times the lines might become blurred. This is especially true when, as in the the case of Israel in the Judges, there is no clearly articulated "national" political will, or as in the early monarchy when the person whose political will stands in for that of the nation, is also the leader in individual battles.

## A. *"Grand Strategy" in the Period of Judges*

In the period of the Judges it is impossible to speak in terms of a "political will" as though that will were an expression of the aspirations of all of the covenant community of Israel *vis-à-vis* the nations surrounding Israel. Corporate concerns, such as they were, were expressed much more in terms of internal matters. We have outlined above the nature of the community and the values of the community during this period, and have characterized it as "strong group/high grid", concerned with limits, protection of its own and avoidance of outside contamination. Such attitudes would result clearly in a strategy of resistance to invasion, and resistance to any attempt by local peoples to disrupt this community. Again, we must be clear that this is not a carefully articulated strategy in von Clausewitz's sense. There is no political will thrust, by the force of arms, on another people. It is rather an ad hoc reaction to a threat of penetration.

This outline gives to the strategy of this period an air of spontaneity. The armed men of Israel reacted to invasion, so in this sense, their strategy was not a planned one, except insofar as it can be called defensive. But here again we have to make qualifications. The defence of Israel in this period, unlike the people of the monarchy, was not organized into a system of border-fortresses. It was a strategy of meeting, and engaging the invader in battle after the penetration had taken place. But the strategy was not completely spontaneous. Some preparations had already taken place since it is clear that membership in the covenant community implied an agreement for mutual military aid in times of crisis. This is the presupposition behind the warnings given to the tribes east of the Jordan in Josh. 22. Returning from battle, they were to remain loyal to the God of the covenant, and their fellows. It is also the background behind the poetic version of the battle between the Canaanite forces of Jabin and Sisera and the Israelites under Barak. Some tribes, notably Dan, Reuben (E), Gilead (=E. Manasseh) and Asher, refused to become involved in the battle (Jud. 5.12-18). Enforcing this arrangement, however, is impossible, and short of open warfare between the tribes, the policy seems to be shaming them in the poetic record. Tensions between tribes did exist, leadership accepted in one tribe, even reluctantly, is rejected in another. In the case of the Ephraimites, who upbraid Gideon for his policy of not inviting them to participate early in the fight against Midian (Jud. 8.1), Gideon has to argue his position and explain his actions. Later, in the same story, the men of Penuel and Succoth reject outright any request for help (Jud. 8.4-9), with severe consequences. Ephraimites are again involved in a dispute with other Israelites, this time Jephthah of Gilead, who was appointed leader of the forces on the east side of the Jordan to deal with the threat of the Ammonites (Jud. 11). The Ammonite intention was to dislodge the Israelites from the eastern side of the Jordan. Using the same reason as before, the Ephraimites complain to Jephthah about his unwillingness to involve them in his struggle against Ammon. Each of these incidents illustrates the problem of co-ordinating a "national" policy for Israel at this time.

Resistance to invasion and disruption of the covenant community is the general stance of the tribes. Therefore, Ehud takes the lead in reacting to the invasion of Moab (3.12-30), inviting other "people . . . from the hill country" to join him in the rout of the Moabites. Deborah and Barak join forces to stem an incursion of the chariot army of Jabin, presumably intent on forcing the Israelites out of the north (Jud. 4-5). Gideon calls up a special force of men to expel the Midianites from the north, then pursues them across the Jordan to finally crush their army (Jud. 6-9). Some Israelites from other tribes take part in this.

The same motivation, namely the preservation of the covenant community, propels the tribes to mass against Benjamin after the men of Gibeah had abused communal standards of behaviour and hospitality (Jud. 19-21).

The political wish of Israel is to be a community organized according to the principles of the covenant. No strategy is developed to actively enforce this political will on others. Instead, during the period of the Judges, when the covenant community is threatened, from without or within, small armies are mustered, men are called up to face the threat. Supplies are organized for the precise moment, and the threat is faced. The borders of the community, physical and symbolic, are maintained.

## B. *"Grand Strategy" During the Monarchy*

If, as we have accepted, that warfare is the imposition of the political will upon the enemy by force, and strategy is conducted in accordance with that political will, then we can properly speak of "grand strategy" in ancient Israel only at the time when that political will is able to be formulated and expressed clearly. That brings us to the period of the monarchy. With the monarchy we have to reckon with the shift of the political will to the newly formed centre of the society. But more than this, that political will is now concentrated in one person, the king. By attracting to himself the trappings of ancient Near Eastern kingship, and by developing the "royal traditions" of Israel, by forming a continuity with the people's past, the king now stands in a position between the people and God. Symbolically, he is the "son of God", through whom the people are blessed, and for whom they pray (Ps. 72). In reality he is the focus of the political power of the people. Decisions can now be made affecting the whole nation, and as the monarchy develops, these decisions can be enforced. It is only under these circumstances that we can conceive of a "grand strategy" which implicates the whole people. The political will can now be expressed from the centre, and the expression of that political will takes on a different form. The reactive, defensive position that characterised the time before the monarchy is abandoned in favour of the opposite. Israel now goes on the offensive.

At this level of discussion we are not concerned with the numerous historical explanations which can be, and have been offered for this phenomenon. The period of transition of Israel from tribal society to centralised bureaucracy (ca. 1100—1000 BC) was a period of confusion in the ancient Near East. Great nations, such as the Hittites, the early Assyrians and the Egyptians had temporarily lost the status they once had and a "power vacuum" existed in the Levant. Numerous smaller states emerged, each jostling for territory and stability. Such a state of international affairs is undoubtedly the broader context for the rise of the monarchy in Israel. It could be argued that only under this new political system could Israel compete, and only by adopting an aggressive stance could she survive. These points are debatable, and certainly worthy of notice, but they belong properly in a broader history of the region. Our concern is to concentrate on the military developments of the period. Conditions such as these could explain, in part, the moves made by Israel, but they explain only in part. The affairs of nations are not determined solely by external conditions. Faced with such conditions, those in positions of power make certain decisions, and these decisions bring about circumstances in which new decisions have to be made. As one historian has stated it, "Causes in the form of events, conditions and consequences (intended and unintended) in the world, cannot have social effects except via human perception and evaluation of them."[2] In the events and conditions which pertained at this period of transition, Israel chose to react politically by changing its political (and social) structures, and militarily by becoming an aggressor against her neighbours. It is this effect that we want to look at and its consequences.

During the reign of Saul it is unlikely that Israel's strategy involved aggressive movements against her neighbours to the extent it did later. From what we know of the reign of Saul, Israel was hard pressed by the continuing pressure exerted by the Philistines in the south and west. As his reign opens the tribe of Dan had been dislodged, and military activity in the region of the Judaean Shephelah is focused in the story of Samson. In the period immediately before the appointment of Saul as king, the Philistines are continuing their aggression along the coast to the north of the Shephelah, and a major confrontation takes place at Eben-ezer at which Israel is defeated and the Ark captured. Within the reign of Saul the new king had to contend with the serious

[2]So I. Hodder *Reading the Past: Current Approaches to Interpretation in Archaeology* (Cambridge: University Press, 1986 ) 13.

threat of the Philistines entrenched in the "Benjamin saddle" area with garrisons at Michmash and the surrounding villages. The Philistine strategy is clear from the geography. The land is cut in two. Opinions about the precise motive for this strategy vary, but it is an attempt to dislodge the new society from the hill country. It is an invasive strategy reminiscent of the attack of Jabin into the Galilean highlands (Josh. 11). The reaction is defensive, to rid the new society of this threat by expelling it. This is done through clever tactics on the part of Jonathan (1 Sam. 14) and the Philistines are once again confined to the coastal plain and a measure of peace and security is restored in the hill country.

The setting of the story of David and Goliath is the attempt of the Philistines to move inland again from the coastal plain into the fertile region of the Judaean Shephelah, and eventually on to the hill country of Judah, possibly via Hebron or Bethlehem which are situated a little to the east. Again, the Israelite strategy is to stem this invasion. It now has an organised army which "lines up" for battle in the Elah valley and stalls the Philistine advance for days. The stalemate is a fair indication of the level of the organisational developments within the Israelite army, and of the measure of sophistication of the strategic measures adopted by Saul. This time the invasion is stemmed through the outcome of the conflict between David and Goliath.

The reign of Saul ends with an attempt to repeat the expulsion of the Philistines, who by now present a much more serious threat to the new kingdom. Instead of attacking the heartland of the kingdom, the Philistines move along the coastal road, the Via Maris, and east across the Jezreel valley into the area near Beth Shean. The ease with which they are apparently able to do this is due, no doubt, to the control they still exercised over the coastal road. The earlier battle at Aphek/Eben-ezer had done nothing to break the Philistine control of this area, and there is nothing in the account of the reign of Saul to suggest that he ever had any effect on the Philistine exercise of power in the west. The Philistines were able to call together a large army at Aphek for the move to the north. The effect of this incursion to Beth Shean was, on the one hand to encircle the central and southern hill country, barring any exits to the west, north and possibly south, and on the other hand, to sever the northern territories occupied by Asher, Zebulun, Issachar and Naftali from the south. Such a serious state of affairs could not be allowed to continue, and Saul chose to confront the Philistines at the foot of Mount Gilboa near the important city of Beth Shean. The attempt was a failure.

The Philistine threat to Israel was the most important problem throughout Saul's reign. The possible motivation for the Philistine activity was the wish to control the agriculture of the hill tribes, and to break any attempt at organisation, such as the fledgling monarchy represented. However, this was not the only problem Saul dealt with. I Sam. 14:47-48 offers the following summary of this other military activity of Saul:

> When Saul had taken the kingship over all Israel, he fought against all his enemies on every side, against Moab, against the Ammonites, against Edom, against the kings of Zobah, and against the Philistines; wherever he turned he put them to the worse. And he did valiantly, and he smote the Amalekites, *and delivered Israel out of the hands of those who plundered them.*

The text is not to be understood as portraying an aggressive foreign policy on the part of Saul. The language suggests otherwise, namely that much of Saul's activity as king was devoted to the protection of Israel from the invasions of the forces of the neighbouring territories including Moab, Ammon, Edom, Zobah. The fact that these are linked with the Philistines, whose plan was to invade, suggests that these other nations followed the same plan. This text can be compared with 2 Sam. 8, which offers a picture of the distinctly different activity of David. The language in 1 Sam. 14.47-48 is the same as the language of the book of Judges (Jud. 2.16), and one may assume that the military activity of Saul was seen as a continuation of the activities of the judges.

The exception to this defensive strategy is invasion of the territory of the Amalekites (1 Sam. 15), and we should note that this kind of activity demands a completely different kind of justification than the defence of home territory and one's own people. The Amalekites appear to be a group of southern desert dwellers, akin to and allied with the Midanites on occasion (Jud. 6.3), and prone to invade the settled territories to the north. They are expelled from Israel by Gideon, but they are not condemned to annihilation because of their previous invasions of Israelite territory. The justification is found in their past sins because they ". . . opposed Israel in the way when they came up out of Egypt" (1 Sam. 15.2). The incident is found in Exod. 17.8-16 and has become part of the national memory and national history.

The summary of the military activity of David found in 2 Sam. 8 shows that David's grand strategy was an offensive one. Invasions of the Philistines into the hill country, after the occupation of the city of Jerusalem, are quickly dealt with (2 Sam. 5.17-25), and for the rest of his reign the Philistines present no further danger to Israel. But it appears that David goes beyond the expulsion of the Philistines from Israelite territory, because he ". . . subdued them, and took Methegh-ammah out of the hand of the Philistines" (2 Sam. 8.1). The language implies invasion, subjugation of a local population, and the seizing of territory. The exact interpretation of "Methegh-ammah" is not clear. The literal meaning is "Bridle of the mother", which has been understood by some to refer to a capital city of the Philistines. 1 Chron. 18.1 interprets it as Gath. This is a possibility, but not certain. However, it must refer to some territory which the Philistines controlled. This control is wrested from them by David.

Invasion of Moab is certainly implied in the following sentences (2 Sam. 8.2), since one of the outcomes of the conflict is the paying of tribute (see also 2 Kings 3), something which only defeated and occupied nations are required to do. The treatment of Moabite prisoners of war is striking in its cruelty and arbitrariness, especially in the light of earlier help given by Moab to David in his outlaw days (1 Sam. 22.3-4). The reason for this action is clear, and is linked to the broader aggressive strategy of David. It robs Moab of fighting men and the means for effective retaliation.

In 2 Sam. 8.3-7 the attention of David is turned to north and east to face two of the Aramean states which emerged on the scene approximately the same time as did Israel. Aram-Zobah was one of the powerful Aramean kingdoms which, at this time, controlled the regions to north of Israel from the southern reaches of the Valley of Lebanon to the banks of the Euphrates. To its north and west was Hamath, and to its south was Aram-Damascus. By the end of the second millennium BC Aram-Zobah was a major force in the Levant, and it appears that David took advantage of some disturbances to the northeast of Zobah's domain to attack and defeat its army, capturing several thousands of prisoners and horses. It is not clear exactly when these campaigns took place in David's reign since the sources are not written in chronological order. By this time David's army must have reached a considerable size and level of expertise in the field and possibly contained a large chariot force. An Aramean ally, Aram-Damascus, came to Zobah's aid and was also defeated by David. This effectively gave David control over these territories. Both provided him with considerable booty, including gold and bronze (2 Sam. 8.7-8). The victories were consolidated by the staffing of garrisons in Aram to ensure loyalty and stability.

These successful campaigns in the north inadvertently bring into David's camp the nation and the king of Hamath, with whom Hadadezer of Damascus had often been at war (2 Sam. 9.10). The alliance made between the two demonstrates the power now achieved by David because Toi of Hamath willingly sends to David precious gestures of his submission. Following the campaigns in the north David returns to the south and eventually subdues the southern neighbour, Edom, in whose territory he also placed garrisons. (2 Sam. 8.13-14). David's subjugation of Edom was particularly brutal and excessive. Following the battles to control the territory, when the army remained behind to bury its dead, Joab set his soldiers loose on the country and for six months they terrorized Edom until all eligible men were slaughtered (1 Kings 11.14-16). Such action reflects the more deliberate massacre of the Moabites, and undoubtedly had the same effect. Edom's army was no more, and rebuilding one would now take decades. "All Israel" (v. 15) over which David now reigns is greatly increased in size. Within a few decades, Israel on the defensive has become Israel the aggressor, and eventual controller of most of the territory between the Red Sea in the south to the "entrance of Hamath" in the north. These campaigns and their subsequent results are a new phenomenon in Israel's history. They are not defensive wars in the sense that the battles of the period of the judges and Saul were defensive, so there is no implied justification of them from this perspective. They are not justified either by appeal to some past misdeed or wrong which must be redressed, as was the case with the Amalekites. Nor do they fall into the category of "holy war", in which the battle is fought for the sole purpose of the annihilation of the enemy and his possessions as "dedicated" to Yahweh. On the contrary, these campaigns result in territorial and material gain for David. They are part of an aggressive grand strategy, no doubt brilliantly planned and executed, judging by the results, but nevertheless an aggressive grand strategy designed to build an empire beyond the borders of Israel itself.

By the middle of the reign of David, Israel had entered the world of international military politics. In this world at this time the players were "minor league". It is highly unlikely that David could have done what he did in the face of the powerful and well-armed Egypt of a century or two before. Nor could he have been victorious over the north if the Hittites or Assyrians had maintained their impressive military structures intact. He fought instead against emerging nations like his own: Arameans, Edomites, Ammonites and Moabites, or against the declining power of an outdated city-state system like the Philistines. Against these he could compete, and could win, and for a while the empire enjoyed a period of prosperity and power never experienced before or since. It remained to be seen whether this empire, forged out of conquest and oppression, could hold its own when the "major league" players came back into the game: players like Egypt and Assyria. For the time being, however, the empire was maintained through the reign of David and consolidated by his son, Solomon, but by the middle of the ninth century BC, after the major division of the kingdoms of Israel and Judah in 930 BC, and the wars which followed, things were different. David had bequeathed to his successors a legacy of militarism. Whether they could maintain this legacy was now open to question. Already by the reign of David's son, Solomon, the memory of these events in Edom and Zobah caused some repercussions in the persons of Hadad of Edom, now married into the royal family of Egypt, and Rezon of Zobah, who formed a guerrilla band and created a nuisance for Israel (1 Kings 11.14-24). He eventually became king in Damascus (vs. 24b-25), an act which demonstrates that David's hold over his empire was not strong enough to maintain it intact.

It is impossible to deal with all the battles and campaigns Israel and/or Judah fought from the death of David and Solomon until the collapse of the north in 722 BC and the destruction of Jerusalem in the south in 586 BC. We look now only at scattered, but typical, examples of the way in which subsequent monarchs dealt with their task. With the closing of the reign of David, the limits of the empire are established, and the successors of David have now inherited something they must maintain, and maintain by force of arms. David bequeathed vast territories to Solomon and Rehoboam and the others who followed, but they were territories *under occupation*, and this established a set of rules quite different from those that pertained to the period of judges. Local populations have to be maintained to keep up levels of productivity, but these local populations also become a liability, because they have to be controlled. The Hadads and Rezons of Solomon's reign could reappear, and, in fact did. So the legacy of David was, at first glance a boon, but was, on closer examination, a burden.

Solomon, through careful building up of the administrative structure of the empire was able to maintain and strengthen what David had left him. These careful administrative moves were supported by financial and political alliances with neighbouring nations, through trade and marriage. But his successsors were not so astute, nor so fortunate. With the death of Solomon a civil war broke out which resulted eventually in the secession of the north from the south and the formation of two separate nations, Israel and Judah. At this stage it is not our intention to deal with the religious implications of this split, nor to deal with the way in which it was viewed theologically by the biblical writer. We concentrate instead on the form of military strategy these events produced.

In the south, following the split of the kingdoms, Rehoboam, the king, made an attempt to win back the north through invasion, but the plan was aborted on the advice of a prophet, Shemaiah (1 Kings 12.21-24). No military reason is given. Instead the prophet justifies his advice from a religious perspective. It is a moot point, however, whether Rehoboam would have had the resources from the population of one (or two) tribe(s) to mount a successful campaign against the ten northern tribes with their tradition of warfare. We leave aside for the moment the suggestion of many that in anticipation of (or in reaction to) the invasion of Shishak of Egypt, Rehoboam established a defensive system of fortresses in the south (see 2 Chron. 11.5-12). This is a matter of domestic policy ". . . there was war between Rehoboam and Jeroboam continually" (1 Kings 14.30). In other words, the north and south, once they had separated turn on each other. For what reason?

The answer can be found in the accounts of reigns of subsequent kings, Asa and Baasha (1 Kings 15.16-34). The wars continue, and the object of the conflict is the strip of land north of Jerusalem granted to Benjamin (Josh. 18.11-28). It is the strategically important, and lucrative "saddle" which links the Via Maris with the Jordan Valley via Gezer, Gibeon, Bethel and Jericho, and which provides access from the north into Jerusalem, and from the south into the heartland of Samaria. Numerous cities and fortifications change hands throughout this early period of the monarchy, among which are Ramah, Geba and Mizpah (1 Kings 15.22-23), all of which are "built" (i.e. rebuilt) to protect access either way. Warring between Israel and Judah is no less costly than warring between Israel and Syria, except that the lines of communication and supply are not as stretched. The texts referred to clearly indicate that conflict on the border between Israel and Judah was a permanent state of affairs during this period. Yet it was, in a sense, local, perhaps diverting energies and supplies away from the task of maintaining an empire. It is against this background that the ease with which the Egyptian Pharaoh, Shishak, marched through both Judah and Israel, plundering as he went in ca. 925 BC, must be seen. The Bible mentions his attack on Jerusalem and his plundering of the treasures there, but his own records indicate that his invasion was far more extensive. A side-expedition was mounted into the Negev, presumably against the newly formed farming settlements. But the main force of his army went through the Shephelah, up the Beth-horon pass to Jerusalem, then north through Israel, turning toward the Jordan crossing at Adam, then continuing north on to the Beth Shean and Jezreel Valleys, returning home via the coast. The invasion was, according to the accounts, unopposed.

In the decades which follow the death of Rehoboam and Jeroboam the two kingdoms chart their separate courses, although at times these paths cross to create alliances, or violent conflict. The hostile state of affairs which characterised the reign of Rehoboam continued into the reigns of his successors Abijam (1 Kings 15.7), Asa (1 Kings 15.15), with continual wars between north and south, presumably over the control of the Benjamin saddle (1 Kings 15.22). A new development takes place during these wars which was to repeat itself in subsequent conflicts, and that was the creation of military alliances with one-time enemies against former partners. Asa of Judah (ca. 911-871 BC) bought the help of Ben-Hadad of Damascus against Baasha of Israel (ca. 909-886 BC). But this gesture on the part of the southern king was made to break up an already existing alliance between Ben-Hadad and the king of Israel! (1 Kings 15.19). The effect of this new alliance was the invasion of the north against a (presumably) unsuspecting new enemy, along the Upper Jordan Valley (1 Kings 15.20). The result was as Asa desired and Baasha withdrew from his southern border, leaving it to Judah (1 Kings 15.22). Ideologically motivated conflict now gives way to the pragmatism of international politics.

A further complication in the north was the unstable nature of the monarchy. Unlike Judah, Israel was a coalition of a large number of separate units, ten tribes in all, and the difficulties of maintaining some kind of stable central control are exemplified in the numerous *coups d' état* and counter *coups*, which toppled one regime after another. Jeroboam's son Nadab was deposed after a short reign (910-909 BC) by Baasha, who reigned for twenty-four years (909-886 BC). His successor, Elah, was quickly deposed by one of his chariot generals, Zimri. In turn he was challenged for the throne by Omri, his commander-in-chief, and Zimri committed suicide (1 Kings 16.17). A brief civil war followed between Omri and Tibni, another pretender to the throne, and finally Omri was established as king. At times the conflicts appear as struggles between tribal groups—Baasha is of the "house of Issachar"—and at other times the conflicts are seen as struggles between power groups within the royal bureaucracy, or more precisely, within the army. For example, Zimri commanded one half of the royal chariots, while Omri was commander-in-chief.

Omri established the "Omride dynasty", a succession of four kings, Omri (885-874 BC), Ahab (874-853 BC), Ahaziah (853-852 BC) and Jehoram (852-842 BC). Before his seizing of the throne, the founder of this dynasty, Omri, was occupied with the Philistines at Gibbethon, in the southwest of the country, presumably protecting his access to and control of the Via Maris. But for the duration of his reign and that of his successor, Ahab, attention is turned eastwards, in a struggle against the old enemy Syria. The object of the conflict is to keep open access to the east, most likely to the eastern trading route, the so-called "Kings' Highway". From the non-biblical source, the commemorative stone of Mesha of Moab, it is clear that Omri had secured his hold on the southern extension of this route across the Moabite plateau, building fortresses and settling Israelites there. If the same strategy is being enacted in the northern Transjordan, it is understandable then that Ramoth Gilead is a constant location for fighting.

A Syrian attack on Samaria was repulsed (1 Kings 20.1-21), and a subsequent battle planned by Syria on the heights of southern Golan at Aphek proved disastrous for the Syrians. The benefits for Israel were large. Ahab regained many of the Syrian cities conquered earlier by Omri, and was allowed to trade in the lucrative Damascus markets (1 Kings 20.34). After a brief lull in the fighting (1 Kings 22.1), Israel once again planned an attack on Ramoth Gilead. This time Ahab's ally was the king of Judah, presumably Jehoshaphat (870-849 BC). The battle was the last for Ahab, who died in it (1 Kings 22.29-36), but there is no follow-up by Syria, indicating perhaps that the Syrians had been placed firmly on the defensive in the latter years of Ahab's reign, and was the recipient of Israelite aggression.

The wars between Syria and Israel were overshadowed by a much larger threat to them both in the person of the restless new Assyrian monarch, Shalmaneser III (ca. 858-824 BC).[3] Shalmaneser turned his sights to the west and embarked on a series of campaigns with the intention of reaching the coast of the Mediterranean, and of conquering all those who stood in his way. According to his own record, he reached his objective, and one effect of this was to force the establishment of a coalition of twelve western kings, led by Hadadezer of Damascus. The coalition included Ahab of Israel, who contributed one of the largest contingents of troops—two thousand chariots and ten thousand infantry. A further campaign by Shalmaneser in 853 BC was met at Qarqar by the forces of the coalition, and the battle, in which Shalmaneser claimed to have killed between 14,000 and 25,000 of the coalition's soldiers, was indecisive. Shalmaneser retreated, regrouped, and four years later marched westward again. Over the next ten years he conducted at least five such western campaigns and on each occasion was met by the coalition forces consisting of the armies of between twelve and fifteen kings. Since Shalmaneser continually refers to them as "... twelve kings of Hatti (the Assyrian name for the Levant) ..." or "... twelve kings of the upper and lower sea (i.e. the length of the eastern Mediterranean coast) ..."[4]

---

[3]On this period see the still valuable article by W. Hallo "From Qarqar to Carchemish: Assyria and Israel in the Light of New Discoveries" *BA* 23 (1960): 34-61.

[4]*ANET*: 279-280.

it seems that Ahab and his successors were involved in these wars. The brunt of the Assyrian pressure, however, fell upon the Aramean, Hadadezer. None of this is mentioned in the Bible, nor is the tribute which Jehu, the overthrower of the Omride dynasty, paid to Shalmaneser. All the information comes from the records of the Assyrian himself.

In the light of this pressure, and the resultant coalition between Israel and Aram-Damascus, it is somewhat surprising to find records of continued warfare between the two western neighbours throughout the remainder of the ninth and into the first half of the eighth century BC. There are, of course, periods of relative peace between the two nations. Naaman, the commander-in-chief of the Syrian king, is able to visit Israel, and diplomatic correspondence passes between the two nations (2 Kings 5). However, the reaction of the Israelite king, presumably Jehoram (ca. 852-842 BC), shows that the peace between them was very fragile (2 Kings 5.6-7). Elisha is able to visit Ben Hadad in Damascus, and the relationship between the two seems quite close (2 Kings 8), but often, in the Bible, campaigns are conducted into each other's territories. Elisha is the cause of a siege of Samaria by the Aramean (2 Kings 6.15-31), which is eventually lifted, and soon after the Israelites, now allied once again to their southern neighbours, Judah, attack Ramoth Gilead (2 Kings 7.28). But by the end of the reign of Jehu, most of the territory east of the Jordan is lost to Damascus (2 Kings 10.32-33), and after the reform of Joash in the south, the Judaean king is forced to pay off the Aramean successor to Ben Hadad, Hazael, before the gates of Jerusalem (2 Kings 12.17-18). In much of the fighting Damascus gains the upper hand (2 Kings 13.3). Part of the explanation of this conflict between Israel and Aram-Damascus is the decline which Assyria experienced after the death of Adad-nirari III (ca. 811-784 BC), however, this does not explain all, since the squabbling is not limited to this period alone. What emerges from the reconstruction of the history of this period is a series of wars and campaigns which involve a number of different enemies and allies, with partners changing on a number of occasions. Israel is allied for a while with Aram-Damascus against the greater Assyrian threat, but then fights against her with the help of Judah. On occasion Judah and Israel fight, but ally themselves to defeat a common potential enemy, Moab. Motivation comes at times, but rarely, from defence of territory. However, successful defence is followed by renewed attack on the territory of an enemy, either in revenge , or to perpetuate subjugation. If there be a strategy visible, it is to win against whatever foe is chosen, and Israel fights one war after another. The net result is disappointing because her territory gets whittled away at the same time. All of the expenditure of manpower, energy and wealth is virtually meaningless in the long run. Taking advantage of the Assyrian weakness in the first half of the eighth century BC both Israel and Judah expand their control over the old limits of the Davidic empire and enjoy an extended period of prosperity, possibly a couple of decades. It is shortlived, and when it is destroyed it is never regained.

The turning point came with the ascension to the Assyrian throne of one of the most successful campaigners in the west, Tiglath Pileser III (745-727 BC), and with his success begins the next period of Assyrian expansion. The victories he won in the west profoundly affect the northern nation of Israel. Soon after his reign began (ca. 741 BC) he was invited by the usurper Israelite king Menahem to help consolidate his power. The cost of hiring the "biggest boy on the block" as a mercenary was great (2 Kings 15.17-20). Eight years later Tiglath Pileser returned, picking off the valuable territories in eastern Galilee, (2 Kings 15.29) among other lands along the coast, and Aram-Damascus in a series of successful campaigns. If any strategy can be detected in this period on the part of Israel, it is a, rather unsuccessful, defensive one designed to deal with the kind of warfare the Assyrians had perfected into a brutal art, the siege.

In general the same posture is adopted in the south. There are the occasional pitched battles (2 Kings 14), but with the advent of the Assyrian presence into the region in the latter half of the eighth century, Judah, now depleted, launches no more campagins into neighbouring territory. In the face of an Israelite and Aramean coalition in 735 BC, the Judean king Ahaz, calls on the help of Tiglath Pileser III, who returns to defeat Damascus, and eventually secure Galilee for himself. Judah, it appears, escaped the ravages of 722 when the northern nation fell, but was invaded by Sennacherib in 701 BC, and suffered the horrendous privations of siege warfare. Manasseh's reign was remarkably peaceful, presumably as a tribute-paying vassal of Assyria, and the next important venture outside Judah was conducted by Josiah in 609 in his abortive attempt to stop an Egyptian army moving north. He fought a pitched battle at Megiddo, and suffered the same fate as the Canaanites over eight and a half centuries before, against Thutmosis III at the same place. He was killed and his army defeated. The freedom with which the Egyptian Necho returned to Judah, attacking cities and deposing their king demonstrates the state to which the Judaean army had fallen. Resistance was impossible. In the major changeover from the Assyrian empire to the Babylonian control of the world, Judah remained a spectator, and to a large extent became a victim of the actions of others.

In the closing years of the nation of Judah, after the death of Josiah, Babylon became master of the eastern Mediterranean. Deposed by Egypt, Jehoahaz, the son of Josiah was succeeded by his brother, Eliakim/Jehoiakim (2 Kings 23.31-35). During his eleven-year reign (ca. 609-597 BC) Babylon incorporated Judah into her empire, and Jehoiakim became a tribute-paying vassal. Toward the end of his reign Jehoiakim rebelled, and suffered at the hands of raiding bands of Ammonites, Syrians and Moabites encouraged by the Babylonians to attack. It appears that Jehoiakim was powerless to resist, and when the Babylonian army invaded in 597 BC Jehoiakim's regime collapsed. He died (suicide)? and was succeeded for a brief time by his son, Jehoiachin, who endured a siege, surrendered and was exiled. For the next eleven years Judah was ruled by the puppet, Zedekiah, who also rebelled, bringing the next invasion of the Babylonians. In 586 BC, after an effective campaign of siege warfare throughout Judah, "against her fortified citites", Nebuchadnezzar succeeded in bringing the nation of Judah to an end. With the administrative and governing ability of the nation torn away, it died. But long before this it was impossible to speak of a battle-ready army. The raids of the eastern neighbours were endured, not met with counter measures, and before the Babylonian army nothing could stand. Like its northern neighbour, the Judaean policy was resistance to siege.

A major strategic policy was introduced at the beginning of the monarchy, and continued throughout most of its duration. That policy was the construction and maintenance of fortresses, not only in the territories occupied by Israel and Judah beyond their borders, but also along and within the borders themselves. There are comments in the Old Testament to this effect, and also a growing body of archaeological data, which show that successive kings of Israel and Judah planned and executed a policy of building fortresses. The Iron Age in Palestine was a period of which such fortresses and fortified cities were built at an unprecedented rate.

Control of an occupied territory demands the garrisoning of that territory with troops and a suitable habitation for those troops. Such garrisons would serve many purposes. At the symbolic level they would represent the occupying power, and be a constant reminder to the locals of their status. They would also serve as administrative centres, from which the local region could be governed and taxes or tribute collected. Militarily, they would act in case of rebellion by locals and suppress any dissent. The size of the fortresses would depend on which of the above purposes, or combination thereof, was being served. An additional purpose of establishing such fortresses was to encourage settlement in these territories of Israelites or Judaeans.

The literary evidence for this practice consists, first, of references to the presence of Philistine garrisons in Israel in the period before the monarchy, leading up to the anointing of Saul as king (1 Sam. 10.5; 13.3; 14.1,6; 2 Sam. 23.14). These garrisons were located at strategically important towns of Israel, mainly on the plateau to the north of Jerusalem. Second, following his defeat of Syria and Edom, David built garrisons in their territories for purposes of control of the local population. David's wish was twofold, to gain tribute from the locals, and to ensure that the locals would not rise up against him. Therefore, he built garrisons in Syria and Edom (2 Sam. 8.6,13), and, although it is not expressly stated, it is clear that his policy regarding Moab would demand a similar strategy.

Israelite presence in Moab is attested, not expressly in the Bible, but in a Moabite account of the revolt of Mesha of Moab against Israelite rule in the mid-ninth century BC.[5] From the Moabite account, Omri had reinforced the occupation of the area by "the men of Gad", and his son, Ahab, had continued the policy. This policy clearly consisted of the building of cities, fortification of strategic areas and sites, and the settlement of sizeable populations of Israelites in the region. Among the cities dominated by Ahab were Medeba, Beth Baal-meon, Kiriathaim, Ataroth, Nebo, Jahaz, several of which Mesha singles out as fortified by the Israelite king. Mesha's strategy was to capture these cities, kill or enslave the populations, and redesignate the land for his own people. Following the successful revolt which gave Mesha control of the entire Moabite plateau, he embarked on an extensive rebuilding and public works programme. The policy of Mesha is mirrored in the activity of king Uzziah, described in 2 Chron. 26.6-15. The possibility of this description being anachronistic must be taken into account, and it probably reflects the activity of David at a time when the Philistines were more of a threat than they would have been in the reign of Uzziah. This, however, is irrelevant because it does describe a general strategy of defeating an enemy, occupying his territory, and building there fortresses and cities of one's own—an early form of colonization. There is one additional clue to this policy, and it is found in the story of Elijah. Elijah is described, in most English translations, as "... from Tishbe in Gilead" (1 Kings 17.1). The phrase has received much attention in scholarly literature because it is so problematic. As a place of origin, "Tishbe" is unknown, and the precise grammatical form "... from Tishbe in Gilead" is very awkward in the Hebrew. A simple suggestion has been made (see the footnote in the RSV) that the phrase be rendered "... from the settlers of Gilead." This is possible

---

[5]For a good translation of the Mesha Stele see J.C.L. Gibson *Syrian Semitic Inscriptions* vol. 1 (Oxford University Press, 1971): 71-82, and the literature cited.

with a change of vowel, and it also removes the awkwardness of the phrase. Elijah's origin then is quite probably from the colonisers who settled in the upper Transjordan, encouraged by the strategy we have been describing.

During the period of the demise of the Omride dynasty, and the reign of Jehu which followed, many of Israel's territories in the Transjordan were lost through the activity of men like Mesha. However, archaeological research has provided evidence for a strategy of fortifications in the south, along the border with Edom, in what is today known as the central Negev hill-country. Fortified settlements existed in this area to as far west as Beer Sheva, as far north as Arad and as far south as Kadesh Barnea and Har Ramon. Many of these settlements were founded in the early Iron Age, corresponding with the advent of the monarchy in Israel and Judah. Others, like Arad, were rebuilt at strategic places which had long since been abandoned. The forts are not of a uniform size, nor shape, nor were they all in existence at one time. Additionally, identification of some of them as fortresses has recently been questioned. However, the opinion of one of the original excavators and examiners, Yohanan Aharoni, remains intact: ". . . Archaeological survey proves that full control of the Negev and of the roads through it was secured by a system of fortresses and settlements founded in their vicinity."[6] The purpose of this system was, according to Aharoni, to control the important roads through the Negev which led eventually to the southern port of Elath. In fact, the purpose can be broadened to include defence against the Edomite incursions which increased during the latter part of the monarchy in Judah. Amaziah of Judah (ca 795-767 BC) fought Edomites in "the Valley of Salt", which could be identified with Nahal Malhata, the very location of some of these fortresses (2 Kings 14.7), and his son regained control

---

[6]Y. Aharoni "Forerunner of the Limes: Iron Age Fortresses in the Negev" *IEJ* 17 (1967): 1-17. There is still a vigorous debate on the precise significance of these structures. See R. Cohen "The Fortresses King Solomon Built to Protect His Southern Border" *BAR* 11 (1985): 56-70; idem "Solomon's Negev Defense Line Contained Three Fewer Fortresses" *BAR* 12 (1986): 40-45; I. Finkelstein "The Iron Age Sites in the Negev Highlands" *BAR* 12 (1986): 46-53.

of Elath for a short time (2 Kings 14.22). Edom, it appears, was a perpetual nuisance during the late monarchy (see e.g. 2 Kings 16.6), and it is clear that this region was a hotly disputed one throughout the monarchy, and such a system of fortresses would have assisted in its control.

We gain some insight into the purpose of these desert fortresses from the extensive and important excavations conducted at Arad. Arad is at the northeast end of the "chain" and because of its size and history was an administrative and command centre of the system. It is located on the old Early Bronze Age ruins of Arad, and it sits on the northeast hill of the site. The geographical location of the site is important. From the fortresses one can see, therefore guard, the road which winds off through Nahal Malhata and Nahal Beer Sheva to the west. In the east, the ridge before the drop to the Arabah Valley and the "Way of Edom" (2 Kings 3.8) is clearly visible. To the south the range of Negev hills on which the other fortresses are situated can be seen, and behind the fortresses to the north is a road into the heartland of Judah via Maon and Eshtemoa. The strategic value of the site is unmistakable. The first Israelite fortress was built there in the tenth century BC, probably during the time of Solomon. After its destruction by Pharaoh Shishak in 925 BC, it was rebuilt and redesigned over the course of the monarchy no less than six times, attesting to the important strategic location of the site. During the excavations in the 1970s over eighty Hebrew ostraca were found containing records of the activities of the fort and letters written to its commander, Eliashib. Eliashib's archive provides us with an excellent summary of the commander's duties, and the role of the garrison at Arad.[7]

Some of the ostraca are lists of names (#39), and others appear to be receipts of provisions sent in from places in Judah, such as Anim and Maon (#25). Still others contain lists of provisions of flour or bread, wine and oil, which were to be handed over to the "Kittim" usually on a daily basis.

[7] Y. Aharoni *Arad Inscriptions* (Jerusalem: Israel Exploration Society, 1984) contains full descriptions and translations of these inscriptions.

The Kittim referred to in these texts are to be identified as Aegean mercenaries in the service of the king of Judah, and they probably staffed the outlying forts in the system. Of special interest is ostracon #24, which throws light on the historical circumstances of the fortress at Arad at the end of the monarchy in Judah. The obverse is badly preserved and contains just a few decipherable words and phrases, such as "To Eliashib . . .", ". . . king . . .", ". . . force (or troop) . . .", ". . . money . . .", ". . . passed . . ." The reverse, however is an easily readable text containing the second part of the letter. In full the reverse reads:

> . . . From Arad 50 and from Kin[ah] and you shall send them to Ramat Negeb by the hand of Malkyahu, ben Qerab'ur, and he shall hand them over to Elisha ben Yirmyahu in Ramat-Negeb, lest anything should happen to the city. The word of the king [is incumbent] upon you for your life! See I have sent to warn you today. [Get] the men to Elisha: lest Edom should come there.

Arad clearly functions as the strategic centre of the fortress system, dispatching men to other sites in the face of the Edomite raids which were common at the end of the period of the monarchy.

We have come almost full circle in this survey of strategy. Israel, as a tribal society, was encouraged to adopt a defensive position against the instructions of outsiders. The life of the covenant community was dependent upon a measure of stability and peace. When the monarchy was established an offensive, colonial strategy was adopted, and the machinery of state needed to keep this strategy alive absorbed so much in energy and manpower, that the whole nature of society was changed. In the world of "major league" international politics, Israel and Judah survived for a while, but eventually became absorbed in the plans of nations and empires greater than themselves. Their territories shrank, robbing them of valuable resources, and at the same time the pressure from the outside increased. It came in the form of former colonies, or allies, or in the form of giant imperial armies, the likes of which the Levant had not seen before. Once again, a defensive strategy was adopted, but one which proved ineffective. Successive invaders and conquerors were able, albeit at some cost, to take and eventually control the region. In the final analysis, Israel, then Judah proved powerless to resist to save themselves.

## C. Battle Tactics

From the broader canvas on grand strategy we now turn to the detail of tactical use of troops in the field. Descriptions of what a good tactician is vary, but most of them are variations of the theme attributed to a number of generals, "To get there the fastest, with the mostest!" There is truth to this, but being there first, with the most soldiers is no guarantee of victory in antiquity or today. When Napoleon was being offered the services of a commander whose reputation was well-known and admired, he asked a simple, profound question, "Yes, but is he lucky?". "Luck" in Napoleon's words would be what von Clausewitz called "genius". It is, in part, the ability to master the organization of the troops under his command, to deploy them to the best advantage, to understand the terrain on which he is fighting, to employ the troops as efficiently as possible against an enemy—the strongest against his weakest—but above all, what Machiavelli called "invention", the flexibility to adapt to new circumstances as they arise, and to use them as creatively as possible. In the words of one commentator of Sun Tzu's masterpiece, "... the supreme requirements of generalship are clear perception, the harmony of his host, a profound strategy coupled with far-reaching plans, an understanding of the seasons and an ability to examine the human factors."[8] The tactical skills of a Thutmoses, an Alexander, a Caesar or a Robert E. Lee exemplify these qualities to the full, and demonstrate the complexity of the use of tactics on the field of battle. Of course, so much depends also on the mistakes of one's enemy,

---

[8]Sun Tzu *The Art of War* (Oxford University Press, 1963): 87.

but it is the victorious general who can take full advantage of them, while recovering from his own.

Only on rare occasions does the Old Testament inform us of the tactical details of a battle, and on many others it is content to record that "David smote the Philistines at ...", or "Jehoram killed ... Edomites in the Valley of Salt." So for many battles we are at a loss to know exactly what tactical moves were made; at what time in the battle was a line advanced, when were shock troops, or archers brought into play, or what caused the enemy line to break and flee in panic. These things happened, to be sure, but we do not have the precise data to reconstruct the battle plans of Israel's generals. Later armies developed tactical manuals to offer their generals a framework within which certain tactics might work, so if we find in the annals of their history that an army defeated an enemy at a given place and time, we would have a rough idea as to how this happened. With ancient Israel we have little such information. In its earlier period, before the monarchy, there are general outlines of battles which use widely known tactics, but in the period of the monarchy we are, in the majority of cases, left to guess at what might have transpired at a given battle. One form of battle, the siege, followed a fairly predictable pattern since there was only so much one could do. The genius of the attacker lay in a combination of knowing exactly when to attack and the encouragement of patience among his troops. Beyond this, however, we are frequently in the dark. Comparative material is of little help either, since detailed descriptions of battles are lacking there. For example, we know where Thutmoses deployed his troops when he encountered the Canaanites at Megiddo, but we do not know in what proportion. We do not know from his record when, and in what order, he advanced. We learn nothing of why the Canaanites fled in panic, except in self-serving, metaphorical language about the Pharaoh's glory and grandeur. With Assyrian sources we fare no better. As a general strategic comment we can value the sequence of battles outlined in Shalmaneser III's annals[9],

[9]*ANET*: 277ff.

but as a piece of information on the precise tactics used, the comment "... I approached the town of Ki[ ... ]qa, the royal residence of Ahuni, man of Adini. Ahuni, man of Adini, [putting his trust] upon his numerous [army, ro] se for a decisive battle ... I fought with him on a trust [-inspiring] oracle of Ashur ... and inflicted a defeat upon him ... " is quite useless.

In the following pages I shall follow a plan of action which will, on the one hand, avoid anachronistic speculation on Israel's battles, and on the other, enable us to deal with the material within a reasonable scope. We shall look first at the nature of battle in the Old Testament period and examine the likely results of a clash between two lines of soldiers armed in the way we have outlined above. Second, we shall outline some of the tactics suitable to such clashes of arms and offer some known illustrations of these tactics in the pages of the Old Testament. Third, we shall treat separately a distinctive kind of warfare which was suffered by Israel and Judah, but also practised by them. It was the most time-consuming and the most brutal kind of conflict in the ancient world. We speak, of course, of the siege.

The "Face of Battle" in the Old Testament period was shaped by many factors, and some of these factors have been dealt with in earlier pages. They include the kinds of weapons used, and the effectiveness of them. Tactics appropriate to men armed with swords, spears and shields, supported by the occasional bow or sling, would differ not only from tactics appropriate to mechanised warfare with weapons delivering high rates of fire and destructive power, but also from tactics appropriate to warfare which involved the organised use of chariots and other mounted warriors. However, one thing was common in the use of the standard weaponry of the day, and that is that the majority of men killed on the field of battle in the Old Testament period met their demise in what we would call today "hand-to-hand" fighting. In other words, opposing forces would really have to meet each other on the field. Another feature of these ancient battles was the nature of their communications, once the battle was joined. Did all depend upon the original deployment of the troops, or was there room for manoeuvre, for feint and counterattack in a co-ordinated manner? The third feature would be the weight of forces on either side. The skillful commander would seek first to ensure that he had larger numbers than his opponent, but if that were not possible and the battle was inevitable, then he would ensure that the precise nature of the battle would be to his advantage.

Given these preliminaries about the nature of the weaponry and the limitations of communication, we can suppose that most conflicts involving the armies of Judah and Israel were deadly clashes of lines of infantry armed with spear, shield and sword. To win a battle, one line had to force the other to turn at the flank, or to break in the middle, but to do either of these they could not depend upon the firepower of sling or bow indefinitely, the lines had to meet.

In the period of the Judges, in the days before an organized army and co-ordination of weaponry of various kinds, other factors play a prominent role in conflicts, and they are the intimate knowlege of the terrain used to the advantage of the Israelites, and the element of surprise. These were, of course, not always used to good effect because in its selectivity the Bible only records those incidents in which they were used to good effect. There were undoubtedly many other conflicts throughout this period which Israel lost and became subject to various oppressors for different lengths of time. On these incidents the Bible is silent.

From the period of the Judges there are several battles (little more than skirmishes, in fact), which provide us with some idea of the tactics used by an "irregular" force against a more organized army. The "elements of the art of war" listed by Sun Tzu are measurement of space, estimation of quantities, calculations, comparisons, and chances of victory. But such elements can be afforded by organized armies fighting against each other. Irregular forces need additional skills and knowledge because often they are destined to fight against far superior numbers, and armies more regimented and organized than themselves. Therefore, from the "people's army" of the ancient Israelites to the kommando of the Boer, intimate knowledge of the land, ability to fight in an unconventional manner, and absolute dedication to the task of survival tip the scales in favour of the local.

In the case of Ehud and his battle against the Moabites, he used the simple tactic of demoralization of the enemy. Israel had been invaded by a force of Moabites, led by a warrior-king, and the warrior-kings of the ancient Near East provided not only an organizational, but also a symbolic centre for the army. The sight of Thutmosis III marching at the head of his army through the Aruna Pass inspired his troops, as did the personal bravery of Ramses II at Kadesh some centuries later. It is the same attitude toward the leader that encouraged Joab to persuade David to remain out of the heat of battle (2 Sam. 10-11), and the death of Ahab, in front of his army at Ramoth Gilead demoralized them, and caused them to desert the field (1 Kings 22.29-36). Ehud's plan was simple: demoralize the enemy by assassinating their warrior-king. Then, in this state of confusion the invaders would be an easy target. Together with men from the hill country of Ephraim, he swept down on the Moabites at Jericho, and drove them back over the Jordan.

In the story of Gideon (Jud. 6-8) the tactics used against "the Midianites, the Amalekites and the people of the east" were more inventive, since the local Israelites were seriously outnumbered. In the tradition of what came to be known later as "Holy War", in which the soldiers went to war with the belief that victory was promised by Yahweh and him alone, Gideon cut down his army to a manageable three hundred soldiers. These he divided into three companies and attacked the Midianite camp at night. The tactic was to spread panic throughout the camp, and this was done by noise (horns) and the display of lights. The surprise was complete. The Midianites panicked at the sound and sight and, no doubt thinking that they were faced with a large force, fled eastwards, pursued by the Israelites, now reinforced by men from the southern Galilean tribes (Jud. 7.23).

In the stories of Abimelech and Jephthah, we have additional details on the precise tactics used in their battles. In the case of the former, the activities of the inhabitants of Shechem when they fell out with Abimelech amount to little more than banditry, ambushing the soldiers and partisans of Abimelech (Jud. 9.22-25), but the record of Abimelech's response (Jud. 9.30-49) is full of detailed information with several implications. To put down the "rebellion" of Shechem under Ga'al ben Ebed, Abimelech employed sophisticated tactics. First, he had a spy in the city itself in the person of Zebul, the city governor (Jud. 9.30-33). Second, on the advice of this spy he organized a night advance on the city (Jud. 9.34), and split his force originally into four companies (Jud. 9.35). He used the element of surprise, planning to attack at dawn. The attack as Ga'al left the city and fell into an ambush was completely successful. The following day he repeated the process, but this time manoeuvered some of his troops, now divided into three companies, behind the Shechemites and barred their retreat (Jud. 9.42-49). With the bulk of the armed men of the city now dead or captured, the city quickly fell to the siege set by Abimelech (Jud. 9.45-49). The attempt to repeat the process at Thebes was less than successful because Abimelech was mortally wounded in the attack on the city.

In the record of the "campaign" of Jephthah to rid the Israelites in the east from the oppression of the Ammonites, we find little reference to tactics. He was able to break the Ammonite hold by campaigning across the territory and attacking their settlements. With "very great slaughter" he was victorious. The record does not state whether his campaign consisted of sieges or pitched battles.

With Deborah and Barak (Jud. 4-5) the key to the success of their fight against the much heavier armed Canaanites was the creative use of the terrain. The Canaanite army of Jabin under the command of Sisera was composed mainly of chariot forces, used as mobile platforms for infantry armed with bows or spears. Against such forces conventional infantry lines would be quite ineffective. They could neither hold nor counterattack. The weight of a rush of chariots would prove too much for a standing line, unless armed with lengthy pike-like spears, but such weapons are unknown from this early period. Counterattack was useless because the chariots could retreat and manoeuvre at a much faster rate. Given these circumstances Barak took appropriate measures. He retreated up the heavily wooded slopes of Mount Tabor and waited for the chariot army to make the first move. The chariots were encamped at the nearby city of Megiddo, famous for the scene of Thutmosis III's defeat of the Canaanite chariotry some four hundred years before. The reference to "by Taanach at the Waters of Megiddo" (Jud. 5.19) is to be understood probably as the sight of the final defeat of the Canaanites since it is some distance across the Plain of Jezreel from Tabor. Tempting the Canaanite chariotry into the lower slopes of Tabor was a shrewd move on the part of Barak, and the fact that Sisera allowed himself to be so tempted shows his lack of good generalship. Once on the slopes the chariots lost their manoeuverability and their system of command. At this point the Israelites attacked. Their attack would certainly not have been in an ordered line of advance, but a rush down the hill at the stalled vehicles. This is certainly the impression gained from the account of the battle call in Jud. 4.14. The Canaanite line broke, and fled in panic, only to be defeated by another feature of the terrain, the floods of the River Kishon.

The Kishon is one of the few perpetual streams in Palestine, the others being the Jordan and the Yarkon. In the summer the Kishon is a small trickle of water flowing across the Plain of Jezreel almost its whole length, then exiting near Helkath and joining the swamps of the Plain of Acco. In the winter the stream gathers the run-off from the Carmel Range, the western end of Gilboa and the foothills of southern Galilee, and overflows its banks. The red dust of summer turns into a quagmire and is quite unsuitable for wheeled traffic. One can only surmise that the scattered chariots bogged down in the mud, enabling the Israelites to overtake them, and kill their occupants. Sisera himself fled down the field—in the opposite direction from Megiddo, indicating the nature of the panic in the Canaanite ranks—and was murdered by an enterprising young Kenite woman from Za'ananim near lower Kedesh.

These three episodes illustrate well the innovation which an irregular army, pitched against an organised force, was compelled to use. Demoralizing of the enemy by the removal of their leader; surprise causing panic; inventive use of terrain and season, all were part of the added arsenal of the early Israelites. The organized forces of Abimelech, which gained the upper hand over Ga'al of Shechem would appear to contradict our point here, but this is not so. To be sure, the centralization of power under Abimelech, however crude, resulted in an organised and near-regimented army—the kind that fell victim to the irregulars in these other battles. The tactic of siege warfare which Abimelech used was one which the troops of Gideon, Barak and Ehud could not have hoped to use with any success. The arms and resources needed for such an approach were not available to them, but Abimelech was successful because of his use of two of the elements outlined above, surprise and terrain. With his unexpected dawn attack on Shechem he put the locals off balance, and the fight on the following day saw him use the terrain to his advantage. He sealed off any means of escape and surrounded the Shechemites so that they were forced to fight on his terms. They inevitably lost.

The same variation of tactics is found in the stories of the Israelites in the early chapters of 1 Samuel. Whatever religious interpretation is placed on the story of the loss of the Ark of the Covenant at Ebenezer/Aphek, it is clear that the Israelites were no match for the Philistines. The Philistine army was clearly a well-disciplined fighting force which, when tackled on its ground, was difficult to defeat. This was the mistake the Israelites made. Against the ordered line of the well-armed Philistines, the Israelites—with little, if any battle organisation and few useful weapons—attacked. They relied instead on the psychological value of the presence of the Ark of the Covenant. Against the Philistine line which was fighting on its kind of ground, the Israelites were smashed.

Yet a subsequent battle involving the same antagonists ended with the opposite result. Saul's initial success against a Philistine garrison resulted in a strong force of chariots being brought up from the coast to police the region north of Jerusalem, and to be stationed at Michmash (1 Sam. 13.2-7). The reaction of the locals was one of cowering fright. The Philistines gained an economic, as well as a military hold on the region (1 Sam 13.19-22), and the situation was hopeless for the Israelites. The break came when Jonathan, Saul's son attacked the Philistine camp at Michmash and caused panic in the ranks. The Philistines, now in disarray, were pursued back down to the coastal plain losing many soldiers in the process (1 Sam. 14). Two features are at play here. First, in

Gideon-like fashion, Jonathan introduced the element of surprise and panic into the camp of the Philistines. Second, in
Barak-like fashion, the Israelites took advantage of the terrain they knew well. The descent from the plateau north of
Jerusalem to the coastal plain is via one narrow, and treacher-
ous route, the pass of Beth-horon. In the story of Joshua
(Josh. 9), the battle under discussion (1 Sam. 14), the early
days of David (2 Sam. 6) and the struggle of the Maccabees
against the Seleucids (1 Macc. 7), the antagonists in battles
at this location are similar—irregulars against a well-armed
opponent, and the results are identical—the irregulars win.
The explanation is found in Josephus's description of a
similar fight during the early days of the Jewish Revolt
against Rome (Nov. AD 66). The powerful force of Cestius
Gallus was routed by the Jewish rebels at precisely the same
spot and retreated in panic with horrendous losses. Josephus,
correctly, blames the debacle partly on the nature of the
terrain, and partly on the poor generalship that could not
inspire the troops under its command, nor take decisive
action to halt the growing panic.

In the period of the judges there is one further conflict we
need to look at and that is the "civil war" between Benjamin
and the other tribes. The scene is Gibeah, a town atop a hill
about five kilometres north of Jerusalem and at the south
eastern edge of the plateau. The background to the story is
well-known. The numerical odds were against the Benjaminites. The lone tribe mustered twenty six *'elafim*, plus seven
hundred excellent slingers. They faced four hundred *'elafim*
from the other tribes. According to our earlier calculations
the tribes had in the field approximately 3600 men, against
the 900 Benjaminites. It is clear from the record that the
Benjaminites had a strong position at Gibeah, which they
were not willing to relinquish, and against which the only
tactic of the Israelites was to storm it. On the first day the
Israelites lost about 200 men, and on the second, 160. The
tactic of the Benjaminites was simply to withstand the storm,
aided by their expert slingers, then advance and rout the
remainder of the line.

On the third day, the tactic of the rest of the tribes changed.
As before, they attacked, but when the Benjaminites came

out to counterattack, as they had done on previous days, the Israelites withdrew to the northeast in the direction of the small town of Geba. When the Benjaminites were in hot pursuit a division of Israelites attacked the undefended city and torched it. At that signal the fleeing Israelites turned to make a stand, and the men who had attacked the city, now entered the field behind the Benjaminites. Under this pressure, the Benjaminites were crushed, losing almost all of their fighting men (Jud. 20.1-47). Now undefended, the cities of Benjamin fell prey to the avenging Israelites and "... all the towns which they found they set on fire" (Jud. 20.48). The tactic of the Israelites here is a repetition of the tactic recorded in the book of Joshua against Ai, and is similar to the one used by Abimelech against Shechem. It is the feint/ ambush, catching the unsuspecting pursuers in a pincer from which they rarely escape.

In the time of the monarchy the battlefield tactics of the armies of Israel and Judah must have been modified. Command structures were now in place, officers were trained, men were recruited, trained and equipped for war. Weaponry was improved, and each fighting man was now equipped with standard issue—sword, shield and spear. In addition to the slingers, bowmen appear providing additional firepower, and by early in the monarchy Israel had adopted the weapon introduced into the ancient wars by the Hittites, and which was used by the Canaanites, Philistines, Assyrians and the Egyptians, namely the chariot. Although not used in such abundance, it is known that eventually the Israelites developed another "arm of service", namely the cavalry. We have looked briefly at the development of the chariotry in Israel, and it is clear that by the mid-ninth century BC Israel placed great emphasis upon her chariots. From the victory of David over Hadadezer after which he hamstrung all but 100 chariots horses, to the battle of Qarqar in 853 BC great developments had taken place. The presence of such large numbers of chariots in the Israelite army would, of necessity change the nature of the tactics used.

First, the chariot is an offensive, not a defensive weapon. Its value is its ability to manoeuvre quickly on the field of battle, and to bring pressure to bear on a weak point of an infantry line when necessary. It is not completely invincible, since its drivers and passengers can be struck by arrows and slings, as was the case with Ahab, and it needs a suitable terrain in which to manoeuvre. Swampy, soft ground, or ground with large numbers of field stones is useless, as are woods and hills. The terrain of a chariot must be reasonably flat and firm. This explains the attempt of the king of Syria to entice the Israelites on to the plain near Aphek (Upper) so that he, with his chariots, could defeat them (1 Kings 20.23-25). The Syrian war gods were, after all, "gods of the plain", not the valley (vs. 23).

Second, the chariot is not a siege weapon. It is a weapon of the pitched battle, such as was the case at Qarqar. Soldiers waiting in siege positions can wait on foot just as well as on board a chariot, and the use of chariots in this way would be severely limited. Parades of chariot squadrons around walls of besieged cities might provide a measure of propaganda against the inhabitants, but of more value to the besiegers are the foot soldiers who can scale walls with ladders, the sappers who can undermine the walls and the steady-footed archers and slingers who can harass defenders. A chariot might be useful for transport of troops from one siege position to another, but this is a severely limited use.

The same limitations are found with cavalry, and the Qarqar figures demonstrate that the use of cavalry in these early battles was not extensive. At Qarqar almost 85% of the allied troops were infantry, 11% were chariotry (allowing for two men per chariot), 1.4% were camel riders and only 2.6% were cavalry. The reason for the low use of cavalry was the instability of the mount without stirrups and saddles, and the unpredictable nature of the horse against a line of infantry. Chariot horses carried a measure of protection, were more easily controlled and many wore blinders.

However, the nature of battle would have changed with the innovations of the monarchy. Troops in line, now in uniform, carrying uniform weapons would be regimented in lines for the advance (cf. 1 Sam. 17). Individual behaviour would be controlled by the need to do things in concert, and the reliance on the stability of one's fellows in line gave an added sense of security, but increased the level of insecurity and potential panic when the line broke. The early monarchical army was an army designed for pitched battles, in which it met the forces of opposing nations and countries. The order of the state becomes reflected in the order of the field, and the centralisation of the state is reflected in the central command, seen for a while in the person of the king, later in the person of his commander-in-chief. Control then becomes important, and coupled with that is the need for conformity on the battle field. Innovation now becomes dangerous because it upsets the line, and the lone warrior, like the hapless cuckold, Uriah the Hittite, is doomed.

We can only guess what precise tactics would have been used on the field in such circumstances. The infantry would have advanced in lines, against one softened by the slingers and archers. The chariotry in battle would be used to harass the flank of an opponent's line, and the cavalry might have had the same, but perhaps relatively more limited role. In the final analysis the victory depended upon the infantry lines moving towards each other, in a basic formation which armies adopted for the next 2500 years. When these lines met much is left to chance. If spears were used then they were of limited effectiveness. As Machiavelli reflected many centuries later, "... the enemy has nothing to do but to receive their [spears] upon his shields and to rush in upon them sword in hand."[10] Once this stage had passed then the front lines engaged each other with sword, dagger, shield, fist, rock, club or hand in an attempt to inflict as much injury, pain and death on the enemy as possible. The object was to move the enemy's line back until it gave way. For the front line there was no chance of retreat because behind would be one's colleagues, eager to engage the enemy, and forming a barrier almost as impenetrable as the one in front. The only way to go was forward against a line as determined as yours to withstand the onslaught and hold. Once the line broke, with men falling back or being killed, the message would be quickly relayed down the line, and only the most

[10]N. Macchiavelli *The Art of War* [Eng. trans. by E. Farnsworth] (Indianapolis: Bobbs-Merrill, 1965): 50.

resolute would dare stay and continue the fight. Without the support—real or imaginary—of one's fellows in line, it demanded more strength of will than most could muster to fight. The tendency would be for self-preservation, and it would appear that the most direct route to safety was away from the line of fighting. The problem with this was that escape from the front line not only added to the sense of disorder and panic, but was extremely difficult since it was back through one's own lines. While the organization of infantry lines, when properly controlled, presented a formidable and sometimes unbeatable opponent, these lines only remained so as long as they retained their form and discipline. Once these were lost, the battle quickly turned into a rout, and soldiers would turn on their own men in the interests of getting to a place of personal safety. Thus it is that in the Bible an army's panic is sometimes described as "turning the sword on one's neighbour" (2 Kings 3.23).

As we have shown earlier, once this panic set in, it spread like the proverbial grass fire. As one historian has described it, "Once a panic gets under way it develops a frenetic momentum of its own. Indeed, those involved seem to lose many of their human characteristics, and become animals, given over to the hysteria of the herd."[11] A less prosaic description of an army in a panic is found in the biblical prayer, "Let them be turned back and confounded, who devise evil against me. Let them be like chaff before the wind" (Ps. 35.4-5). In the flight many would trust only those things they could control, namely the legs, and items that hindered a soldier's flight would be discarded, but the irony is that they often included those very things which would protect him against a determined and pursuing foe, such as weapons and protective armour, or those items which would speed his retreat, such as mounts and chariots (2 Kings 7.7).

But the back turned away from the enemy is a vulnerable and exposed one. The shield, if not yet discarded, protects

[11]R. Holmes *Acts of War: The Behaviour of Men in Battle* (New York: Free Press, 1985): 227-228.

the front, and few soldiers in line would wear extensive protective armour. A well-aimed arrow could wound, a sling stone could stun or slow down, and a thrust of the sword or javelin could seriously maim or kill.

## D. Siege

"The worst policy is to attack cities. Attack cities only when there is no alternative".[12] For Sun Tzu, who regarded good generalship as an exercise in the craft of deception on the field of battle, siege warfare was the lowest form of warfare. But it was so judged not because of high moral ideals about the killing of civilians, but rather because it was time-consuming and potentially costly. It robbed the skillful commander of the initiative and bogged him down in an activity which wasted time, resources and manpower. But Sun Tzu was an exception. Although many war leaders in antiquity preferred to attack the enemy's army on the field of battle, just as many were tempted into the kind of warfare where the greatest need was not so much skill as patience, and where the rewards were more or less assured. That was the siege.

Siege warfare is an ancient kind of warfare, and the first recorded battle in history, Thutmosis III's battle at Megiddo, was concluded by a lengthy siege of the city after the Canaanites had fled from the field, and the Egyptian army had lost its discipline and not pursued them. Instead, they had become distracted by the promise of loot from the abandoned Canaanite chariots. Siege warfare was the model for the story of the conquest of Canaan by Joshua, at least in the southern and central regions. It was practised by Abimelech at Shechem, with desired results and adopted by Jephthah in his campaign across Ammon. With the beginning of the monarchy there is a revival in the building of fortified cities,

[12]Sun Tzu *The Art of War.* 78.

and this, in turn, shaped much of the kind of warfare which developed and in which Israel and Judah took part. Shishak's invasion (ca. 925 BC) was a campaign of sieges; Mesha's struggle to rid the Moabite plateau of Israelite influence was a siege campaign, and the retaliatory campaign by Israel, Judah and Edom was the same. In fact, in the period of the monarchy many of the "battle campaigns" of the ancient monarchs more closely resembled the *chevauchée* of the Hundred Years' War, with its endless succession of sieges, than they did the battle campaigns of the seventeenth, eighteenth and nineteenth centuries.

Not only did local nations fight in this manner, as is seen many times in the Old Testament, but the great empires of the ancient Near East perfected this type of warfare. None were more expert at it than the Assyrians, who developed specialized storm troops, regiments of sappers, and equipped their armies with new siege weapons, such as covered battering rams and mining tools.

Siege warfare was practiced because in the long run the costs in equipment and manpower were less than those of the pitched battle, and some armies, like the Assyrians, mounted several sieges at once. The effects on an enemy were devastating and the rewards were certain and large. What the attacker needed most of all was a near inexhaustible supply of patience. Control of one's troops was difficult, but made easier by the promise of the loot awaiting them, and a strong application of discipline. Premature attack on the city could result in the decimation of one's forces by a determined and still able defender. Such was the case with the tribal attack on Gibeah. Two days of slaughter taught the attackers to change their tactics, and only when the enemy was forced into the open was he defeated.[13] Cities were attacked because they comprised the "nerve centres" of the developing urban societies. It was here, behind the walls, that the administrators lived, and with them rested the con-

<hr>

[13]On this see Machiavelli *The Art of War.* 194-195.

trol of the regions round about. With the development of this bureaucratic "middle class" came an increase in the wealth and power of the cities, so harshly condemned by the prophets. Here an attacker could control a region by controlling its centre. Here he could gain, not only the wealth of the urban powerful, but also their skills, their families as slaves, and their women.

Siege warfare would involve the "sealing off" of a city under attack by encircling it with an army. In a prominent place, the attacker's tent would be pitched as a symbol of the threatening power. Assyrian reliefs reflect this practice, as does the biblical expression of "setting up one's throne" at the gate of an enemy city (Jer. 1.18). The army would then be encamped (Isa. 29.3) and siegeworks would be built. These consisted of a surrounding earthen wall into which guard towers would be built. Siege ramps would be put in place when the time was ripe for the rams to be brought up to attack the city walls. But for the most part the siege would be a game of waiting. The besiegers would need patience, and the besieged courage. On occasion, local campaigns into the surrounding countryside would lessen the boredom for the attackers, and keep their skills sharp. The outcome of the siege was inevitable. Unless relief came in the form of a column of allied soldiers to attack the besiegers, the inhabitants of the city were doomed.

There are numerous references in the Bible to the fate of besieged citizens, and they could look forward to three things: famine, disease and the sword (Jer. 13.13-17). Since most cities were built on or near a permanent water source, water supply was not a major problem. Extensions were made to the supply tunnels, as has been seen at Gibeon, Hazor, Megiddo and Jerusalem. Access to the water from inside the city was assured by the system of channels and steps. However, food supplies were limited. Cities were not designed to store an inexhaustible supply of food. Domestic silos were small, and easily exhausted, and the level of public works was not sufficient to store large amounts of food. One can assume from the request made to the king in 2 Kings 6.26, that either he, or the *sar ha'ir* was responsible for the distribution of food during a siege. On this occasion, certainly not an isolated one, he was unable to fulfill that responsibility. Hunger, famine and starvation would be inevitable during a long siege. The old and the weak would die first, and as starvation increased, people would be pushed to extremes of self-preservation. The tragic depiction of the siege of Samaria (2 Kings 6.28-30) shows that cannibalism was certainly common in such circumstances. A description of judgment in the prophet Jeremiah is certainly inspired by the knowledge of the nature of a siege:

> ... I will make them eat the flesh of their sons and their daughters, and everyone shall eat the flesh of his neighbour in the siege (Jer. 19.9).

The painful deaths resulting from the starvation of the inhabitants of the city under siege would create a problem of sanitation. Burial would normally be outside the city, an area now in the control of the besiegers. As they died the corpses of the victims of famine would pile up in the streets:

> ... the people ... shall be cast out in the streets of Jerusalem, victims of famine and sword, with none to bury them ... (Jer. 14.16).
> ... their corpses were as refuse in the midst of the streets ... (Isa. 5.25).

And the bodies would rot, spreading disease to all who came in contact with them, and eventually contaminating the water supply itself. At the moment when the defenders were too weak to lift the sword, the attackers would break the walls and enter the city. The frustration of the besiegers, building up over weeks and months of waiting, would be let loose, and few commanders had the discipline, or even the inclination to hold back their troops. Now they came to claim the reward for waiting. Items of value that could be moved were taken, the rest were smashed or burned. Men still alive were slaughtered; children were cruelly butchered; pregnant women brutally murdered and other women raped and claimed by the intruder. The city itself would be razed to the ground (2 Kings 8.12). The catalogue of evil found in the prophetic tirade against the neighbours of Israel and Judah (Amos 1-2) is a list of actions committed by soldiers after siege. The cruelty is grotesque, but taken for granted. The punishment of those who perpetrated these crimes is to suffer the same fate themselves. The indelible impression that siege warfare left on the collective memories of the inhabitants of the ancient Near East, and especially Judah and Israel, cannot be underestimated. It brought the conflict of nations to the very hearts of those nations (Jer. 4.10). No longer could battle be spoken of in the abstract as though it were confined to the defeat of enemy armies on the distant fields of battle. The scribes who now wrote the histories suffered themselves with their families, and the descriptions contain a sense of immediacy and vividness which the battlefield encounters do not have. Thus it is that the three things suffered most in siege—famine, plague and sword—are combined with the fourth, death, and become a symbol of universal judgment in the later tradition of apocalyptic (Rev. 6.1-8).

# 6

# War and Old Testament Literature

In this chapter we are not concerned with what some would call the "Bible's teaching" about war. The literature on that topic is quite substantial, and we shall speak more about it in the final chapter. Our concern in this chapter is to sketch some of the implications of what we have seen so far for an understanding of the literature of the Old Testament. We shall explore the different kinds of literature one can expect from different historical contexts as they relate to the question of warfare. It is important in this endeavour to look at the anthology of literature which we know as the Old Testament, as the product of an increasingly complex society which practised warfare. Biblical studies have long since argued that a text can be understood only in its social, political, historical context. As one scholar recently put it:

> "... there is broad concurrence that the biblical writings were rooted in interacting groups of people organized in social structures that controlled the chief aspects of public life, such as family, economy, government, law, war, ritual and religious belief ... The guiding question ... becomes, 'What social structures and social processes are explicit or implicit in the biblical literature...?'"[1]

[1]N.K. Gottwald *The Hebrew Scriptures: A Socio-Literary Introduction* (Philadelphia: Fortress Press, 1980): 26.

Sensitivity to these issues is a first step to understanding the Old Testament's presentation of war. Given this state of affairs it would then make a difference whether the stories, attitudes about warfare are found in pre-monarchical or monarchical literature, at the historical level, or whether they come from the supporters or critics of the centralized monarchy at another. I am not concerned so much with specific literary genres which are produced under different circumstances and from different interest groups, but rather with the general tone which can be detected in the literature. Nor am I concerned with those texts and passages which can be brought together which present an opposite viewpoint, especially during the time of the monarchy and empire. During times of aggressive warfare dissent is common, so such passages are not out of place, nor do they destroy my basic approach.

In his work *The Shape of the Past: Models and Antiquity*, T.F. Carney[2] examined the way in which military institutions affect their host societies. His object of study was the introduction of the military innovation of the hoplite into Greek society, and his findings provide a valuable model for the examination of similar social changes. Carney noted that the main thrust of change was through the new use of natural resources (manpower and materiel), the shifts in the social and economic structure to accommodate this, and the formation of politico-military institutions. In turn this "main thrust" of change has a profound effect upon technology, population structure, socialization and personality, foreign affairs, culture, and belief systems. Some of these we have observed in previous chapters. We have noted that in the interests of a militarization of Israelite and Judaean society natural resources are reallocated, the socio-economic structure changes, foreign affairs are affected. What we have only touched upon in a previous section are the shifts in cultural and belief systems. This was seen in the excursus "David and the Invention of Tradition". Since the literary product of a society emerges from culture and belief systems, which are in turn dependent upon matters of socialization and personality, it is this which we shall explore in the following pages. We shall pose the questions, What is the presentation of warfare in certain bodies of literature? and, Why? We have begun an answer in our chapters which outlined the political and social changes Israel underwent when it moved from a tribalised society to a centralised bureaucracy. We shall now move deeper into these areas.

Whether we adopt a "conquest model", an "infiltration model" or a "revolutionary model" of Israel's beginnings in Canaan, the basic profile of the settled community in Canaan, as portrayed in the book of Judges remains much the same. Ideally, it is an "egalitarian", tribalized community, with power scattered throughout the community. Within the community any form of centralization is resisted firmly and decisively by the tribes, and any attempt to disrupt the community from within is dealt with in a harsh manner. The poetic shaming of the tribes who did not participate in the battles against the Canaanites in the north offers some hints at the ideal of a mutually dependent community. The severe reaction to centralization of power in the story of Abimelech (Jud. 9-10) makes clear the aversion to a move which would upset the balance and be a threat to the very nature of the community. Similarly, the stories surrounding the civil war with Benjamin show the lengths to which the community will go to preserve its identity as an "alternative community" to the Canaanite city-state system which it sought to replace, or at least resist.

The stories which have come out of this context have, of course, been incorporated into a larger work known as the Deuteronomistic History, which in its final form comes from the end of the period of the monarchy, so allowance must be made for a certain amount of overwriting of these earlier tales. However, the war stories of the period of the Judges have a distinctive flavour. They are stories concerned with the *preservation* of the order of the old covenant community. Set in a religious/theological context of the relationship of the people to Yahweh through obedience to the Torah—a perspective which provides the early chapters of the book of Judges with its "rhythm" of apostasy-judgment-deliverance—these stories tell of the defence of that community against aggressors who are almost always portrayed as "kings", that is, embodiments of centralised and organised power. The stories repeat a fundamental theme of survival against the attempts of despots to destroy the style of life they had fashioned under the rubric of Yahwism. The consistent model in these stories is of the underdog struggling to survive against the odds. A poorly armed, but cleverly led army of Barak outwits the more powerful Canaanites, and the denouement of the tale is the death of the once powerful Canaanite general at the hands of a woman. Gideon's relatively small band set the strong invaders into confusion and panic, and the early Samson is set—one against thousands—in opposition to the Philistines. This material is, in Brueggemann's words, applied to the early David, ". . . the trustful truth of the tribe . . . " which is ". . . an alternative sketching of reality that serves the interests of a community in deep tension with the dominant rulers and rules of the day."[3] In this material the tribes survive against all odds, and against all threats, internal and external. Thus formulated, the stories in the book of Judges become an *apologia* for the tribal order, a testimony to the validity of the order, and a legitimation of it.

The preservation of the tribal order, the covenant community, which stands as a new experiment over against the existing centralized systems represented by the Canaanites and Philistines, is conducted entirely through defensive wars. On no occasion is Israel the aggressor, but a defender and protector of its borders, physical and symbolic. The nature of these stories is *saga*, stories usually of victory and triumph in the affairs of human beings. They originated in the oral tradition of the tribes, and eventually were incorporated in the larger framework of the Deuteronomistic History. But they retain their primitive excitement and confidence.

---

[3] W. Brueggemann *David's Truth in Israel's Imagination and Memory* (Philadelphia: Fortress Press, 1985): 22.

To help us understand some of the dynamic of change that Israel and Judah underwent with the advent of the monarchy and the development of an empire, we need to understand the nature of such an empire, especially as it concerns the development of a supportive *ideology*. For a working definition of ideology we shall adopt that of Edward Shils:

> "Ideologies contend ... for a purer, fuller or more ideal realization of particular cognitive or moral values that exists in the society which the ideology obtains."[4]

In other words, ideology has a homiletic, or propagandistic intent, and we have seen something of this in the Excursus on "David and the Invention of Tradition." We also hinted there at the effects this would have on the literature of the period. Now we look closer at this. For a summary of the link between ideology and empire, we follow the recent work of historian and Assyriologist, Prof. Mario Liverani. In 1979 Prof. Liverani published a paper entitled, "The Ideology of the Assyrian Empire" in a symposium volume, *Power and Propaganda*.[5] In this paper he looked at some of the characteristics of the Assyrian empire as examples of the "centre-periphery" structural model. In much the same way as Eisenstadt, in his book *The Political Systems of Empires*, Liverani sketches general characteristics, and particularizes them in Assyrian historical examples. Since Israel/Judah developed an empire, albeit small and shortlived compared to the Assyrian, it should be possible to detect some of the same characteristics there. I shall first summarize Liverani's position.

Empire is the domination of the few (centre) over the many (periphery), it is the surrender of wealth (and we should add, power) by classes or groups of producers in favour of non-producing consumers (in the case of Israel, the bureau-

---

[4]E. Shils "Ideology" in *The Constitution of Society* (Chicago: University of Chicago Press, 1982): 202-223.

[5]T. Larsen [ed.] *Power and Propaganda: A Symposium on Ancient Empires* (Copenhagen: Akademisk Forlag, 1979). Liverani's contribution is on pp. 297-317.

crats and administration of empire). Empire also involves the delegation of political decisions in favour of groups which have different interests. In the case of Israel/Judah, these interests become identified with the political will of the monarchy. This imbalance extends to the territories conquered. Such a situation requires first the systematization of the imbalance, and the development of an ideology which facilitates this action and overcomes resistance. This ideology would explain the differences between ruler and ruled and how and why other countries exist for the one. In Liverani's words, "... the kernel of the whole ideology is a theory of diversity as justification of the unbalance [sic.] and of exploitation." "Ultimately", he states, "imperialism is founded on one difference only, the one that exists between ruler and ruled."

The ideology of diversity applies to four areas, those of space, time, goods and men. The same general principles apply throughout, namely that the closer one is to the centre, the more stable things are. Within the understanding of space there is an opposition between the "cosmic centre ... and a chaotic periphery". Activity related to this is imperialistic expansion, supported by an ideology of the movement of order into the chaos. With time, the centre is the place of order, and the ordering of creation. Ritual demonstrates that the king knows and controls time and the cosmos. The imperialistic activity which results from this is the creation at the centre of a capital/temple, "... the apex of creation, after which there will not be much more to be done."

As far as goods are concerned, the periphery is the place of the exotic, unprocessed goods, whereas the centre is the place where the unknown is shaped into the known. Therefore the imperialistic activity in this regard is seen in the drawing of taxes and tribute from the periphery to the centre. Finally, the same structure is imposed upon the world of men. Those related to the centre are seen in a positive light, those on the periphery in a negative light. The periphery is a place of a different language, different customs, whose stance is one of potential opposition. They are "strangers" or "foreigners", a term loaded with negative value, and who are generally seen as a threat. The activity related to these peoples of the periphery is elimination or subjugation, and "After war, submission, conquest, and destruction, the peripheral human setting is rebuilt according to the correct pattern." One can see this in the Assyrian policy towards Samaria in 722 (see 1 Kings 17). Conversely, expulsion of an enemy is followed by a rebuilding according to local pattern, as is seen in the Moabite Stone.

Now this rather lengthy diversion into the work of Liverani is important because it offers us, first, a pattern of imperial expansion which the monarchy in Israel seemed to follow, and second, it offers an outline of the kind of ideology which is propagated in support of such expansion. It is an ideology of diversity, a strong diversity of value between the centre and the periphery. In the Old Testament, all of the points made by Liverani are echoed in the ideology which surrounded the Davidic monarchy. Zion becomes not only the essential part of the capital city, but also the place from which "Torah" will go out to the nations, and to which the nations will eventually come (Isa. 2.1-4; Mic. 4.1-4). It is the centre of ritual, and becomes even more so as the monarchy progresses (2 Kings 22-24). To Jerusalem, goods in the form of tribute are brought from afar. All of these points could be expanded and properly applied to the Davidic monarchy in detail, and it would be possible to trace the elements of an Israelite ideology which supported the growth and development of the smaller Davidic empire, but this is not the place for such a study. Sufficient for our purposes will be a closer look at the idea that there is a diversity of men built into this ideology, and we shall look at this in some detail.

Liverani argues that in the Assyrian imperial ideology the qualitative difference between the Assyrians and the foreigners is evident. The Assyrians see themselves, in ethnocentric fashion (to use a concept invented much later), as the standard of what is truly human. Foreigners are strange, speak with strange tongues—not because they are unknowable; quite the contrary. Trade is conducted with the nations, therefore some use of the stranger's language can be presupposed—but because they are different. Foreigners are also characterized, and often caricatured as subhuman, belonging to the animal world, and often compared to animals.

They are inferior in all ways, and are noted for their cowardice and deceit. Beyond this, the one nation (Assyria) is pitted against a host of enemies. "... in the last analysis the Assyrian king on his own ... prevail [sic!] over the many representatives of the chaotic world." The king, trusting in his deity, however, is always victorious.

The action of centre to periphery, of order to chaos, or of natural to unnatural, is to eliminate or subjugate. Resistance to this is not tolerated, and rebellion, often described in "religious" terms, such as "sin", is a further example of the unnatural nature of the peripheral nations. When resistance is confronted with power, the enemy's courage fails and he runs. "If there is a clash ... , it is a one-sided massacre ... not a clash between two armies," and the enemy is destroyed through a combination of his own stupidity and deceit, and the over-whelming power of the conquering king. The king is often depicted, in understandable fashion, as a hunter searching out and destroying his prey. All of this is supported by an appeal to, and citation from, the primary sources of the Assyrian empire.

It is naive, of course, to expect all of this to be necessarily repeated in the ideology of the Davidic monarchy in Israel and Judah. Between Assyria and monarchial Israel there were many differences. But, one cannot avoid the similarities either. Since Liverani is developing a general framework in which the many activities of the Assyrian empire can be understood, in other words, a model, it is theoretically possible to see at least some of these characteristics in the development of the Israelite monarchy, especially in its imperialistic stage. For our purposes, the stark ideological differences seen between men affects the nature of warfare in this period directly, and would affect the nature of the literature that comes from the central institutions of the period. But a word of correction is needed at this point. In outlining these characteristics as they appear in Israelite and Judaean literature, I am not suggesting that ancient Israel and Judah be seen as precisely the same as Assyria. What appears to be unique among the literature of the Old Testament is that the same epithets which are applied to the enemies of Israel are also, eventually applied to Israel and Judah, generally by the prophets. This is an important point and it cannot be overlooked. The behaviour of Israel and Judah deserving of these epithets leads eventually to judgment and exile, so it does provide a context of meaning for the exile, and provide the basis for what some have called a "theology of defeat". This is unusual, if not, unique. But having said this, I must stress that in applying these same epithets and characterisitics to the peoples of Israel and Judah the prophets are doing no more than comparing them with the nations, from whom one expects such activity. It presupposes a view of "strangers from a foreign land" which is generally negative. The title of the volume on ancient empires in which Liverani's essay appeared is important, *Power and Propaganda*, and many of the statements which perpetuate this ideology of the imbalance of power come under the category of propaganda.

First, let us look at the use of the term "stranger" (Heb: *naker*, *nokri*) in some texts in the Old Testament. The meaning of the term in early stories is well illustrated by Gen. 31.15. Here the context is the dispute between Jacob and Laban over the latter's daughters. Jacob has been cheated by Laban out of his wages and the daughters of Laban have lost their inheritance through Laban's deceit. Their complaint is that they have been "treated like foreigners (*nokrim*)", in other words, like nonmembers of the family or group. The same meaning is found in Exod. 21.8, and clearly in Deut. 14.21. In this latter text the dietary laws, which distinguish Israel from all others, are not applicable to the "alien" (*ger*) or to the "foreigner" (*nokri*). The term in these representative texts means a person outside the group, one not entitled to the benefits of group membership, nor under the obligations of group membership. Thus it is that in the law of the King in Deut. 17.15 the king is to be chosen from among the Israelites, and is not to be *'ish nokri*, ". . . who is not your kinsman." One must also notice that the *ger*, (often used as a synonym in Deuteronomy of the term *nokri*) is to be well treated, and is placed on the same level as the widow or the orphan. In the prophets the term is frequently applied to gods whom the Israelites and Judaeans are not to worship, or of wives whom the king is supposed not to marry (Jer. 5.19; 1 Kings 11.1,8).

For representative texts from the period of the monarchy we will take two psalms, acknowledged to be "royal psalms", but which also are concerned with warfare and battle. They are Ps. 18, which we have looked at in another context, and Ps. 144. In both, the term is used with added nuance. The first of these psalms is a well-known battle psalm in which the king praises God for victory and deliverance on the field of battle. With the help of God he has soundly defeated an enemy (vss. 31-42). The enemy, however, is identified as "the nations" (*goim*), over whom the king is victorious:

> Thou didst deliver me from strife with the people; thou didst make me the head of the nations; people whom I had not known served me.
> As soon as they heard of me they obeyed me; *foreigners came cringing to me. Foreigners lost heart, and came trembling out of their fastness.*

In other words, over these "foreigners" the king rules. They become subject to him.

Ps. 144 takes the attitude to foreigners one step further. From the opening verse it is clear that the psalm is a battle-psalm, in which the psalmist blesses God for skill in battle, and for being a protector in battle ". . . who subdues the peoples under him" (vs. 2). But in vss. 5-10 the depiction of foreigners is extremely negative, and absolute. The foreigners are caricatured as perpetual liars and utterly corrupt. This is a general hyperbolic characterization which is not provable, but was never intended to be, since these are stereotypes, the stuff of propaganda.

This brings us to another element in the view of foreigners as enemies in the latter period, and that is the depiction of them as not only corrupt humans, but at times as subhuman. According to Liverani this is done in Assyrian literature, and it is also present within the pages of the Old Testament. We have already mentioned the depiction of the enemy in Ps. 35.5 as "chaff before the wind". Similar sentiments are expressed in Ps. 18.42 where the enemy is ". . . like dust before the wind . . . like mud (Heb: *tit*) in the streets." This latter term is always used as a term of contempt in the Old Testament, and its meaning is clear. It can be walked upon with immunity. With such descriptions of the enemy, ill-treatment of them is taken out of the realm of morality, and regarded as a matter of course.

Coupled with this complete dehumanizing of the enemy is the depiction of the enemy as a dangerous animal, bent on destruction, against which one must fight. Favourite images for this are fierce animals or fire, both of which "devour". Thus the pursuing enemy of Ps. 7 is a persistent lion which tears its prey, a theme echoed in Ps. 17.12; 22.13 and 91.13. Moabites are "lionlike" in 2 Sam. 23.20, and the prophets borrow this imagery in their descriptions of judgment upon Judah (Jer. 4.7; 5.6; 8.16). By implication, what is "truly human", is found in Israel, who (supposedly) "know God" and are "holy to the Lord".

Finally, Liverani points out the tendency in the time of an expanding empire to describe battles in ways which we might call "one-sided". In his words "If there is a clash . . . it is a one-sided massacre . . . not a clash between two armies" (p. 311). From the point of view of form-criticism, what he is describing is the bureaucratic record of battles, listed as though on a scoreboard with a kind of detachment common to administrators. The purpose is not so much to whitewash the nature of battle, as to enhance the reputation of the victor. Numerous Assyrian texts listing the conquests of kings repeat in a formulaic way the defeat of resisting enemies, and offer numerous figures of the enemy dead. Realistically, no victory is ever won without cost to the victor, but nowhere in these texts do we hear of Assyrian dead, nor in the numerous battle reliefs placed on palace walls do we see Assyrian dead. The same is true of Egypt and other ancient Near Eastern nations. It is a hallmark of imperial battle reporting. The obvious, but often overlooked fact must now be stated. In the numerous reports of David's imperial campaigns we find records of enemy dead. He kills half of the Moabite prisoners captured in battle with his neighbour, captures 1700 cavalry and 20,000 infantry from Hadadezer of Zobah, kills 22,000 Syrians in the same campaign and in a battle with Edom kills 18,000 soldiers (2 Sam. 8). In the following chapter

David defeats and kills the crews of 700 chariots and 40,000 cavalry. But not once do we hear of an Israelite casualty. It is only in those passages which have a different motive from battle reporting, such as 2 Sam. 11.17, that Israelite fallen are mentioned, but no precise figures are given. Even civil wars are recorded in favour of the victor, such as was the case of David's fight with the Ephraimites who followed Absalom (2 Sam. 18.7). In the early, expansionist wars of David and Israel against the neighbours, the victories are decisive, and—if the records are to be taken at their face value—completely without cost to the Israelites. The point is, of course, that they are not to be taken at their face value, but fall into the category of imperial literature which perpetuates an ideology of an invincible leader.

In sharp contrast, the stories of the period of the Judges are much more "honest", in the sense that the loss of soldiers in battle is not so much of an embarrassment to the tradition. If they died, they died defending their home and their own; or even died because of the bad tactics and general stupidity of their leaders, such as in the defeat at the hands of the Philistines in 1 Sam. 4. On more than one occasion they died because the tribal confederacy was in danger of fragmenting, or even because of petty jealousies among the tribes. But never is there the need to protect the reputation of the central figure, the king.

This is by no means an exhaustive study of the literature of the two periods, pre-monarchy and monarchy, and indeed no such exhaustive study can be attempted within the confines of this short chapter. However, in some important instances it has been shown that there is a change in perspective as regards warfare and the object of warfare between the period of the judges and the time of the monarchy. In the latter period many of the attitudes of imperial expansionist policies found elsewhere are present within the Old Testament.

Before we sum up some of the implications of these differences in attitude, one final question needs to be addressed, and that is the question of resistance to what we can call the "royalist perspective" on warfare. Was there an alternative viewpoint, both to the expansionist policies of the early monarchy, and the attitudes it engendered? The answer to this is difficult to detect since so much of the literature of the monarchical period, as we have seen, emanates from the very cultural and political centre itself. One would hardly expect to find any clearly articulated, and endorsed, alternative viewpoint from this literature. However, it would be worth investigating the attitudes of the literature which comes out of those circles which often present an alternative to the royalist ideology, and those are the prophetic circles. At the founding of the monarchy the record shows that there was some ambiguity in the prophetic response—seen in the figure of Samuel—to the new institution. The prophetic response to monarchy was guarded. There was acceptance, but acceptance under strict conditions. If we follow one recently aired, and widely accepted viewpoint, the conditions of the monarchy are set out in the book of Deuteronomy in the section which incorporates the "law of the king", namely Deut. 17.14ff. In the words of this recent study:

> "The legislation of Deut. 17.8-18.22 ... establishes a national political constitution with historical and literary links to the institution of the monarchy. In erecting a central judiciary, a priestly order, and a prophetic office as positions independent of the monarchy, this remarkable document serves the end of the "law of the king": it limits the monarch's power to arrogate to himself all authority in the national regime."[6]

Within this "constitution" the prophet had a key role to play. It was he who imposed limitations on the use of power by the king, and "... it was the prophet's duty to protect the divine covenant against human infringement." In other words, the prophet's role is, ideally, to protect the values and ideals of the covenant community.

[6]B. Halpern *The Constitution of the Monarchy in Israel* (Missoula: Scholars Press, 1980): 234-235. See also S. Talmon "The Rule of the King—1 Sam. 8.4-22" in *King, Cult and Calendar in Ancient Israel* (Jerusalem: Magnes Press, 1986): 53-67.

In general terms the prophets see themselves as continuing the office established by Moses. I have argued in another context that the key to the prophetic consciousness is the figure of Moses.[7] Whether this Moses is the Moses of history or of tradition is not vitally important at this stage. What emerges, however, from the picture of Moses presented to us is a character who stands against the current ethos, in his case, of Pharaonic imperial Egypt. He confronts and challenges, and offers alternatives. He stands against the dominant culture. This, too, is the prophetic mode of behaviour, and when some of them are challenged, they resort to descriptions of themselves and their calling in terms of the Mosaic call (see Jer. 1.4-10; Amos 7.10-17; Isa. 6 etc.). Not all of the prophets express themselves in precisely the same way. There are differences of historical and geographical location which must be taken into account, and there are some differences of social status which must also be taken into account. But the general stance of the pre-exilic prophets regarding the monarchy is to stand for a higher code of behaviour, the covenant ideal. Numerous individual examples can be found for this position, but we do not want to move too far away from our topic of warfare. So we shall restrict ourselves to two elements related directly to warfare, and in which the prophets play a prominent role. Both concern transformations of existing attitudes to warfare. The one is the "war oracle" and the other the relationship of Yahweh to warfare.

The so-called "war oracle" has received extensive study in the scholarly literature, and one of the most comprehensive treatments has been that of D.L. Christensen in his work *Transformations of the War Oracle in the Old Testament Prophecy*,[8] published in 1975. Christensen traces the development of early "war oracles", or "oracular divination", which promise victory for the armies of early Israel. An example is

[7]T.R. Hobbs "The Search for Prophetic Consciousness: Some Comments on Method" *BTB* 15 (1985): 136-141.

[8]D.L. Christensen *The Transformation of the War Oracle in Old Testament Prophecy* (Missoula: Scholars Press, 1975).

Jud. 1.2-6. Linked with this are the promises of defeat in battle for Israel's enemies, such as Exod. 17.14. A third type is the summons to battle in defense of the tribal confederacy, and a fourth type is the summons to flight, which, Christensen acknowledged, is not common before Amos. These formulaic sayings are rooted in the early history of Israel, and linked, according to many scholars, in the Holy War tradition of the Exodus and Conquest. Within the royalist ideology, such sentiments are preserved in Ps. 83, with its request for God to destroy the surrounding enemies of Israel.

What happens within prophecy is that these ancient war oracles, used as oratory tools to encourage Israel's soldiers against Israel's enemies, are transformed in part into weapons against Israel. In the 9th century, in the prophetic ministry of Elisha, prophetic words of judgment begin to be spoken against the nation of Israel itself, it is also during this time that Israel begins to lose territory (a sign of judgment); first Moab, then Libnah, Edom and eventually the whole of the Transjordan by the time of the death of Jehu.

In the so-called "classical" tradition of prophecy, this war oracle is redirected against Israel on numerous occasions. In a clever fashion the opening chapters of Amos include Israel, and perhaps Judah in the universal judgment of God. The tradition continues in the pre-exilic prophets until a climax is reached in the prophecies of Jeremiah. Here Yahweh the warrior fights against His own people, and it is He who eventually "hands over" Jerusalem and Judah into the control of the Babylonians. In highly dramatic fashion Jeremiah adopts ancient forms and war songs, not to depict the aggression of Israel against her neighbours, but to show with relentless clarity the destruction of Judah, its fortified cities and Jerusalem, because of the "fierce anger of Yahweh" itself (Jer. 4.26). As the former enemies of Israel were powerless before the armies of Israel, so now Judah and Jerusalem are powerless to resist the newly adopted armies of Yahweh, the Babylonians (Jer. 32.26-36).

I am not arguing here that the prophets are against warfare as such. The evidence would not support that, and like most of their contemporaries, the prophets accept warfare as a part of life. But what is evident is that the prophets do not seem to support warfare as an instrument of the expansionist policies of the monarchy. Nathan and Gad, the prophetic advisers of David, do not express themselves on the issue. But if Micaiah ben Imlah is typical of the "true" prophet, then he provides a good illustration of this position (1 Kings 22). Conversely, like their predecessors, the prophets of the monarchy endorse warfare as a means of preservation of the covenant ideals. In the interests of these ideals, Ahijah from Shiloh plays an active role in the secession of the north from Judah (1 Kings 12). Later, Shemaiah prohibits Rehoboam from invading the north to regain the lost territory. Elisha takes part in the bloody destruction of the dynasty of Omri (2 Kings 9) and in the accession of Hazael (2 Kings 8), an event which was to have dire consequences for the apostate Israel.

Coupled with this attitude, and in direct contrast to the triumphalist tone of the royalist ideology, is another telling side of the prophetic proclamation. In the face of the denial of defeat and destruction, of the denial of the pain of the vanquished, of the repetition of the false "peace" of the monarchy, the prophets "offer symbols that are adequate to the horror and massiveness of the experience which evokes numbness."[9] In other words, through the use of words and language and symbolic action, the prophet confronts his audience with the awful, terrible reality of warfare. In stark contrast to the stereotyped, official accounts of battle on foreign soil found so frequently in the historical annals of the monarchy, the prophet presents the people with vivid, heart-rending visions of a devastated land, a slaughtered and humiliated people, the sword, which reaches the very heart of Judah. It is in the prophetic books that we find poetic depictions of the horrendous conditions of siege warfare (see above ch. 5) when bodies line the streets, people faint through lack of food, and the fear of the doomed inhabitants gives way to absolute despair.

We have then sketched three reactions to warfare in the Old Testament reflected in the literature. In the period before

---

[9] W. Brueggemann *Prophetic Imagination* (Philadelphia: Fortress Press, 1978): 49.

the monarchy, warfare was necessary to the survival of the covenant community. This is reflected in the stories of the great deeds of Israel's early heroes. In the period of the monarchy itself warfare became an instrument of policy and this is seen in the attitudes towards enemies engendered by the royalist ideology, and in the detached records of distant battles in which the king is the victor without cost. In that same period the prophetic champions of the covenant order reacted to the monarchical use of warfare by transforming its conventional literary war poems.

# Excursus

# Joshua's Battles and "Holy War"

This is not the place to rehearse the arguments for and against the so-called "historicity" of the account of the conquest of Canaan in the book of Joshua, nor to recapitulate on the state of the archaeological "evidence" for the conquest. This has been done on a much larger scale by many writers. In this section our purpose is much more limited. It is to come to some understanding of the book of Joshua, and the story it tells, in the light of the scope of the military-historical concerns which emerge in our study. To accomplish this we shall enter into a discussion with an important article written by Abraham Malamat and entitled, "The Israelite Conduct of War in the Conquest of Canaan."[1]

Malamat is mainly concerned, as we are, with the question of "historiography" rather than "history", and he acknowledges some of the difficulties surrounding the matter of the conquest. It is entirely unnoticed in nonbiblical documents, and we are dependent solely upon the biblical account itself. This account, which is the book of Joshua, has two important characteristics. It is the subject of "reflection" or "contemplation", in which the invasion becomes transformed into an action of Yahweh; and the events are "telescoped". The result is what Malamat calls the "official" or "canonical" tradition which portrays a swift, unified, and complete attack upon

---

[1] A. Malamat "The Israelite Conduct of War in the Conquest of Canaan" in *Symposium: Celebrating the Seventy Fifth Anniversary of the American Schools of Oriental Research (1900-1975)* (Philadelphia: ASOR, 1979): 35-56.

the land of Canaan by the tribes under the command of Joshua. To use Malamat's [unfortunate] word, a *Blitzkrieg*. The variant account in Jud. 1 is regarded as a "deviant" version. The conclusion drawn is that the events were actually much more complex than is portrayed in the biblical account. But Malamat does not want to distinguish what is "historical" from what is "traditional". Instead, he asserts that the biblical "evidence" is

> ". . . an ancient theoretical model depicting the conquest as if the Israelites themselves (especially the "official" tradition) sought to form an articulate concept of their inheritance and domination of Canaan."[2]

To understand this "model" he adopts a "typological approach" which examines its broader characteristics. Five such characteristics emerge:

1. Canaan is inherited by force.

2. Entry was not via a direct route.

3. The population of western Canaan had no overall military organization.

4. Israel was not prevented from gaining a foothold in Canaan via the Jordan, due to the lack of suitable defences.

5. In the "first stage" of the conquest, Israel was successful only in the hill country.

The important military question which is raised by this outline is, How? The answer is that Israel knew and exploited the heterogeneity of the local population by using certain well-tested military skills. These skills were the use of intelligence (Num. 13.18-20), sound logistics through the bridgehead established at Gilgal, and the "indirect military ap-

---

[2] Malamat *Ibid*: 36.

proach" which would place even a superior defender at a disadvantage. To lend support to this outline, Malamat notes that in the attack on Ai there was a failure of intelligence, mainly because the intelligence operatives overstepped their mark and became involved in operational decisions.

The same kinds of skills were used in the attack on cities, such as the neutralizing of a city's defence through the use of a "fifth column", as at Jericho, and the enticement of the defenders into the open through the use of the feint. Added to this arsenal of military skills are the use of the surprise attack, and nighttime operations. Malamat's conclusion states:

> The early Israelites encountered an adversary much superior to them in military strength. By preserving a clear view of the objective and applying means unanticipated by the enemy, a bold and imaginative Israelite leadership was successful in translating what we today would call a specific military doctrine into spontaneous victory. An overriding factor was the Israelite soldier's basic motivation—his deep sense of national purpose. It was this blend which engendered the momentum of the Israelite conquest.[3]

Malamat's study offers some important insights on the narrative of the conquest, and is one of the few studies on the topic which tries to use military-historical categories to understand what is after all a matter of military history. There are some implications of his study which are worth pondering. First, he makes plain (as many others have done) that the biblical account of the conquest is a literary creation for purposes quite other than historical "reporting." This is reinforced by the discrepancy between the Joshua account and the first chapter of Judges—called unfairly a "deviant chapter—and also between the rarely quoted passage in Exod. 23.23-33, which clearly supports a gradual takeover of Canaan by the Israelites:

<hr/>

[3] Malamat *Ibid*: 54.

> And I will send hornets before you, which shall drive out
> the Hivite, Canaanite and Hittite from before you. *I will
> not drive them out from before you in one year ... Little
> by little I will drive them out from before you, until you
> are increased and possess the land* (Exod. 23.29-30).

The account in Joshua is seen as a "theoretical model" of the takeover.

The implications extend further, however. Malamat is never precisely clear on the socio-political use of the term "Israel" in his paper, and, as we have seen from our study of the period of the judges, the impression of unity of order and purpose attributed to "Israel", especially in his conclusion, is a far cry from the impression given in the book of Judges itself. We have seen that the period of the Judges was not characterised by a central political motivation for military strategy. The military strategy, which in turn reflects the political set-up is more "ad hoc", a defensive reaction to invasion, an instinctive protection of the social limits which involved some, though never all of the tribes. The blend of the "deep sense of national purpose" and the strategic military doctrine, so much a hallmark of the story in Joshua, disappears when we read the stories in the book of Judges.

Malamat hints at a broader motivation for the presentation of the stories of Joshua's battles with his use of the word "official", or "canonical". But what does he mean by this? No explanation is given, but there appear to be two options. The first is the "revolution-model" which suggests that the Yahwistic tribes of Canaan revolted against their Canaanite overlords (city-states), and formed an alternative community. The conquest tradition then becomes a kind of coded story presenting a rapid, unified conquest of the land with the expulsion of the Canaanite inhabitants. This position has been persuasively argued by George Mendenhall, and expounded in a slightly different form by Norman Gottwald.[4] The position has caused a considerable debate, and been

---

[4]G.E. Mendenhall "The Hebrew Conquest of Palestine" *BA* 25 (1962): 66-87; N.K. Gottwald *The Tribes of Yahweh* (New York: Orbis Books, 1979).

fully discussed in other contexts. For our purposes the main drawback would be the temporal proximity of the newly formed religious community of "Israel" and the invented traditions of the conquest. The difficulty is especially acute in the light of the nonliterate character of premonarchical Israel, and of the enormous discrepancy between what is experienced (Judges) and what is propagated (Joshua). To create such a unified view of the past a real unified present is needed. Our reading of the book of Judges has shown that this was not the case. A second alternative is to move the creation of this unified image to a later period. The stories of Joshua's battles presuppose 1) a central system of command and policy, under the generalship of Joshua; 2) a clear, and generally agreed strategy, namely the systematic conquest of Canaan, and; 3) a clear motivation shared by all, namely a national "all-Israel" policy. It seems to me that such a picture is more appropriate to the time of the monarchy. It suits most clearly the model developed by Liverani,[5] namely the center-periphery model, in which deliberate, enforceable, unified political goals are supported by the necessary military organization and skill.

The whole matter of early warfare in ancient Israel has been linked to the concept of "holy war", especially since the publication in 1949 of the study by Gerhard von Rad, *Der heilige Krieg im alten Israel.*[6] Adopting a "form-critical" approach to the text, von Rad detected several common characteristics in the accounts of early warfare, which he organized into the following scheme:

1. The blowing of a trumpet as the announcement of the holy war;

2. The naming of the army as the "people of Yahweh";

3. The sanctification of the participants;

---

[5]See the discussion in the previous chapter.

[6]G. von Rad *Der heilige Krieg im alten Israel* (Göttingen: Vandenhoeck & Ruprecht, 1949=1962).

4. The sacrificing of an offering and/or the consultation of Yahweh;

5. The announcement of victory by Yahweh "I have given ... into your hands".

6. The announcement that Yahweh "goes out" before the army

7. The claiming of the war as "Yahweh's war" and the enemy as "Yahweh's enemy";

8. The encouragement not to fear, because the enemy will lose courage;

9. The war-shout;

10. The fear of Yahweh among enemy troops;

11. The practice of the "ban", the slaughter of all enemy men, women and children;

12. The dismissal of the troops with the cry "To your tents O Israel."

Von Rad's work has inspired a vast amount of literature, both for and against the theory of "holy war" in ancient Israel. Von Rad expounded an isolated, religious institution, known as Holy War, which was practised during the period of the Judges, and sanctioned by the so-called "amphictyony", the twelve-tribe confederacy. Not all commentators on the war of early Israel agree with von Rad and at the other end of the scale one finds the conclusion that "While war was religious by association, it was no more a cultic and holy act than was sheep-shearing."[7]

In discussing the concept of "holy war" we must bear in mind that it is not a biblical term, so the idea that Israel embarked on holy wars is an inference from the data which is not clearly stated. The origin of the term appears to be Greek, and on occasion ancient Greek writers talk of groups

[7]P.C. Craigie *The Problem of War in the Old Testament* (Grand Rapids: Eerdmans, 1978): 47.

of city-states embarking on "sacred wars"[8] as acts of punishment or vengeance for an overt wrongdoing. The Old Testament, however, does know of "wars of Yahweh" (1 Sam. 25.28), and there is even a collection of ancient poetry to confirm this (Num. 21.14), but this is not widespread. Many scholars have found the concept of an early institution of "Yahweh war" a more profitable avenue of research than a formal "holy war."[9] By the use of the term "Yahweh war" it is suggested that this was not a cultic institution, but rather an early form of warfare done in the name of Yahweh. This form of warfare evolved. Some religious ceremonies were attached to it, and often accompanying the army was an important religious person who was used for consultation. Also on occasion the "ban" was practised, but:

> ... when all the evidence is assembled, no set pattern for Yahweh War emerges; it is not possible to say that when Israel went to war it had to perform a number of rituals according to a given formula.[10]

In the handing on of these traditions of warfare, however, the pattern of warfare blends into a "Holy War scheme", and in the final literary presentation, "... there has been a process of standardizing the Holy War pattern and of schematizing the events."[11] This standardization is not restricted to the wars of conquest under Joshua, but also is noted in Jud. 6, for example, and in some of the stories in 1 and 2 Samuel. However, it is with the book of Joshua that the schematization is most noticeable. The book of Joshua represents "... a more advanced stage in the presentation, and provide(s) a

---

[8]The phrase is used in Thucydides *Peloponnesian War* I:112.

[9]See, for example R. Smend *Yahweh War and Tribal Confederation* [Eng. tr.] (Nashville: Abingdon, 1970); G.H. Jones "Holy War or Yahweh War" *VT* 25 (1975): 642-658; F. Stolz *Yahwe and Israels Kriege* (Zurich: Theologischer Verlag, 1972).

[10]Jones "Holy War or Yahweh War": 651.

[11]Jones *Ibid*: 651.

more formularized account."[12] The schematization follows
three distinct stages:

1. The stories of "Yahweh War",

2. A pre-Deuteronomic adoption of some of these stories
   into a distinct framework,

3. The final incorporation of the scheme of Holy War
   into the Deuteronomic tradition.


This argument is essentially a literary argument, dealing with
the stages of the development of the literary tradition of
Holy War. Jones contents himself by dealing with the historical questions at the level of whether Holy War was ever
practiced as described. His answer is ambiguous. While the
Holy War scheme rests on an historical tradition of Yahweh
War, the scheme does not represent what actually happened
in history. There are, however, other historical questions
which need to be raised, and the main one is why the need to
develop a tradition of the past which sees Israel acting in
concert, according to strict religious customs, and with inevitable success over her enemies? The answer, we suggest, is to
be seen in the context of the same pressures for unity and a
unified image of the past which emerge from our understanding of the military history aspects of the book of Joshua,
namely the monarchy. Such dynamics are the products of an
"imperialistic ideology", which is basically religious in character. In this context war is always holy, if fought by the
protagonist, an evil thing if waged by an enemy. It is "holy"
by virtue of the fact that it corresponds to the social values
and ideology of the Israelite monarchy. In this interest the
past is reshaped to conform. As Joshua is now seen, an-
achronistically, as employing a strategy and tactics more at
home in a centrally controlled society, so he is seen as the

[12]Jones *Ibid*: 653.

perfect warrior-leader of this unified society. In addition to the strictly military questions in this picture are the ideological tendencies of the centralized monarchy we have noted elsewhere, especially the attitudes to foreigners. In other words, Joshua emerges as a man who most of Israel's kings would like to have been.

From a literary-historical point of view, I would add another stage to Jones' development of the Holy War scheme. The original wars were probably less organized than the book of Joshua leads us to believe. The traditions of the wars were reshaped, first in the interests of the tribalized society (see Ch. 6), and then in the interests of the monarchy. This latter stage tended to concentrate more on the traditions which adhered to the figure of Joshua. The final incorporation of these traditions into the deuteronomistic history presents a dramatic tension between what was seen as an ideal—the ideal law (Deuteronomy) and the ideal occupation (Joshua)—and what was reality, namely the apostasy-judgment-deliverance pattern which is established in the book of Judges, and which continues throughout the subsequent history of the monarchy.

# 7

## Old Testament Warfare and New Testament Insights

It is time now to try and piece together some of the implications of the preceding pages for Christian Theology. We began our study with a sketch of the basic problem of warfare in the Old Testament from a Christian perspective, and we must now try to see whether what we have found on our journey addresses any aspect of the problem. Our attempt in this book has been to see warfare in ancient Israel in its proper historical perspective. We looked first at the period before the founding of the monarchy, the so-called period of the judges, and then we examined some of the social, political and economic changes that took place with the advent of the monarchy. With this background we examined the topic of warfare, looking at the types of warfare, the changes in organization, questions of leadership and motivation, use and manufacture of weapons and finally questions of strategy and tactics. Our final attempt was to see how these historical data are reflected in the stories and literature which were produced in Israel, and how the different periods of early Israel's history viewed warfare and conquest. We have tried throughout to make some historical sense of the topic of warfare, as a prerequisite for any ethical or theological reflections which might be made on the general topic. Now, it is time to attempt to show some of the ways in which this material can be appropriated when we talk of "Old Testament

Warfare and New Testament Insights." As with many of the preceding chapters, this is not an exhaustive treatise on the topic. It is more in the nature of a collection of "signposts" to show directions of study and reflection which will prove helpful. The discussion on warfare in the Old Testament is littered with all kinds of different approaches to the matter. Some of these we hinted at in the introduction to this book. On the one hand, the so-called "Peace churches" and, on the other, those sincere people with equally strong Christian convictions who see warfare as necessary, are poles apart ideologically, and between them with varying degrees of support for one side or the other are thousands upon thousands of readers of the Bible. What I find interesting is that in their use of the Old Testament both sides show some strong similarities. There is a tendency among all, no matter what their committed position might be, to explain *away* those elements in the Bible which disagree with their position, or to ignore them altogether. It is sometimes a source of amusement to see the way in which two different and opposing ideologies will use the same passage of the Bible in support of their viewpoint. I must confess, however, that it is also a source of irritation and annoyance that this is done so easily and almost unconsciously.

In the final analysis it comes down to how the biblical material about warfare is used. Every reader of the Bible, of course, thinks that she or he is an interpreter with an opinion to be aired and listened to. That these same people would not claim to be interpreters of other ancient writers does not worry them. With the Bible there always seems to be a "direct" line of understanding between the reader and the text. Of course, what most of us do when we read the Bible "cold", is to bring to it all our presuppositions and prejudices. What we find there, is often what we look for in the first place. Now none of us can come to the text without presuppositions, but it is important for us to acknowledge first, that we have them, and second, what they are. Many who are brought up in a Christian tradition which shows great respect for the Bible as a guide for "faith and practice", or as a source of meditation and spirituality, are often ignorant of, or avoid the historical dimension of warfare within its pages. Terms like "victory", "deliverance", and even "salvation" are "war-words", grounded in the historical reality of war and conquest, which includes killing, loot-taking and raping. Since they have been adopted (and, one must add, transformed) by the New Testament in its Gospel-language, those same readers tend to "spiritualise" these words and concepts, when they appear in the Old Testament and to interpret them often in a very personal way. It is reminiscent of the royalist tendency to record battles without cost, which we noted in the preceding chapter. What we are dealing with here are ways of reading and understanding, and it might be helpful first to sketch some of the approaches which we should try to avoid.

## A. Anachronism

In historical studies of ethical issues such as warfare there is often a tendency to read back into the past the concerns of the present. Sir Moses Finley, in writing on the important question of slavery in antiquity, called this the "teleological fallacy" which:

> ". . . consists in assuming the existence from the beginning of time . . . of the writer's values . . . and then examining all earlier thought and practice as if they were, or ought to have been, on the road to this realization; as if [writers] in other periods were asking the questions and facing the same problems as those of the [modern] historian and his world."[1]

This is a common approach in what is known as the "History of Ideas". Facts about the past are not sought out and examined in their own context, but used to illustrate ideas which have come about in quite different circumstances and for

[1] M. Finley *Ancient Slavery and Modern Ideology* (Harmondsworth: Penguin Books, 1982): 17.

very different reasons. The literature of the past is then forced to answer questions which are imposed on, and often alien to the literature itself, or it is drawn into a historical scheme which is more "propagandistic" than historical. It is, to quote Finley again, a "... habit of using the ancient world as a springboard for a larger [modern] polemic." As we have seen, the title of Peter Craigie's book, *The Problem of War in the Old Testament*,[2] appears to understand warfare in the Old Testament as an ancient problem, which, of course, it was not, it was taken for granted. Further, the subtitle of Millard Lind's important work *The Theology of Warfare in Ancient Israel*[3] falls into something of the same trap by talking about a "Theology" of warfare in the Old Testament. It is difficult to speak in this way about a social institution which was so much a part of life. Part of the problem is that so much that has passed for "Theology" or "Biblical Theology" has been done in this fashion. What we are dealing with here is not a "theology" of warfare, or of anything else, for that matter, but shared and sometimes conflicting attitudes to the social institution of warfare.

Another aspect of this approach is to read back into the past what are indeed valid concerns and attitudes of the present. The motivation of this approach is often the very highest, but it is nevertheless misguided in its treatment of the Old Testament text. I will offer three common illustrations of this point. The first can be dispensed with quickly since it does not have to do directly with warfare, although it is often brought into the discussion.

The commandment "Do not kill" is used today in discussion of two topics, that of capital punishment (on both sides) and in connection with warfare. In the first case, since the Bible prohibits killing of another, then capital punishment is wrong, *or*, since killing of another is prohibited, then the penalty for breaking that law must be exacted. In many,

[2]P. Craigie *The Problem of War in the Old Testament* (Grand Rapids: Eerdmans, 1978).

[3]M.C. Lind *Yahweh is a Warrior: The Theology of Warfare in Ancient Israel* (Scottsdale, PA: Herald Press, 1980).

though not all cases in the Bible, that penalty is death. For the opponents of capital punishment to use the text in this way is a misuse of the text. In its context, this text does not refer to officially imposed penalties, and in the same collection of laws, the death penalty is invoked frequently. However, for the proponents of capital punishment to use the same law in this absolute way in support of their position is equally misguided. When the complete picture of the laws on murder in the Old Testament is examined, the issue becomes more complicated. The law is changed, on occasion, to accommodate different social circumstances. There are examples of murderers who were not punished, and there are a number of crimes in the canon of Old Testament law which also call for the death penalty, such as slandering one's parents. Yet few would advocate the imposition of such penalties for disrespectful behaviour in the modern world. What I am pointing out is that the issue is extremely complicated, and to use the text simply as a prop for one's own disposition and attitude is an abuse of the text.

This is no less true for the use of this text in the context of warfare for the simple reason that it did not apply to warfare in ancient Israel. The Hebrew verb used in the commandment is *ratsach,* one of several words used for killing in the Old Testament, but this is a word which is applied to the murder of a fellow Israelite. This law applies to internal relationships between Israelites (the closely bonded community) *at a time when there was no war.* When war was waged, a different set of rules applied. We have already seen the tendency to denigrate the enemy, and to treat his soldiers as something less than human. The death of enemy soldiers was what a *gibbor chayil* was trained for, and something upon which he built his reputation. Joab, we are reminded, is punished for murder not for the act itself, but because the act was committed *at the wrong time.* He was avenging blood shed in war, in this case in a "civil war", and chose a time of no war to act. In war, it seems, killing was accepted, and even encouraged, but in time of peace different rules applied.

Similar problems emerge with literature which expounds ideas of "peace" in the Old Testament, or which seeks, as one volume puts it, "The roots of pacifism within the Old Testament".[4] The difficulty with such treatments is that they so often read back into the biblical material modern ideas of what peace is, or, in the second case, "pacifism". Now whatever the merits of pacificism in the modern world, and I must go on record as expressing my strong sympathies for the ideal, the term cannot be found in the OT, and any attempt to find it there is bound to come up against serious problems. Unfortunately, what frequently happens is that historical events or actions are interpreted as though they were of relevance to this ideal. So, in Enz's book, the prophetic criticism of the monarchy is understood as a criticism of warfare, whereas we have seen that the prophets see warfare as a tool of judgment on Israel and Judah—and also on the enemies of Israel and Judah in the oracles against the foreign nations. What the prophets object to is the use of warfare as a tool of imperial expansion. This has little or nothing to do with "pacifism", but a lot to do with the misuse of power. Further, in this discussion refuge is often taken in the theme of "Yahweh's wars", interpreted to mean wars fought miraculously by Yahweh. Thus it is stated: ". . . the great defeat of Egypt which reverberates through all the Bible was a weaponless victory!"[5] But this is really nonsense since it does not dispense with warfare as such, but instead reminisces about certain kinds of warfare.

One final illustration is offered, and we refer to a fine article entitled "War, Peace and Justice in Early Israel",[6] written by P.D. Hanson. There is so much in this article with which we can concur, but there is also so much here that we must challenge. Having offered a good interpretation of some of the early war poetry of the Old Testament, Hanson concludes that the victory over Egypt ". . . is a demonstration of the validity of the principle of *universal justice* over the principle of special privilege" [italics mine]. Of course it is nothing

[4]J.J. Enz *The Christian and Warfare: The Roots of Pacifism in the Old Testament* (Scottsdale, PA: Herald Press, 1972).

[5]Enz *The Christian and Warfare*: 52.

[6]P.D. Hanson "War, Peace and Justice in Early Israel" *Brev* 3 (1987): 32-45.

of the sort, and to argue in this way is to indulge in Finley's "teleological fallacy" in which, in this case, a modern political ideology is thrust back into the past.

## B. Selectivity

Closely related to this anachronistic approach to the text is one which indulges in a highly selective reading of the Old Testament, either deliberately or unconsciously, so that the main issues are side-stepped. In the first case there are those works which avoid any discussion of the basic issues of the topic by choice. Such are those studies which take "religious themes" and trace them through the Old Testament, more or less as an exercise in "form-" or "tradition-criticism". A case in point is the study by E.W. Conrad entitled *Fear Not Warrior*[7] which is a form-critical study of the use of this expression throughout the Old Testament, with some comparisons made with contemporary foreign material. It is a disappointing study, not because it does not do what Conrad set out to do, but rather because of what he set out to do is far too limited. He informs the reader that "This volume does not attempt to look at origins or institutions behind 'formulae' but only at the 'rhetorical features of the text.'" And the conclusion is about as far-reaching as such a programme of study will allow it to be, "... 'fear not' is part of stereotypical language used to address a warrior, to give comfort and assurance before an impending battle or an envisaged war." But divorcing the "rhetorical features" from the institution which gave it birth tells only half the story. From such a study we learn nothing of warfare in the Old Testament on the one hand, and an important aspect of interpretation is lost on the other. The painting "Guerenica" by Picasso can be studied in isolation from history, and merely as an example of the changing techniques of the artist, but it lives when placed in the context of the Spanish

---

[7]E.W. Conrad *Fear Not Warrior: A Study of the "'al tira'" Pericopes in the Hebrew Scriptures* [Brown Judaic Studies: 75] (Chico, CA: Scholars Press, 1985).

Civil War and the obvious outrage felt by the artist at the bombing of innocent civilians.

Similarly, Craigie's conclusions on warfare in the Old Testament disappoint. While he disapproved of "historical reductionism" which would destroy the concept of revelation, he himself indulged in what can only be described as "theological reductionism" which takes away any historical sense from the text. The metaphor of God as warrior is a limited tool ". . . to say that God participates in human history, through sinful human beings, and through what have become the 'normal' forms of human activity."[8] Such participation by God reveals, not his being, but his action which takes place in a world as it is. Now this seems all well and good until it is analyzed closely. There is much more at stake here which ought to be acknowledged. For one, why does God's activity have to be seen in terms of human violence? Granted the world is populated by sinful and imperfect human beings, but those same human beings create beauty, harmony and poetry. To be sure, some kill each other, but others love each other and care for each other, and simply generalizing the problem away like this does not solve the questions. Nor does the de-sacralizing of the concept of "Holy War" in the Old Testament, so that it becomes a kind of cautionary tale showing how bad war can be.[9] The fact of the matter is that war *need* not be that bad. Entire populations of cities, including women and children *need* not be slaughtered, and the reputation of kings and leaders *need* not be built upon the piles of bodies of their slain foes. To say that this is a reflection of the world "as it is" destroys the principle of revelation which Craigie set out to preserve in the first place. With the (much) later attempts by theorists and practitioners of war to limit the effects of war, and to make it more efficient, one could well argue that the world of today is a better place than the world of the ancient mid-Orient.

Introduction of comparative questions is always dangerous for the historian since historical questions are always "open-

[8]Craigie *The Problem of War in the Old Testament*: 41.
[9]Craigie *Ibid*: 47ff.

ended", that is, through more reflection and research, the answer might change or be modified. It was customary in the 1940s and 1950s (and it seems, the 60s, 70s) to compare ancient Israel's institutions with those of her neighbours, with the intention of demonstrating the higher values represented in Israel's institutions, and of seeking thereby the locus of revelation through the Old Testament. Such a course of study is fraught with difficulties, not the least being the possibility that Israel's institutions will be seen to be not as good as those of her neighbours. It is, to use an old illustration, like peeling off the successive skins of an onion, each skin representing something which Israel has in common with her neighbours. The danger is obvious—you eventually run out of onion! In the case of warfare and violence, it also allows for the convenient side-stepping of the main problem. Thus it is in a treatise of violence from a Christian point of view, that one reads the following treatment of the Old Testament material:

> "The Old Testament, especially the books of history, has a dark, blood-red streak of violence that mars the image of Yahweh and Israel. *But this violence is Israel's borrowing from her neighbours.* The heart of the Old Testament message is found in Israel's and Yahweh's difference from their neighbours.[10]

Even a casual reading of the Old Testament shows that this is not the case. To be sure, Israel was condemned for being "like the nations" and for practising the "abominations of the nations", but nowhere are these abominations equated with warfare. Even kings who are condemned for violence are condemned because their violence is directed against "innocent", or undeserving Judaean subjects, as was the case with Manasseh. (2 Kings 21.16).

---

[10] P.W. McKay *Violence, Right or Wrong?* (Waco, TX: Word Publishing, 1973): 63.

## C. The "Prophetic Vision of Peace"

Is there no place then for what is called in some literature "the prophetic vision of peace"?[11] Do not the prophets look forward to a time of universal peace when all warfare will cease, and are they not, in fact, forerunners of the modern peacemaker? Now there are many questions here, and some of them do not necessarily follow on from the others. The first thing to acknowledge is that there are indeed passages in the prophetic literature of the Old Testament in which a vision of a peaceful future is seen. One of the most famous is the passage which appears in both Isa. 2.1-4 and Mic. 4.1-4. Parts of it are also repeated in Joel 3.10, but in reverse order! What we have to do with these passages is to interpret them in their proper contexts, not simply the immediate literary context, but in the context of the *complete* vision of the future which is found in the prophets. Like any other part of the Old Testament we must adopt the more demanding approach of looking at the fullest context possible, and not to select according to whim and prejudice. Without a doubt, Mic. 4.1-4 and Isa. 2.1-4 are part of the prophetic proclamation, but they are only part of it, and we should fill out as much as possible the complete picture of their future vision.

One point we should address at this stage is the understanding of the word *shalom*, which is often translated "peace". This tends to confuse the issue if we are not as clear as we should be about the word. In the first place there is an irritating modern tendency to interpret the word with a modern *psychological* understanding, so that it is seen as an ancient counterpart to the Jungian idea of integration, or of the pop-psychological idea of "wholeness". Now these notions are not wrong in themselves, but again we must beware of thrusting them back into a context which was decidedly non-psychological. The so-called "false prophets" who prophesied "Peace, peace, when there was no peace" (Jer. 6.14; 8.11) were not commenting on the state of mind of individual

---

[11]For example, see J.L. McKenzie "Peace: A Biblical Concept" in *New Testament Themes for Contemporary Man* [R.M. Ryan ed.] (Englewood Cliffs: Prentice-Hall, 1969): 156-160.

members of the Jerusalem community, but making a comment about the immediate state of Judaean society. Further, in spite of numerous claims to the contrary, "peace" in many of the prophetic statements *is* an absence of war (Jer. 8.15; 12.5,12; 14.19).

The word *shalom* has a very wide range of meanings in Hebrew, and it cannot be forced into one mold easily. For example, it can be used as a simple greeting (2 Kings 9.17, 19), and it need not be translated so clumsily as it is in the RSV: "Is it peace?" It would be no more significant than the phrases "Hello" and "Goodbye" in English.

The word is also used, in a verbal form, with the meaning of "to pay", as in the property laws of Exod. 21 and 22. For damage to a property—whether it be animals, land or other goods—through the misuse or inattention of a neighbour then payment must be made. The word used is a verbal form of *shalome—shillem*. Similarly, in Mic. 7.3, judges are accused of judging *"bashillum"*; since this is an accusation we can hardly interpret it as "judging in peace"! It is judging for a payment, and accepting bribes. With this understanding of payment the word is used well over sixty times in the Old Testament. This use is important because it unveils what is a basic meaning for the word, that of *repayment*, *recompense*, or *restoration* of something damaged.

It is a small step from this to another use of the root of the word in the Old Testament, and that is "to avenge", often with the use of force. Thus it is, in the visions of the future, Isa. 34.8 speaks of "a day of vengeance (*gemulim*), a year of recompense (*shelumim*)" during which time the sword of Yahweh becomes "sated with blood" in the destruction of Edom. Almost exactly the same expression is used of the impending judgment upon Israel in Hos. 9.7, in keeping with the affirmation in Deut. 32.35 that "Vengeance (*nakam*) is mine, and recompense (*shillem*)." Human activity in this regard is seen in the attempt of some of the young men from the Judaean court to avenge the death of Ahaziah, their "brother", at the hands of Jehu (2 Kings 10.13).[12]

---

[12]On the text see T.R. Hobbs *2 Kings* [Word Biblical Commentary 13] (Waco, TX: Word Publishing, 1985) in loc.

It would be difficult with this range of meaning before us to understand the term in the way it is frequently used by those in the present age who are concerned with peace. Unfortunately this is the most popular victim of what Finley termed the "teleological fallacy." In so many treatments the results express the modern wish for (and understanding of) peace rather than the ancient reality. Such a reality can only be discovered by looking at the broader picture of the prophetic vision of restoration.

## D. The Restoration Vision of the Prophets

The prophetic tradition spoke much about the judgment of Yahweh on His people for their apostasy and social evils. The blame for this state of affairs in the two and one-half centuries leading up to the Babylonian invasion and destruction of Judah and Jerusalem was laid squarely on the shoulders of the leaders of society. Micah's repeated appeals to the "heads" of Judah and Israel (Mic. 3.1,9) and Jeremiah's opposition to the rulers and administrators from the outset of his ministry (Jer. 1.17-19) are illustrations of this posture (see also Jer. 5.1ff). This judgment receives an awful reality with the Assyrian destruction of the north in 722 BC and the Babylonian invasion of the south in 598 and 587 BC. However, beyond this destruction and judgment most of the prophets looked forward to a period of restoration, when Israel (now the *religious* community, not the nation), will be restored, granted rest from aggressive neighbours and will embark on a period of blessing and prosperity. Although the term is used infrequently in these visions of the future, this is the "peace" to which they look forward. It is a period of the restoration of a damaged people, or, to use another appropriate metaphor, a period when the balances will be righted again for Israel. On closer examination, however, the way in which this is achieved is far from "peaceful".

Let us look at the structure of the future vision as found in the book of Isaiah. We do this mainly because Isaiah is the most quoted of the prophets, and because he can be taken as typical. What we find in this vision is that the restoration is localized in Zion, is particularized for Israel, and is achieved at the expense—or subjugation—of Israel's neighbours. In other words in the vision of the book of Isaiah for the future we have a projection of the imperial, "centre-periphery" model. The centre is Zion, the beneficiaries of the blessings brought to the centre are the restored Israel, and the non-Israelite nations surrounding Israel are perceived as a threat and are dealt with by often brutal subjugation.

Frequently, the "day of vengeance, the year of recompense" comes for the benefit of Zion alone (Isa. 34.6; 27.7-13; 29.8; 33.1-12; 17-24; 35.1-10), and the familiar passage borrowed by Handel for his oratorio "Messiah", illustrates this well. It is Jerusalem which will be purified, clean and free (Isa. 52.1-2). It is to Zion that Yahweh returns (vs. 8) in triumph, and the observer nations and kings will be dumbfounded because of this restoration (vv. 13-15).

Further, the recipients of the blessings of the restoration in the future are Israelites alone. It is Israel which will increase and enlarge its borders (Isa. 26.15), and it is "my people" who will be protected in the renewed land (Isa. 32.8). The people are not to fear because ". . . your God will come with vengeance (*nakam*), with divine vengeance (*shelumim*) he will come and save you" (Isa. 35.4). Through Cyrus, the achievement of peace is for Israel alone (Isa. 44.24-28), all is done for the sake of Jacob (Isa. 45.4), and in the restoration Israel ". . . will spread abroad to the right and to the left, and your descendants will possess the nations and will people the desolate cities" (Isa. 54.3). In these sentiments we see what later observers would call nationalism.

Nowhere is this "nationalistic" and "imperial" spirit seen more clearly than in the attitude to foreigners in this future vision. There is no improvement on the attitude we detected in the royalist ideology of the earlier monarchy, and in fact, there is justification in describing the attitude now as more harsh. Israel's salvation, according to Isa. 25.10-12, is brought about by the subjugation of her neighbour Moab, who:

> ". . . shall be trodden down in his place as straw is trodden down in the dung pit . . . and the high fortifications of his walls he will bring down, lay low, and cast to the ground, even to the dust."

The general attitude to foreigners is well illustrated by Isa. 14.1-2 in which Israel will capture and enslave neighbouring populations, annihilating their children lest any should be left to rebel against them. Peace for Israel means utter destruction, through invasion and siege, of Babylon (Isa. 43.14; 47). Former enemies will ". . . see and rise; princes, they shall prostrate themselves" (Isa. 49.5-7), and further:

> "Kings shall be your foster fathers, and queens your nursing mothers. With their faces to the ground they shall bow down to you, and lick the dust of your feet. Then you will know that I am the Lord" (Isa. 49.22-23).

Foreigners shall build walls, and their kings will become slaves (Isa. 60), and do other menial tasks for their new masters:

> "Aliens (*gerim*) shall stand and feed your flocks, foreigners shall be your plowmen and vine-dressers; but you shall be called priests of the LORD, men shall speak of you as the ministers of our God; you shall devour the wealth of nations, and in their riches you shall glory." (Isa. 61.4-5)

In the future, former enemies are still dehumanized or ridiculed (Isa. 9.12a; 19.16, and 29.5) and fit for menial tasks, subjugation and death. The final vision of the book is of an Israel glorying in the new-found faithfulness of God, but at the same time gazing at the bodies of the slain, whose violent deaths are the cost of the restoration (Isa. 66.22-24).

It is difficult to appreciate the violent nature of this vision of the prophets. Even appeal to the more gentle nature of the so-called "Servant Songs" does little to detract from the overall impression of the violence of the vision. If these songs are removed from their context and interpreted according to the New Testament and early Christian use of them, then they stand in sharp contrast to the surrounding vision. But this kind of interpretation is highly selective (not to say, speculative) and nonhistorical. It does not see these poems in the literary context of Deutero-Isaiah (Isa. 40-55), nor does it find for them a proper setting within the complete vision of the future. Whatever the identity of the servant in the poems may be, he is a symbol of forsakenness, a person who has suffered violence. But the tables are to be turned. The suffering is to be vindicated, but not without violence and warfare. In the Old Testament context it is not through suffering that the restoration comes, but rather through an overthrow of the enemies of Israel that the suffering is given meaning.

Let us recapitulate what we have seen. Warfare was part of the ancient world, and very much a part of the life and history of ancient Israel. In the period of the Judges warfare was used as a legitimate means of defense of the community against aggression. Certain attitudes of and actions by Israel's leaders, such as Gideon, reflect the tradition of fighting with Yahweh at one's side, and of the unimportance of human strength or numbers. Nevertheless, these were not days without violence or warfare, rather they were days with limited, but real use of violence.

In the period of the monarchy we saw that warfare ceased to be used mainly as a means of defense, but instead became a tool of aggression against the political neighbours of Israel and Judah. The expansionist policy of David and his successors demanded an aggressive foreign policy and the armed means for enforcing that policy. At the same time, through the use, and even mimicking of the language of warfare, the prophetic voices were raised in protest against such self-aggrandisement. Yet in the post-exilic visions of restoration, the prophets also resorted to the same language of empire to envision a restored Judah and Jerusalem. This is a Jerusalem restored at the cost of the subjugation of the traditional enemies of Israel, at times their enslavement, and at times their annihilation. To be sure, this subjugation is seen as the work of Yahweh, but it is not a miraculous, "weaponless" victory. It is a victory for the exiles brought about through warfare in a kind of international *lex talionis*.

The important hermeneutical question here is: How does the Christian view this material?[13] When the question is

---

[13]This is not the place to get involved in the debate over the "just war" theory, although, of course, it does have relevance for later Christian thought and practice.

brought into the context of the view of the Scriptures as authoritative in matters of faith and practice, then the difficulty is clear. Is this violent behaviour depicted in the Old Testament presented as an example for us to follow? Does it provide a license to kill in the name of God, or in the defense of what we hold dear? Can we adopt the stance of the military leaders of the period of the Judges who mustered men who fought, killed and died for the sake of the covenant community? Can we adopt the stance of David or his successors, who expanded this covenant community through conquest, and for their support developed stories and traditions of a violent beginning, and a country either rid of outsiders or an empire lauding it over outsiders? Do we mimic such a stance, and follow the line of the prophets who preached against the self-interest of the kings, and who even advised Judaeans themselves to submit to the invading Babylonians? Or do we continue the later prophetic/apocalyptic stance and look to the future and to a fully restored empire whose borders have expanded, whose neighbours cower in submission and whose wealth is unlimited—the difference from the earlier one being the more active participation of Yahweh in the preceedings?

When the different modes of Old Testament behaviour and Old Testament attitudes are set out in this way, one thing becomes clear. The Old Testament does not present a uniform pattern of behaviour with regards to warfare. If we wish to adopt an Old Testament model as a standard of behaviour on this important issue, then we have to make a choice between these three models. It has been customary to speak of the period of the Patriarchs as a time of pacifism.[14] But the so-called "pacifism" of the Patriarchs is no pacifism at all, but rather a case of making a virtue out of a necessity. The social and political conditions of the patriarchs hardly encouraged warfare on a scale seen later. But when pressed, and when the opportunity did present itself, characters from this period did resort quickly and easily to violence to retrieve

The literature on the topic is vast. For a balanced treatment see M. Walzer *Just and Unjust Wars: A Moral Argument with Historical Illustration* (New York: Harper Torchbooks, 1977).

[14]See Lind *Yahweh is a Warrior:* 35-45.

what they had lost, as in the case of Abraham's rescue of Lot (Gen. 14), or to redress a balance of lost honour, as in the case of the treatment of the men of Shechem (Gen. 34). This period does not represent an alternative to any of the other three options. But let us take the historical dimension farther. If we are to make such a choice, and to adopt a policy from the past, then it would be best if not only the policy, but the very conditions in which that policy was viable could be reproduced. Let us, for the moment, take this out of the context of a discussion on warfare, and look at the question when dealing with another matter of social ethics, that of the family.

On this matter it is evident that if I wanted to reproduce in my own life and practice the Old Testament presentation of the "ideal family", then it would be best to do it in conjunction with the ideal conditions in which such a family could function, namely pre-Christian, eastern Mediterranean life which was based on agriculture. Of course, these conditions did not remain static, but the more realistically these conditions could be reproduced, the better chance there would be of reproducing the ideal "Old Testament family." This would be a family in which the father was the absolute ruler, the owner of the family; and in which the wife, along with the "house ... the male slave, the female slave, the ox, the ass" (Exod. 21.17), was the property of the father, and treated as such. It is in this historical and cultural context that the Old Testament laws on adultery make sense, or the regulations on other illicit sexual relations make sense. It is in this context that the questions over the right of women to inherit the father's property make sense (Num. 27.1-11), and that an attempt is made to expand on these rights (Num. 36.1-12). It is also in this context that the absolute obedience demanded of a son by his father makes sense. It is trite, but also true, that times have changed. Definitions of the word "family" have changed, as have the social and cultural conditions in which a family can function. Already in the story of the daughters of Zelophehad room is allowed for such changes in law and custom to accommodate new circumstances. Sometime during the history of Israel the family unit changed from a polygamous unit to a monogamous unit, and by the time of the New Testament, what is meant by the word "family" would have been unrecognizable to a Jeremiah or a Moses. The Hebrew word which often stands behind the translation "family", *mishpachah*, is something quite unknown in modern western society. What this illustration shows is that as a social institution, the "family" changes shape throughout history, and these changes are brought about sometimes for quite mundane reasons, such as use of space or shifts in economic structure. But the basic principle that "one should not be alone" is not affected seriously by these changes. The race continues, companionship is maintained, the race reproduces, and society is organized throughout.

As in any developing society, social and political institutions change, and this is no less true of the institution of warfare in ancient Israel. Its organization changed because of different circumstances, its purposes changed because of different circumstances, and in one period there was a strong difference of opinion on the use of warfare. At times there were periods of peace (few and far between) and even advice on non-resistance, but the times of peace were achieved by force and the subjugation of neighbouring states, or because of the noninvolvement of the greater states of the ancient Near East. Jeremiah's advice on non-resistance to the Babylonians is born not out of a concern for "pacifism", but more out of pragmatism as Jer. 27-29 show. One thing is certain, throughout Israel's history warfare was a given, a fact of life, and it was viewed as an appropriate means for settling disputes between peoples. Israel, like her neighbours, went to war motivated by "... the perceptions by statesmen of the growth of hostile power and the fears for the restriction, if not the extinction, of their own."[15] Without judgment the writer of Ecclesiastes, having observed the activity of the human race, and having reflected on his own experience, states simply, "There is ... a time to slay and a time to heal ... a time for war and a time for peace." Had he lived at a

[15]M. Howard *The Causes of Wars* [2nd ed.] (Cambridge, Mass: Harvard University Press, 1983): 18.

later age he might have agreed with the comment of Thomas Hobbes:

> Hereby it is manifest, that during the time men live without a common Power to keep them all in awe, they are in a condition which is called Warre.[16]

If there is any direct instruction about war in the Old Testament, it is found in Deut. 20.1-20, 21.10-14 and 23.9-14. These instructions are probably from the time of the monarchy, since they deal with campaigns into foreign countries outside Canaan. We shall deal with the third regulation, Deut. 23.9-14, first, since it is quickly dispensed with. It deals with matters of hygiene during a campaign, and where soldiers can defecate. The advice is to do it outside the camp, and to cover it afterwards. This avoids the soiling of the ground within the camp. The first set of instructions in Deut. 20 is designed to weed out potentially uncooperative soldiers who are either preoccupied with domestic matters, or just plain scared (vv.1-9). The interests of the leader here are not for the control of excess in warfare, but for efficiency. There follows a section of instructions on siege warfare and the conduct of Israelite troops in a captured foreign city (vv.10-18). All the males are to be killed, but all else, including the women and children, are regarded as spoils of war and to be enjoyed by the victorious troops. Cities close to home, occupied by non-Israelites are to be slaughtered. This is to be done so that no contamination will affect the Israelites. The regulations governing trees (vv. 19-20) are quite pragmatic. On a campaign far from home, and for a considerable time, the problems of supply would be acute. An excellent source of food would be local fruit trees, so they are not to be cut down either as punishment for the local population, or for use in the making of siegeworks.

The second regulation in Deut. 21.10-14 has a single subject matter, that of the fate of captured women. In wars of this period, women were taken as prizes of war—a practice

---

[16]T. Hobbes *Leviathan* Pt. I, para. #62.

which, though regulated, has not ceased even in the present day. If an Israelite captured a foreign woman, then his kidnap was controlled by this regulation. The woman was allowed to mourn the loss of her family, slain in the siege, for a period of one month. Following that period the captor could have intercourse with her. If he grew tired of her, she was to be released, but not sold as a slave "since you have humiliated her" (vs. 14). Any thought here of the humanizing of war is stretching the argument. The woman is taken away against her will, she is treated as a possession, raped, then allowed to leave. The fate of such a woman in ancient Israelite society, without the benefit of a male, was disastrous. The introduction of such a regulation into Israel might have done something to curb the practice of wholesale rape in the field of battle, but the motivation is ambiguous. Was it in the cause of efficiency—no distraction for the troops, or was it a matter of respecting the rights of the woman?[17] Knowing the attitude to foreigners at this time I suspect the former. The regulation could be enforced to a limited degree during the campaign and siege, but once the soldiers had returned home with their prizes, it would be impossible to police their behaviour. These regulations of soldiers in the field were probably a move in the direction of making warfare more efficient— I cannot use the term more "humanitarian", because the concept is absent from the passage. They represent a standard of warfare morality which the modern world has long since surpassed, although the will to follow that standard may be lacking still.[18]

## E. New Testament Insights

In the final analysis, the Christian believer understands the nature of the Gospel, and the character of living accord-

---

[17]See Walzer *Just and Unjust Wars*: 134-135.

[18]On the modern attempts at moderation in warfare see G. Best *Humanity in Warfare: The Modern History of the International Law of Armed Conflicts* (London: Methuen, 1983).

ing to the Gospel from the New Testament. It is to this section of the Scriptures we must turn for our understanding of the nature of the relationship between warfare in the Old Testament and the Christian. Christian belief and behaviour are drawn from the teaching of and example set by Jesus of Nazareth, and it is at first surprising that the first recorded "sermon" by Jesus is the announcement that with his coming the Kingdom of God is also present (Mk. 1.15). Although the term is never used in the Old Testament, the image conjured up by the use of the term "kingdom" is that of the empire established by David. It was the product of aggression by warfare, yet this is surprising on the lips of the man identified as the "prince of peace". What does it mean?

To answer that question we must sketch briefly the setting of the coming of Jesus.[19] The Old Testament closes with the Persian empire controlling the destiny of the Judaeans. Two hundred years later, when the Persians were replaced by the expanding empire of Alexander the Great, the country of Judaea was brought under the western influence of Hellenistic culture. The death of Alexander in the early fourth century BC saw the country in the hands of the Egyptian heirs of the Macedonian leader; they were known as the Ptolemies. Their eventual rivals, the Seleucids, based in Syria, eventually won the territory in the early second century BC (198 BC). Some thirty or so years later, the Jews in Judaea rebelled against the growing influence of Greek thought and ways in Jerusalem and began a war of independence, known in history as the Maccabean War.

Following this war, which ended in 160 BC, the Jews gained a measure of independence, and embarked on a programme of enlargement under a dynasty of their own people, the Hasmoneans. By the late second century BC much of the old territory had been regained by conquest, and a form of Jewish culture had been imposed on the captured territories. In the early part of the first century BC this new kingdom

---

[19]On this history see E. Schürer *The History of the Jewish People in the Age of Jesus Christ (175 BC—135 AD)*[new, revised edition by G. Vermes and F. Millar] vol. 1 (Edinburgh: T & T Clark, 1973.

began to collapse, and was faced with internal conflicts and great pressure from outside. By 68 BC a new power had arrived in the eastern Mediterranean, that of Rome, and within thirty years Rome had gained firm control over Judaea and ruled through a puppet king, known to history as Herod the Great. After Herod's death (date unknown), there were several serious disturbances and partisan rebellions which were eventually squashed by Roman force. After much squabbling between them, Herod's sons, Archelaus, Antipas, and Philip, received sections of Herod's former kingdom. Philip received the mixed northeast part of the kingdom, including Batanaea, Trachonitis, Gaulanitis, Panias and Ituraea. Antipas received Galilee and Perea, east of the Jordan. The eldest son, Archelaeus, received Judaea and Samaria. Archelaeus died in AD 6, and his territory was incorporated as an annex of Syria with its own governor directly responsible to Rome. The Roman center of administration was at Caesarea Maritima. By the time Jesus' ministry began in approximately AD 30 the presence of Rome was strongly felt. Politically, the land was divided into semi-autonomous regions. Economically, much of the produce and wealth was directed outside the country at the expense of the local farmers and producers, and with the co-operation of many locals who worked in varying capacities for the Romans.

As far as the Jewish population was concerned, it was divided according to class and power and political allegiance. At the heart of Jewish life was its religion, to which concessions were made by the Romans, but within this framework there was a remarkable variety of intensity of religious commitment. Some, such as the Sadducees and their supporters were part of the religious and political establishment. Others, like the Pharisees had a strong following among the common people, and sought to interpret the Torah to these same people. The Essenes appear in literature to be purists who withdrew from society to pursue study of the Torah, and may have formed a community at Qumran. Herodians, who appear occasionally in the New Testament, were probably those who supported a pro-Roman political stance. At the other end of the scale were those, collectively called

Zealots, who advocated violent resistance to the Romans and their supporters. Feeding all of this factionism was a popular religious tradition which is seen most clearly in the large amounts of literature which was produced in the period between 200 BC and AD 100. The dominant theme of this literature is a continuation of the prophetic vision of the future, of a violent, triumphal overthrow of oppressors of God's people and the bringing in of the kingdom of peace and prosperity for God's people. Collectively, this literature is known as apocalyptic, the unveiling. It dominated popular religious thought at the time of Jesus, so much so that one New Testament scholar has depicted it as the "mother of Christian Theology". This created a situation in which there were three possibilities of action, armed resistance, opportunistic accommodation or passive endurance.

It is against this background that the announcement by Jesus of the coming of the Kingdom of God must be seen. The term and the concept behind it would have had explosive political implications. We can see in the New Testament the sense of expectation of common people in the description of Simeon and Anna (Lk. 2.25) who were ". . . looking for the consolation of Israel . . . "; we can see too the sense of disappointment in the words of the disciples who later confess to a stranger that they thought Jesus would have "redeemed Israel" (Lk. 24.21); and we can perhaps understand the presence of a political fanatic (zealot) in the company of disciples, or the frustration of Judas, against this background.

There were several possibilities open to Jesus, but the key to understanding his ministry, his message and his death and eventual resurrection, is the *transformation* which popular and traditional concepts undergo in his teachings. For example, although Jesus used the language of the Kingdom of God, and the phrase was frequently on his lips, he did little to exemplify the popular understanding of it. He did not build up a "power base" as the foundation of rebellion. He preached no revolution against authority, but instead developed what one could call a "subversive" tactic. He associated with both the marginalised and the powerful, treating them all alike. Gaining the world is accomplished by giving up one's life, not in combat, but by serving others (Mk. 8.36;

9.33-35). The true children of God are those who make peace (Matt. 5.9). If his self-consciousness is to be seen in his actions then he took the concept of the "suffering servant" from the Old Testament, and transformed it. The servant is not vindicated through violence, as in Isa. 40-55, but by becoming a redemptive offering himself.

In the Gospel of Mark there is a narrative development of the theme of transformations. At the decisive moment in the Gospel when the Messiahship of Jesus is openly confessed by the disciples, there is an injunction to silence on the part of the disciples, and the beginning of the teaching that Jesus will die. This death will be premature, inevitable, and will be met with no resistance on the part of Jesus (Mk. 8.34-38). The presuppositions of the disciples are now made clear as they question the fate of Jesus, misunderstand the motivation, and eventually desert him. The supreme irony of the Gospel is the scene before Pilate (Mk. 15.1-15). Jesus is beaten and placed before the Roman governor dressed in a purple robe and a crown of thorns. He is powerless, yet when asked by the Roman whether he is in fact the king of the Jews, he answers with a simple affirmative.

Each of the other Gospels has a slightly different version of this incident, which they apparently inherited from Mark's account, but all attest to the powerlessness of Jesus in the final days of His life, and even the remarks attributed to him by the writer of the Fourth Gospel are in keeping with his fundamental position:

> My kingship is not of this world; if my kingship were of this world, my servants would fight, that I might not be handed over to the Jews; but my kingship is not of this world.(John 18.36).

Jesus belongs to an entirely different order of things, and advocates hereby a different way of dealing with human relationships.

The primitive Christian community was in no position to establish a power base from which to launch a strategy of revolution or of conquest, but the records they left behind, the New Testament, are not unanimous on the question of violence, but reflect a sense of ambivalence which has been part of the Christian tradition ever since. It would be an argument of silence to suggest that the New Testament does not advocate fighting as a soldier. The real question here is what would the options have been? The statements attributed to John the Baptist in Luke 3.14 do not condemn the profession of soldiering, but simply ask soldiers to be fair in their dealings with others. Jesus does not demand of the Roman centurion that he renounce his profession, but simply offers help to him (Matt. 8.5-13). Jesus' subsequent statement that "... all who take the sword will perish by the sword" (Matt. 26.52) is not so much an item of teaching or instruction in ethics, but rather a statement of fact. At the arrest, the disciples were outnumbered and resistance would have been quite fruitless.

In the rest of the New Testament there is little direct teaching on the matter. Paul acknowledges the transformation of the struggle against evil on to the cosmic, supranatural level and uses an Old Testament image to encourage the "soldiers" in this fight (Eph. 6.10-17). In Rom. 12.14-21, he offers his clearest instruction of the question of resistance to evil. The matter of revenge is in the hands of God, and in a kind of play on words he concludes, "Do not be overcome by evil, but overcome evil with good" (vs. 21). Before reaching that part, however, he adds an unusual quotation from Prov. 25.21-22. Although something similar is stated in the "sermon on the mount" (Matt. 5.44), the sentiment is not exactly the same. Jesus encourages prayer for those who persecute, and extending love beyond the borders of one's immediate group. Paul's admonition carries with it the element of public humiliation and shame intended in the act of feeding an enemy. Its clearest example is found in 2 Kings 6.20-31. The act of tricking the Syrian soldiers into captivity and of feeding them, brought shame on them. Thus it is that when their king heard about it he declared a full-scale war on the Israelites with disastrous results (vs. 24). In repeating this text from Prov. 25 in the context of Rom. 12.14-21, Paul adds to what otherwise would have reflected the sentiments of Jesus, a note of vindictiveness.

In the last book of the Bible, the Apocalypse of John, two

extremes are represented. On the one hand the language of the apocalypse, in keeping with the common genre of the time, is full of vocabulary of war, victory, destruction of evil and triumph of good. Comparison with contemporary apocalyptic literature shows the seedbed out of which this book grew. On the other hand, there is an added feature not found in any contemporary Jewish apocalyptic. In the vision of the seated God, surrounded by his heavenly courtiers waiting to have the seven seals unfastened from the scroll, "... I saw a lamb, standing as though it had been slain ... " (Rev. 5.6), and the chapter ends on a paradox:

> "Worthy is the lamb who was slain, to receive power, and wealth and wisdom and might and honour and glory and blessing" (Rev. 5.12).

As the book unfolds it becomes a grand synthesis of the triumphalist visions of the prophets and the catastrophic judgment on evil and sin, but at its core, standing as the meaning to history, and as the means by which it is brought to completion is the helpless figure of the slain lamb. It is he, and his own who follow him, who will reign. The transformation is complete.

# Bibliography

## Books

Adair, J. *Effective Leadership*. London. Pan Books, 1983.

Aharoni, Y. *Arad Inscriptions*. Jerusalem. Israel Exploration Society, 1984.

Aharoni, Y. *The Land of the Bible. An Historical Geography* [revised edition]. Philadephia. Westminster Press, 1978.

Anderson, F. *A People's Army. Massachusetts Soldiers and Society in the Seven Years War*. New York. Norton, 1984.

Anderson, J.K. *Ancient Greek Horsemanship*. Berkeley. University of California Pr., 1961.

Best, G. *Humanity in Warfare. The Modern History of the International Law of Armed Conflict*. London. Methuen, 1983.

Bonnet, H. *Die Waffen der Völker des alten Orients*. Leipzig. J.C. Hinrichs, 1926.

Brende, J.O., Parsons, E.R. *Vietnam Veterans. The Road to Recovery*. New York. Signet Books, 1985.

Bright, J. *A History of Israel* [3rd revised edition]. Philadelphia. Westminster Press, 1981.

Bright, J. *Early Israel in Recent History Writing*. London. SCM Press, 1956.

Brueggemann, W. *David's Truth in Israel's Imagination and Memory*. Philadelphia. Fortress Press, 1985.

Brueggemann, W. *Prophetic Imagination*. Philadelphia. Fortress Press, 1978.

Carney, T.F. *The Shape of the Past. Models and Antiquity*. Lawrence, KS. Coronado Press, 1975.

Christensen, D.L. *The Transformation of the War Oracle in Old Testament Prophecy*. Missoula. Scholars Press, 1975.

Clausewitz, C. von. *On War* [with an Introduction by A, Rapoport]. Harmondsworth. Penguin Books, 1968.

Clements, R.E. *Abraham and David. Genesis 15 and Its Meaning in Israelite Tradition*. London. SCM Press, 1967.

Conrad, E.W. *Fear Not Warrior. A Study of the 'al tira' Pericopes in the Hebrew Scriptures*. Chico, CA. Scholars Press, 1985.

Craigie, P.C. *The Problem of War in the Old Testament*. Grand Rapids. Eerdmans, 1978.

Dinter, E. *Hero or Coward. Pressures Facing the Soldier in Battle*. London. Frank Cass, 1986.

Dixon, N.F. *On the Psychology of Military Incompetence*. London. J. Cape, 1976.

Dollard, J. *Fear in Battle*. Westport, Conn. Infantry Assoc, 1944.

Dothan, T. *The Philistines and Their Material Culture*. Jerusalem. Israel Exploration Society, 1982.

Douglas, M. *Purity and Danger. An Examination of the Concepts of Pollution and Taboo*. London. Routledge & Kegan Paul, 1972.

Dupuy, T.N. *The Evolution of Weapons and Warfare.* Indianapolis. Bobbs-Merrill, 1980.

Eisenstadt, S.N. *The Political Systems of Empires. The Rise and Fall of Historic Bureaucratic Societies.* New York. Free Press, 1969.

Enz, J.J. *The Christian and Warfare. The Roots of Pacifism in the Old Testament.* Scottdale. Herald Press, 1972.

Erman, A. *The Ancient Egyptians. A Sourcebook of Their Writings.* New York. Harper Torchbooks, 1961.

Farwell, B. *Mr. Kipling's Army. All the Queen's Men.* New York. Norton, 1986.

Ferrill, A. *The Origins of War. From the Stone Age to Alexander the Great.* London. Thames and Hudson, 1985.

Finley, M.I. *Ancient Slavery and Modern Ideology.* Harmondsworth. Penguin Books, 1980.

Finley, M.I. *Ancient History: Evidence and Models.* New York. Viking Books, 1986.

Fox, R. *Kinship and Marriage.* Harmondsworth. Penguin Books, 1967.

Gale, R. *Great Battles of Biblical History.* London. Hutchinson, 1968.

Gibson, J.C.L. *Syrian Semitic Inscriptions,* vol. 1. Oxford. Oxford University Press, 1982.

Gichon, M., Herzog, C. *Battles of the Bible.* London. Weidenfield and Nicholson, 1978.

Gonen, R. *Weapons of the Ancient World.* London. Cassells, 1975.

Gottwald, N.K. *The Hebrew Scriptures. A Socio-literary Introduction.* Philadelphia. Fortress Press, 1985.

Gottwald, N.K. *The Tribes of Yahweh. A Sociology of Liberated Israel, 1250-1050 BCE.* Maryknoll. Orbis Books, 1979.

Greenhalgh, P.A.L. *Early Greek Warfare.* Cambridge. Cambridge University Press, 1973.

Halpern, B. *The Constitution of the Monarchy in Israel* Missoula. Scholars Press, 1980.

Hardy, R. *Longbow, a Social and Military History.* Portsmouth. The Mary Rose Trust, 1986.

Hobbes, T. *Leviathan.* [with an Introduction by C.B. MacPherson] Harmondsworth. Penguin Books, 1968.

Hobbs, T.R. *2 Kings.* Waco, TX. Word Books, 1985.

Hobsbawm, E., Ranger, T. [eds.] *The Invention of Tradition.* Cambridge. Cambridge University Press, 1983.

Hodder, I. *Reading the Past. Current Approaches to Interpretation in Archaeology.* Cambridge. Cambridge University Press, 1986.

Holmes, R. *Acts of War. The Behaviour of Men in Battle.* [also published as *Firing Line*] New York. Free Press, 1985.

Howard, M. *The Causes of War and Other Essays* [revised edition] Cambridge, Mass. Harvard University Press, 1983.

Ishida, T. *Royal Dynasties in Ancient Israel.* Berlin. W. De Gruyter, 1977.

Keegan, J. *The Mask of Command.* New York. Viking Books, 1987.

Keegan, J. *The Face of Battle. Agincourt to the Somme.* New York. Vintage Books, 1976.

Larsen, M.T., [ed.] *Power and Propaganda. A Symposium on Ancient Empires.* Copenhagen. Akademisk Vorlag, 1979.

Levenson, J.D. *Sinai and Zion. An Entry into the Jewish Bible.* Minneapolis. Winston-Seabury Press, 1985.

Lind, M.C. *Yahweh is a Warrior. The Theology of Warfare in Ancient Israel.* Scottdale. Herald Press, 1980.

Linderman, G. *Embattled Courage. The Experience of Combat in the American Civil War.* New York. Free Press, 1987.

Littauer, M.A., Crouwel, J. *Wheeled Vehicles and Ridden Animals in the Ancient Near East.* Leiden. E.J. Brill, 1976.

Liver, J. [ed.] *The Military History of the Land of Israel in Biblical Times.* Jerusalem. Ma'aracoth, 1964.

Lowenthal, D. *The Past is a Foreign Country.* Cambridge. Cambridge University Press, 1987.

Lumpkin, W.L. *Baptist Confessions of Faith.* Valley Forge. Judson Press, 1969.

Machiavelli, N. *The Art of War* [ETr E. Farnsworth] Indianapolis. Bobbs-Merrill, 1965.

Marshall, S.L.A. *Men Against Fire.* New York. 1947.

McKay, P.W. *Violence. Right or Wrong?* Waco, TX. Word Books, 1973.

Meiggs, R. *Trees and Timber in the Mediterranean World.* Oxford. Clarendon Press, 1982.

Mettinger, T.N.D. *Solomon's State Officials. A Study of the Civil Government Officials of the Israelite Monarchy.* Lund. G.W.K. Gleerup, 1971.

Montagu, A. *The Nature of Human Aggression.* Oxford. Oxford University Press, 1978.

Muhly, J.D., Wertime, T. *The Coming of the Age of Iron.* New Haven, Conn. Yale University Press, 1980.

Pritchard, J.B. [ed.] *Ancient Near Eastern Texts Relating to the Old Testament.* Princeton. Princeton University Press, 1966.

Rost, L. *The Succession to the Throne of David* [ETr.]. Sheffield. Almond Press, 1982.

Sasson, J.M. *The Military Establishment at Mari.* Rome. Pontifical Biblical Inst., 1969.

Simmons, J. *Winning Wars. The Spiritual Dimension in Military Art.* New York. University Press of America, 1986.

Smend, R. *Yahweh War and Tribal Confederation.* [ETr] Nashville. Abingdon Press, 1970.

Snodgrass, A.M. *Arms and Armour of the Greeks.* Edinburgh. University of Edinburgh Press, 1967.

Stolz, F. *Yahwe und Israels Kriege.* Zurich. Theologischer Verlag, 1972.

Sun Tzu. *The Art of War.* [ETr. S.B. Griffith]. Oxford. Oxford University Press, 1963.

Thucydides. *The Peloponnesian War.* Harmondsworth. Penguin Books, 1954.

Turner, V. *The Ritual Passage. Structure and Anti-structure.* Ithaca. Cornell University Press, 1969.

Ussishkin, D. *The Conquest of Lachish by Sennacherib.* Tel Aviv. Institute of Archaeology, 1982.

von Rad, G. *Der heilige Krieg im alten Israel.* Göttingen. Vandenhoeck und Ruprecht, 1962.

Walzer, M. *Just and Unjust Wars. A Moral Argument with Historical Illustrations.* New York. Harper Torchbooks, 1977.

Weber, M. *The Theory of Social and Economic Organization* [ETr Talcott Parsons] New York. Free Press, 1947.

Weber, M. *Ancient Judaism* [ETr H.H. Gerth] New York. Free Press, 1952.

Xenophon. *The Persian Expedition.* Harmondsworth. Penguin Books, 1949.

Yadin, Y. *The Art of Warfare in Biblical Lands*, 2 vols. New York. McGraw-Hill, 1962.

## Journal Articles

Aharoni, Y. "Forerunner of the Limes. Iron Age Fortresses in the Negev." *Israel Exploration Journal* 17 (1967): 1-17.

Balthazar, J.W. "Cypriot Hook-tang Spearheads and Rivetted Daggers—Manufacture and Use." *American Journal of Archaeology* 91 (1987): 321-322.

Cohen, R. "Solomon's Negev Defense Line Contained Three Fewer Fortresses." *Biblical Archaeology Review* 12 (1986): 40-45.

Cohen, R. "The Fortresses King Solomon Built to Protect his Southern Border." *Biblical Archaeology Review* 11 (1985): 56-70.

Craigie, P.C. "War, Religion and Scripture." *Bulletin of the Canadian Society for Biblical Studies* (1986).

Finkelstein, I. "The Iron Age Sites in the Negev Highlands." *Biblical Archaeology Review* 12 (1986): 46-53.

Gordon, D.H. "Swords, Rapiers and Horseriders." *Antiquity* 27 (1955): 67-78.

Hallo, W. "From Qarqar to Carchemish. Assyria and Israel in the Light of New Discoveries." *Biblical Archaeologist* 23 (1960): 34-61.

Hanson, P.D. "War, Peace and Justice in Early Israel." *Biblical Review* 3 (1987): 32-45.

Hobbs, T.R. "The Search for Prophetic Consciousness. Some Comments on Method." *Biblical Theology Bulletin* 15 (1985): 136-141.

Isserlin, B.S.J. "The Israelite Conquest of Canaan. A Comparative Review of the Arguments Applicable." *Palestine Exploration Quarterly* 115 (1983): 85-94.

Jones, G.H. "Holy War or Yahweh War." *Vetus Testamentum* 25 (1975): 642-658.

Korfmann, Y. "The Sling as a Weapon." *Scientific American* 229 (1973): 34-42.

Mendenhall, G.E. "The Hebrew Conquest of Palestine." *Biblical Archaeologist* 25 (1962): 66-87.

Mendenhall, G.E. "The Census Lists in Numbers 1 and 26." *Journal of Biblical Literature* 77 (1958): 52-66.

Millard, A.R. "Saul's Shield Not Anointed With Oil." *Bulletin of the American Schools of Oriental Research* 230 (1978): 70.

Miller, J.M. "Archaeology and the Israelite Conquest of Canaan. Some Methodological Considerations." *Palestine Exploration Quarterly* 109 (1977): 87-93.

Odell, G.H., Cowan, F. "Experiments with Spears and Swords on Animal Targets." *Journal of Field Archaeology* 13 (1986): 195-212.

Rainey, A.F. "The Military Personnel at Ugarit." *Journal of Near Eastern Studies* 24 (1965): 17-27.

Rosen, R. "The Canaanean Blade and the Early Bronze Age." *Israel Exploration Journal* 33 (1983): 15-29.

Schlesinger, D. "A Slingshot from Dor." *Qadmoniot* 15 (1982): 116.

Schlesinger, D. "More on Slingstones." *Qadmoniot* 17 (1984): 89.

Stager, L.E. "The Archaeology of the Family in Ancient Israel." *Bulletin of the American Schools of Oriental Research* 260 (1985): 1-36.

Strange, J. "The Transition from the Bronze Age to the Iron Age in the Eastern Mediterranean and the Emergence of the Israelite State." *Scandinavian Journal of the Old Testament* 1 (1987): 1-19.

Tubb, D. "A Bronze Arrowhead with Engraved Marks from Gezer." *Palestine Exploration Quarterly* 112 (1980): 1-6.

## Collected Essays

Davies, P.E. "Courage." *Interpreter's Dictionary of the Bible*, vol. 1, G.E. Buttrick [ed.] Nashville: Abingdon Press, 1962, 712-713.

Ishida, T. "Solomon's Accession to the Throne of David." *Studies in the Period of David and Solomon.* T. Ishida [ed.] Winona Lake: Eisenbrauns, 1982, 175-188.

Liverani, M. "The Ideology of the Assyrian Empire." *Power and Propaganda. A Symposium on Ancient Empires.* M.T. Larsen [ed.] Copenhagen: Akademisk Vorlag, 1979, 297-317.

Malamat, A. "The Israelite Conduct of War in the Conquest of Canaan." *Symposium. Celebrating the 75th Anniv. of ASOR.* F.M. Cross [ed.] Philadelphia: ASOR, 1979, 35-56.

McKenzie, J.L. "Peace, a Biblical Concept." *New Testament Themes for Contemporary Man.* R.M. Ryan [ed.] Englewood Cliffs, NJ: Prentice-Hall, 1969, 156-160.

Moyer, J. "Weapons and Warfare in the Book of Judges." *Discovering the Bible.* T. Dowley [ed.] Grand Rapids: Eerdmans, 1986, 42-50.

Roberts, J.J.M. "Zion in the Theology of the Davidic-Solomonic Empire." *Studies in the Period of David and Solomon.* T. Ishida [ed.] Winona Lake: Eisenbrauns, 1982, 93-108.

Shils, E. "Ideology." *The Constitution of Society.* E. Shils [ed.] Chicago: University of Chicago Press, 1982, 202-223.

Talmon, S. "The Rule of the King." *King, Cult and Calendar.* S. Talmon [ed.] Jerusalem: Magness Press, 1986, 53-67.

# General Index

243